FROM WORST
TO FIRST

FROM WORST TO FIRST

Behind the Scenes of Continental's Remarkable Comeback

GORDON BETHUNE
WITH SCOTT HULER

John Wiley & Sons, Inc.

NEW YORK • CHICHESTER • WEINHEIM • BRISBANE • SINGAPORE • TORONTO

ISBN 0-471-24835-5

Printed in the United States of America.

10 9 8 7 6 5 4 3 2 1

To the 40,000 men and women
who are Continental Airlines

Letter from a customer and friend

GEORGE BUSH

February 23, 1998

Dear Gordon,

I am very happy that you have written a book that among other things spells out the success you have had with Continental Airlines.

There is a great lesson here. You took on a tough challenge and through true leadership you turned that challenge into a major success story.

I believe your book will resonate far beyond the airline industry. Heaven knows we can all learn from a successful leader.

Sincerely from your customer and friend,

George Bush

CONTENTS

How We Climbed from Worst to First

Is This Any Way to Run an Airline?

Continental Airlines, in early 1994, was going nowhere, and it was going nowhere fast.

If you wanted to get anywhere else fast, like New York or Denver or Cleveland—or, in fact, if you wanted to get anywhere at all and get there on time—you were better off flying almost any other airline.

But nowhere? We were going nowhere like we had an appointment. And nowhere is where we could get you, though we probably would have lost your luggage on the way.

You think I'm exaggerating. I've got to tell you that I'm not.

In February of 1994, I left my comfortable job as a big shot in operations at the Boeing Company in Seattle. I moved to Houston and took over as president and chief operating officer of Continental. The job looked great—president of the fifth-largest airline in the country. I knew Continental had operating problems, but then, I'm an operations guy, and solving problems is the challenge any executive looks for.

Within a few months, however, when United Airlines tempted me to leave Continental and take a similar position there, I looked at that offer as a parachute and was prepared to take it. I would have given anything to get out of Continental, which was, I had no doubt, about to crash and burn. I felt as though I had been handed the controls of an airplane that people admitted was having a little trouble. But nobody had told me both engines had failed. I could pull the yoke, push the rudders, and goose the throttle all I wanted—but, surprise! It turned out I didn't have all the controls, and the controls I had weren't connected to anything. Continental was headed for another financial and operational disaster. And all I could do was watch.

Portrait of a Crisis

Consider these statistics:

- In the years leading up to 1994, Continental was simply the worst among the nation's 10 biggest airlines, which are measured monthly according to several quality indicators by the U.S. Department of Transportation. For example, DOT measures those 10 largest airlines in on-time percentage (the percentage of flights that land within 15 minutes of their scheduled arrival). *Continental was dead last.*

- It measures the number of mishandled-baggage reports filed per 1,000 passengers. *Continental was worst.*

- It measures the number of complaints it receives per 100,000 passengers on each airline. Continental was last. And not just last—in 1994, *Continental got almost three times as many complaints as the industry average* and more than 30 percent more complaints than the ninth-best airline, the runner-up in lousy service. We had a real lock on last place in that category.

- It measures involuntarily denied boarding—passengers with tickets who show up at the gate but because of overbooking or other problems are not allowed to board the plane. That was our big success story: We were only *among* the worst there, not the worst.

We weren't just the worst big airline. *We lapped the field.*

If your planes are showing up whenever they feel like it, if passengers are losing baggage, and if your service is annoying your customers so badly that they feel the need to tell the U.S. government about it, it's going to show up in your financial situation, too.

And let me tell you, it did.

For one thing, Continental had gone into Chapter 11 bankruptcy protection twice in the preceding decade. It had emerged reorganized twice, but somehow in all that time in bankruptcy court it never found the secret to making a profit. Our stock had undergone a steady decline throughout the company's times of troubles, finally settling at around $3.25 a share, where it seemed unalterably stuck. In fact, in early 1995, during our darkest days of financial crisis, we issued a press release describing our tenth consecutive year of losses. We did our best to bury the news that we were in so much trouble that we weren't just trying to reorganize our debts—we were simply going to have to stop paying some of them (temporarily, we hoped). We weren't in bankruptcy, but we wouldn't have had to change planes to get there.

We watched the stock anxiously the next day—not a budge. At first we thought we had done a good job of hiding or softening the news, but then we figured it out. Our stockholders were just betting we'd survive. *Our stock simply couldn't go any lower.* It was at rock bottom.

Just like company morale.

In an organization that had suffered through 10 leaders in 10 years (and as many different management schemes and new buzzwords), remaining employees had learned one survival strategy: Duck. No matter what management told employees they were supposed to do, it was a pretty fair guess that it was a lie. And even if direction was sincerely offered, chances were that long before anybody came around to check on whether employees were following it, some crisis would have caused yet another management change. So employees just did what they could and kept their heads down.

Not that they did it happily. One of the strategies previous management had used to keep the airline together was union busting, so our employees were paid far below industry average. Their repayment for their endurance and ability to hold on was regular layoffs, wage reductions, and broken promises on wage snapbacks and profit sharing. Our on-the-job injury numbers were astronomical; so were turnover and sick time. Employee groups fought each other for scarce resources and wages. When problems occurred, which of course they did almost constantly, covering your ass was a lot more important than solving the problem.

Continental's airport employees actually removed the Continental insignia from their uniforms to avoid having to answer uncomfortable questions from airport coworkers or from customers when off duty. When friends asked where they worked, they'd mumble, "Um, out at the airport."

To put it bluntly, the *Good Ship Lollipop* we weren't.

That's what I joined in 1994: a company with a lousy product, angry employees, low wages, a history of ineffective management, and, I soon learned, an incipient bankruptcy, our third, which would probably kill us.

After I moved to Houston to go to work at Continental corporate headquarters, I didn't sleep real well. But to be honest, sleeping wasn't going to solve this airline's problems.

In fact, it looked like nothing might. I joined Continental in February 1994. In June, when the United offer came, Continental offered me a pile of money to stay instead of jumping. And for reasons I'll never quite understand, I stayed on. Some of it had to do with the fact that I had lured several colleagues whom I deeply trusted and respected to join me at Continental. I couldn't see abandoning them. Some of it had to do with the challenge of trying to save a company in such desperate straits. And some of it had to do with the Continental employees, a disgruntled, angry, mistrustful but straightforward lot. For every employee who would respond to me in an understandably surly, angry fashion—"You're just like all the rest, we've had 10 presidents and we'll have 10 more and I'm sick of promises"—there were a dozen who cut right to the chase: "Help us, Gordon," they said. "Do something." They sure needed me more than a successful company like United ever could.

I decided to stick it out and do something.

It turned out to be the best professional move of my life.

In November, further turmoil landed me the job of chief executive officer, which meant that my hand was finally on the control. To put it in pilot's terms, I was finally sitting in the left-hand seat. I was flying the airplane.

I've been flying Continental for almost four years now, and things are looking a little different.

From Worst to First

Starting early in 1995, a renewed focus on the flight schedule and incentive pay drastically changed our on-time performance, and since then we've been in the top five almost every month, often coming in first. Even when our planes aren't the industry leaders in on-time percentage, our lost-baggage claims are usually among the two or three best. Our consumer complaints are continually below the industry average and usually among the lowest in the industry, and we're the best in the industry at taking care of our customers when the plane is oversold. For 1996, measured as a whole, we were third best or better in all four things the DOT measures, which I liken to hitting a grand slam.

People noticed. Customers began returning, especially the higher-fare business passengers we most wanted on our planes. From a low of 32.2 percent in 1994, businesspeople climbed to 42.8 percent of our customer mix in 1996. And it's not just businesspeople. Now that our product is good, we've found a customer base again, which has made us profitable: In 1994, we lost $204 million; in 1995, we made $202 million; in 1996, we made $556 million. *We've had eleven straight quarters of record profits.*

Not income: *profits.* A company that hadn't made a profit in 10 years has now had 11 straight profitable quarters, each of them surpassing the record of the preceding quarter.

Naturally, our stock has gone through the roof, splitting two-for-one and, even so, now regularly trading at more than $50.

A successful workforce is almost always a happy workforce, and Continental is no exception. However you measure the happiness of a workforce, ours scores high:

- Wages have gone up an average of 25 percent.
- Sick leave has gone down more than 29 percent.

- Turnover is down 45 percent.

- Workers' compensation is down 51 percent.

- On-the-job injuries are down more than half, by 54 percent.

Our employees are better paid and happier, so they show up for work, stay healthy, and pay close attention to what they're doing.

And they're not pulling the Continental insignia off their uniforms anymore. In fact, sales of our logo merchandise to employees have gone up 400 percent.

And more than just passengers and employees have noticed.

As our stock climbed throughout 1995, *Business Week* magazine chose us as their stock of the year for 1995. Reporters from the *Wall Street Journal*, the *New York Times*, *USA Today*, *Fortune*, *Forbes*, and other publications came to Continental to write about what we were doing right. We regularly get requests to talk about how to improve quality and morale from organizations like NASA and companies like Honda.

Best of all, in May 1996, customers surveyed by *Frequent Flyer Magazine* and the J.D. Power and Associates company awarded Continental the J.D. Power Award for customer satisfaction as the best airline for flights of 500 miles or more. In 1997 they chose us again, and we came within a hair of being named the best airline for short flights, too. No airline had ever before won the J.D. Power Award twice in a row, and we had not only done it but had almost won *both* J.D. Power Awards for airlines. In 1996, the J.D. Power folks said they had never before seen an airline go from worst to first in one year. In 1997, they said they had never before seen an airline win two years in a row. We were, frankly, making airline history.

And in January 1997, *Air Transport World*, our industry's leading monthly, put the final stamp on our turnaround: They called us the 1996 Airline of the Year, out of the more than 300 airlines worldwide.

We were a terrible company that did a lousy job of providing service, paid its workforce badly, barely managed to hold onto disgruntled, unhappy employees long enough for them to drop wrenches on their feet and file workers' compensation claims, and lost so much money that we were perilously close to our third (and no-doubt final) bankruptcy.

Now we're the best in our business at providing our service. Our employees are better paid and happy. We're consistently profitable, and we have a billion dollars of cash on hand. We're the darlings of Wall Street, and we've made a lot of stockholders happy and rich. And we were recently the object of a bidding war between two of the largest airlines in the nation—Delta and Northwest. We used our position to avoid being gobbled up by some other corporation. Instead, we were acquired by Northwest in a way that allowed us to keep working as we have learned to work, to keep being the successful airline we have become.

You, Too, Can Save Your Company, with Employees You Probably Have Around the Shop Right Now!

So how did this all happen?

On paper, it doesn't make sense. Other than the big shots, we have all the same people. We're flying pretty much the same airplanes. We're serving pretty much the same cities.

Only now we're more profitable than we've ever been before, and we're only getting better.

Is it me, Gordon Bethune? Am I magic? Am I Vince Lombardi, Ronald Reagan, and the Pied Piper all rolled into one?

I don't think so. But I do think I followed a few extremely simple rules, based on the most obvious understanding of human behavior.

In this book I'm going to tell you what happened between February of 1994 and today—how a company changed from a place where everything went wrong, a place investors, employees, and most of all customers agreed they wanted nothing to do with, into an airline investors love, customers choose, and employees are proud to work for. And in fact, I'll reveal how it did more than just change—how it changed to the best airline flying.

Someplace between an airline going nowhere fast and our second straight J.D. Power award, something went right. I'll tell you what I think it was—what my team and I did, what so many other new managers did, and most of all what the employees of Continental Airlines did once we proved to them we wouldn't sabotage them anymore.

I'm willing to bet you'll be able to see that almost none of what we did here is specific to the airline industry. We're in the business of taking people where they want to go, on time, with their luggage, in a safe, reliable, and predictable way. We needed to give our employees a reason to want to do that. Once we were able to communicate to them that we might actually be willing to just get out of their way and let them do that, our employees were so happy they couldn't believe it. And they showed us how good they were almost instantly.

It took them a while to believe in us—and you can't blame them. But once we got the managers out of their way, once we started helping rather than hindering them, once we started explaining what we wanted them to do and then actually rewarding them for doing that, we found out what I had expected in the first place.

That we have a great airline here, and 40,000 great people.

In this country, one measure of excellence is when somebody wants to buy you, right? Naturally, over the last few years Continental has had a lot of interest from potential purchasers. And in an era of consolidation, we knew we were going to end up connected with somebody. We didn't want to be the last ones at the dance without a partner. But we didn't want to give up what we had fought for so hard.

Finally, at the beginning of 1998 we received competing bids from two different airlines: Delta and Northwest. Delta was going to take us over, in a traditional merger. Northwest was willing to enter into a complex and unprecedented code-sharing alliance with us, by which they'd own us but the two airlines would still function as independent but complementary companies, giving new benefits to the stockholders—and customers—of both airlines but allowing the corporate spirit we'd spent four years developing to continue to flourish. And, incidentally, ensuring that not a single Continental employee would lose a job as a result.

Northwest offered a structure that would deliver significant returns to our shareholders while preserving the things that made us so successful. Delta offered a divisive merger that would have treated our employees unfairly and destroyed shareholder value.

Delta didn't budge, and Northwest worked with us. No surprises: The board chose Northwest.

When Northwest's deal came through at the last minute, the *Wall Street Journal* reported that the chief executive officer of Delta replied, "Labor? You mean this thing fell apart over labor?"

You bet it did. Continental isn't just me, it isn't just our board members and shareholders, and it isn't just our top-level managers with their incentive plans and golden parachutes. It's 40,000 people. It's all of us, working as a team. It's an entire culture, an entire way of being in business together. We fought for that, and we won.

It can be exactly the same for you, whether you're making pizza, fixing watches, or flying airplanes. I'm going to tell you how to find your own great business and great people, no matter how deep they may seem to be buried. The people probably already work for you. And I have to tell you, nothing I can say in this book will be anything you haven't heard before. It has to do with being honest and straightforward. It has to do with hiring the best people in the business to fix big problems. It has to do with understanding your business and what's important to your customers and your employees as well as your stockholders.

It has to do with not just identifying strategies but actually doing something to solve problems.

It has to do with getting good information about your performance and sharing that information with everyone in the company.

It has to do with constant communication.

But most of all, it has to do with common sense, decency, and respect. Those are the most important things Continental has now that it didn't have in 1994, and I've got to tell you that the minute we lose those, we're heading right back to the bottom of the heap. We can go from first to worst as fast as we went from worst to first, so I promise you I'll be practicing everything I preach here. If I don't, my employees will tell me about it—and through their service, they'll sure as hell tell you.

What I'm going to do in this book is explain to you what happened at Continental—the simple, sensible changes we made at the top, how our managers let the employees turn Continental into the best airline flying, how we coped with crisis, and how we moved forward together.

In Part One, I'll tell you how we changed Continental. Chapter 2 will explain how I got control of the airline. Getting the attention of a disgruntled and dispirited group of employees was an equally challenging project, and I'll explain that.

In Chapters 3 through 6, I'll outline our Go Forward Plan, the four-part program that encompasses all aspects of our operations at Continental. It was the blueprint for our turnaround, and to this day it's the plan by which we do every single thing at Continental. No short-lived management mumbo jumbo, the Go Forward Plan was a complete restating of how we would do business at Continental. And we still follow it today, nearly four years later. I'll also tell you how, through all the changes, we've managed to keep things fresh and keep improving, to keep from resting on our laurels.

In Part Two, starting with Chapter 8, I'll tell you what we learned as we took this monumentally broken company and fixed it. We'll go over some of the management lessons I've taken away from my experiences here and some of the lessons I learned before I got here that helped Continental become such a success story.

Chapter 14, which ends the book, provides a chapter-by-chapter summary of all the programs and projects we undertook that caused our success. So if you're in a terrible rush and just want a quick rundown of what we did, Chapter 14 can get you there in a hurry. But don't stop there. If you just read Chapter 14 and your friends read the whole book, when their businesses are experiencing remarkable successes and yours is just showing gentle improvement, you'll have no one but yourself to blame.

I expect you'll find everything I tell you fairly simple and sometimes even obvious. But maybe you'll run across a few things you've forgotten to put into practice or a few ideas you hadn't had explained to you quite right before. But I guarantee you we haven't done anything that you can't do tomorrow (or today) if you're just willing to go ahead and do it. Your employees will love you for it. So will your investors. And so will your customers.

The checklist is complete.

We're cleared for takeoff.

The Last Suppers, or Whose Problem Is It?

On October 24, 1994, I did a very significant thing in the executive suite of Continental Airlines, on the twentieth floor of its Houston headquarters.

I opened the doors.

The doors to the executive suite were locked, and you needed an ID to get through. Security cameras added to the feeling of relaxed charm. The paranoid security may have been a leftover from the days when the conflicts between Frank Lorenzo and the unions made Lorenzo fear for his personal safety—one flight attendant reported that he would not even drink a soda on one of his own airplanes if someone else had opened it for him—but it was still there. The place felt like a snake pit. It was horrible. There were little emergency alarm buttons, panic buttons in case somebody came in to beat somebody up.

Which, looking back, probably seemed fairly likely.

So the day I began running the company, I opened the doors. I wasn't afraid of my employees, and I wanted everybody to know it.

I opened the doors and kicked a wedge underneath. For the first time in a decade, we were genuinely open for business up there.

I had to wonder whether I was a little premature, though, because I wasn't exactly in charge. How that came to be is kind of a long story, but it shows how confused things were at Continental at that point, and it shows one way of getting people's attention.

Anyhow, days after I started there I knew the atmosphere in the executive suite was the first thing I had to change: Working in the executive suite of Continental was like trying to work in a room with a radio tuned halfway between two stations—it was like having a head full of static.

Not because Continental was having financial problems and problems with the quality of its product and its employee relations, though it certainly was. But the truth was just the opposite: Continental's problems were a direct result of that static—of how awful it was to work in the executive suite. Everything at the top at Continental was wrong. That filters down.

And if it was lousy in the executive suite, it sure wasn't going to be any picnic down through the ranks, where people were making a lot less money and constantly in fear for their jobs.

I don't think it took a genius to figure that out.

A Terrible Place to Work

I want to repeat: The executive suite wasn't a lousy place because Continental was in trouble. Continental was in trouble specifically because of the kind of things going on in the executive suite.

I could see Continental's biggest problem the second I walked in the door in February of 1994: This was a crummy place to work. The culture at Continental, after years of layoffs and wage freezes and wage cuts and broken promises, was one of backbiting, mistrust, fear, and loathing. People, to put it mildly, were not happy to come to work. They were surly to customers, surly to each other, and ashamed of their company. And you can't have a good product without people who like coming to work. It just can't be done.

And Continental was the case study for that. In a company where cost cutting was revered, departments fought one another to the death over scarce resources. In a company where management strategies—and management teams—changed overnight, employees schemed above all else to protect themselves, at the cost of their coworkers if necessary. Interdepartmental communication was almost nonexistent, and if you were told something, you had to do some research to make sure it was true. More often than not, it wasn't.

Everybody was screwing over everybody—no wonder the planes were late and the baggage was lost. The product was crummy. The fundamental reasons for that had nothing do with flying planes correctly or being able to clean and fix them. It had to do with an environment where nobody could get their jobs done.

The atmosphere was poisonous; it was the first time in years I didn't like coming to work—and I had just moved my family and my entire life to Houston for this job.

You Don't Change Unless You Want To

When I came to Continental Airlines in February 1994 as chief operating officer and president, I was quickly reminded of one of the most important lessons about making change.

You gotta want to.

My predecessor could see that the airline was in trouble, and his management team had done a lot of thinking about what was wrong with our airline, even identifying some of the most important problems and setting up studies of the problems. Occasionally, strategies had even been defined. But as the months went by, I realized there was something much more important than the specific problems. Except for a few isolated areas in which managers had been left alone to do their jobs, the organization itself was so dysfunctional that it couldn't have implemented the best idea in the world.

There were too many people who were so used to working in Continental's dysfunctional environment that they resisted change. Change is difficult, and people undertake it only if they believe they will be rewarded for it. The current guy at the top wasn't rewarding them for it.

He certainly wasn't rewarding me for it. I had a lot of good ideas, but when I'd float them, he'd shake his head. I came to believe that he really didn't want things to change all that much. Time after time I came up against problems that had nothing to do with the specifics of the airline business. Continental was just a broken company, and I despaired of making any change. We were stuck in our mold of being a cost-cutting airline, and if you weren't talking about cutting costs, nobody at the top wanted to hear you.

I wasn't talking about cutting costs. I was talking about fixing what was wrong with our company.

But you know what? You're not going to change the entire culture of a company from the right-hand seat—from the number two slot, which was where I was sitting as president and chief operating officer. I did what I could. I hired people I trusted to take charge of departments that had the deepest problems—technical operations and purchasing/material services—but I was still swimming against the tide. The chief executive didn't back me up, and he didn't give me the opportunity to make changes I'd come up with. I concluded that coming to Continental was a mistake.

That's why when United Airlines made me an offer only four months after I had started at Continental, I was prepared to accept it. Continental was going nowhere, and I didn't need to be around for the ride. And when Continental made me a handsome financial offer to remain, I said I needed more.

Continental needed some leadership. Even if I wasn't the chief executive, I at least needed an amount of control that would allow me to change some of the biggest problems. I was being asked to restore the operational integrity of a company without the authority to change the environment within which the people worked, and that just wasn't going to happen. That's not the way change works.

So I told the chief executive and the board that I would stay if I could take control of the marketing department and the pricing of the tickets—I couldn't change the way the airline operated if I couldn't control the way the product was presented. I mean, if what we *sold* was not under my jurisdiction, I couldn't change how we made it. You can't have a good operation with a bad product, and unless I had some control over the product and the environment in which it was created, I couldn't do a thing.

Well, Continental wanted me to stay, so I got control over the scheduling, marketing, and pricing of our product. It wasn't another month or so before I knew I still wasn't getting anywhere. We were making some changes, bit by bit, but we weren't getting the support we needed from the top of the company. We got our financials for the peak travel month of August, when everybody on the planet is traveling, and the results were terrible. In the airline business, if you don't make lots of money in August, you don't make money.

Continental Lite, our costly experiment of running a low-cost airline within an airline, was a dismal failure. Today we've got the best in the business, Jim Compton and Bill Brunger, running pricing and yield management, so we don't get into this kind of trouble anymore. But in those days, we were at sea. Different factions at the top had different ideas of what we should do next—we should break our company into pieces; we should sell off assets; we should take all sorts of other unorthodox approaches. To be honest, the deal culture that had started with Frank Lorenzo still existed at Continental. Deal makers look at problems and think deals. As a friend of mine has often said, if you're a hammer, everything is a nail. To deal makers, the solution is always more deals.

Did you ever see a deal maker try to fix a watch? It doesn't work. Deal makers buy and sell watches. If a watch is broken, they usually try to sell it. Or they buy more watches to divert attention from the broken watch—to bury its problems while they're making money on other watches. They wanted to play "Let's Make a Deal" with Continental, which had been playing "Let's Make a Deal" for a decade, but we weren't winning the big prize.

I didn't think more deals were going to work. We're an airline, and the solutions to our problems were airline solutions, not deals. We were making some strides with our pricing and schedule changes, but Continental was not going to change unless the entire environment changed, and that change has to start from the top.

But it wasn't happening.

"Let's Try It a While with No Pilot": The Wrong Way to Take Over an Airline

In late October 1994, our board (itself a combination of investor groups and creditors) finally decided a change had to be made at the top. But probably as a symptom of the way Continental did things at that time, it wanted to make sort of half a change.

Our board decided that it wanted to remove the chief executive, but not tell anybody about it. The chief would say he was taking a six-month leave, and he'd just never come back. We were going to run without a chief executive for a while as we quietly looked for yet another person to take over. I was supposed to run the company for those six months, but not become the chief executive. To me, not having me become the chief executive was kind of like flying an airplane with no pilot. It wasn't going to work.

People need to be motivated to make change, and you motivate them by explaining the consequences of resisting. And a new person at the top who's going to stick around can make that simple. *Because I said so, and I'm the guy at the top, and that's how it's going to be.* You do what the top guy says because if you don't he might whack your head off. It's pretty simple. Suddenly resisting change has a pretty high price, and if nothing else, you have people's attention.

But do what the temporary top guy says, because if you don't, well, he's probably going to be gone in six months anyhow, so what of it? People don't believe in it, and they don't trust it. If you want change, you have to have a strong leader—an identifiable person at the top, where change begins in a highly visible way. It can't be done by a committee of this or an office of that. It's got to be done by somebody.

Still, when push came to shove, the board had the power. It was the kingmaker, and it kind of said to me, it's this way or no way. Take over for six months under subterfuge, or don't take over.

But my predecessor surprised the board: He didn't want to pretend to step aside—and who could blame him. He had the job, he believed he could get the job done, and he wanted the chance to do it. If not, he wanted his walking papers. He took a smart strategy: Don't get kicked out the back door. If you're going to get kicked out, go out the front, with your dignity.

The board came back to me and told me the situation. My predecessor wouldn't take the deal. "So," they said, "Gordon, we want you to take over."

I said great, I get to be chief executive.

They said no, we just want you to take over, and we won't have a chief executive. Once again, I said that just wasn't going to work. I wanted the job, and I wanted the responsibility, but I didn't want some kind of interim position with no future.

And I figured out something important. Continental had a problem. I could see that. But a very important characteristic of that problem suddenly became clear.

It wasn't *my* problem.

The 10-Day Chief Executive, or Whose Problem Is It?

The first step in solving any problem is deciding whose problem it is. If it's not yours, you can go watch your favorite program on TV and let the people whose problem it is solve it. And I could see that this problem was not mine.

If Continental didn't want to give me the reins of the company, I would be able to live with that. I would be fine being the chief operating officer. You tell me to set a course for 270 degrees and go ahead two-thirds speed? Fine, I'll do that. I'll push the organization in whatever direction you want me to push it. But I've got to tell you, I don't think we're going to be going long, because the direction we're headed is dead wrong. But if they didn't want me to be the guy setting the direction, I still had a great job for great pay and I was willing to keep showing up for work and doing my best.

No, the problem wasn't mine. The problem belonged to our board members, who found themselves without a chief executive. So they hedged. The chairman told me I'd be in charge for the moment, but we had a board meeting coming up in 10 days and I'd have a chance to address the board, after which some kind of decision would be made.

I figured, fine, I have 10 days—that's 10 more days of straightforward leadership than Continental's had in a decade.

That was October 24, 1994. I went out and stuck a wedge under those once-locked doors, the equivalent of an "under new management" sign in the window of a restaurant. It wasn't much, and until I had complete control I couldn't do much more. But it was a start.

So the doors were open and I was in charge, for 10 days at least.

It was time to figure out what to do next. We had 10 days to prepare a presentation that would make the Continental board of directors not only recognize the dire straits the company was in but also see that I (along with Greg Brenneman, now Continental's president and chief operating officer but then still a consultant working with Continental) was the right person to steer the company away from the brink. Ten days to not only make the usual financial and operations presentations but to design a plan that would completely change the direction of a $6 billion corporation.

Ten days.

Which is how Greg and I ended up sitting at my dining room table trying to figure out what to do next.

The Last Suppers

Greg, a partner for Bain and Company and cofounder of its Dallas office, had been working for Continental for months before I showed up. He was a whiz at turning companies around, as well as one of the sharpest guys I've ever met. Unlike most consultants, Greg gets things done. He'd been hired to turn around Continental's maintenance operations, which had the highest cost but the lowest aircraft dispatch reliability in the industry. His work in maintenance was one of the few bright spots in the company.

Greg had known the company needed a new direction for the previous year. He was someone I came to trust deeply. After the events with my predecessor and the board, I went to Greg and said I was going to have a chance to run this company, and I wanted him to be my partner.

We went to my house and sat down for dinner. We called the meeting the last supper, as we did subsequent meetings, because we never knew when one of them might turn out to be truly the last—we never knew when a couple bad days might kick the company's precarious finances over the edge or what the result of the upcoming board meeting would be. But we knew we had 10 days to get ready, and we put everything we had into it.

We met at my house because we both knew we wouldn't accomplish anything meeting in the Continental executive suite. We drank wine as we worked. When things looked bleakest, we drank scotch.

The most important thing we needed to do was to put together a board presentation for the 1995 budget. The company had been losing money for a decade, and we knew we needed to find a way for it to make some money in 1995. If it didn't, we weren't going to have to worry about 1996, because we weren't going to be around.

But I've been in the aviation business my whole life, in one way or another. Although I could see airline-related and people-focused problems in our company, Greg had the broad perspective of someone who had worked fixing troubled companies across the board. In spite of our different backgrounds, we saw the situation very much the same. And before long we found ourselves discussing a lot more than just how to squeeze a profit out of Continental in 1995. During 1994, Continental had lost $204 million. That sounds like a lot of money, and it is, but when you figure we were running $6 billion through our profit and loss statement, it's not that big a percentage. It's kind of like swimming up all the way from the bottom of the Marianas Trench and then drowning a few feet from the surface. You wouldn't have to make too huge an adjustment to fix that somehow.

The way we saw it, though Continental had extreme cash woes, that wasn't the real problem. The problem was that every solution to every problem got lost in a maelstrom of anger, backbiting, and plain old dispirited disgust.

We were trying to come up with a plan that would change the entire company.

So we started talking about a plan. We discussed the name for the plan—something about turnaround, something about recovery, we thought. But when we discussed it with David Bonderman, then the chairman of the board, he made an excellent point. He said those names all took as their starting point the mess Continental was in. More appropriate would be a name about moving ahead, going forward. We didn't want to be looking back at what had gone wrong.

So we chose the Go Forward Plan as our title. It was just a simple way of saying let's knock off all this crap. The runway behind us isn't important any more. There are no rearview mirrors in the cockpit. We're going to cut the cord to the past, and we're going to go forward.

The Go Forward Plan

Remember how Vince Lombardi is supposed to have said, "Winning isn't everything, it's the *only* thing"? The Go Forward Plan wasn't the most important thing that we did—it was *everything* we did. It's the difference between Continental in 1994 and Continental today. Every company in trouble develops marketing and financial plans—Continental had more than most. And the Go Forward Plan, which Greg and I hatched in a few evenings around my dinner table, had both of those, of course. But it also had two other elements, and they made the difference. It had a plan to improve the Continental product—to fix what was wrong with what we were trying to sell in the first place. And it had a plan to utterly change the culture at Continental. And as I said, that was what was causing all the trouble in the first place.

We broke the plan into four parts: a market plan, a financial plan, a product plan, and, most important, a people plan. Chapters 3 through 6 will give you complete details on each element of this plan. But let me give you a quick overview now so you know what we were working on. I want to make clear that these were not *sequential* steps. Because the Go Forward Plan addressed every element of our business, it couldn't be undertaken one step at a time any more than you could decide to spend one month working on maintenance and the next month paying your employees. You always have to work on every aspect of your business. All four of these steps were being undertaken constantly and simultaneously. They're more like ingredients in a cake than sequential steps. You kind of need them all.

Fly to Win: The Market Plan

The market plan we called Fly to Win that was Greg's idea—we wanted to talk about winning, about achievement. We had to come up with words that denoted hope. So we took a pretty simple strategy: We decided to stop doing things that didn't make money. Greg said that in a meeting once, and I really liked the sound of it. It sounds simple, even obvious. After all, why would you do things that don't make money?

But we had been doing that for years, so we had to look hard at our schedule. We decided (again, it seems pretty obvious) to concentrate on our market strengths. We were losing money flying all kinds of point-to-point routes for ridiculously low fares in markets where we were at best a minor player. We decided to drop those routes and fly only to places it seemed people actually wanted to go. We realized that we simply had too many seats out there—like the farmer who tries to sell more tomatoes in a glutted market at depressed prices. Removing capacity would keep the same revenue while reducing our cost.

We also decided to contact the major travel agents and approach them hat in hand. The way Continental had been doing business, we had alienated everybody in the travel business. Around 80 percent of our business comes through travel agents, so we figured it would help to go to those people and apologize, work with them to reestablish commissions that were fair to them and to us, and generally do whatever it took to get our flights back on their radar screens. The agents had been booking clients on Continental only when they had to, and who could blame them? By going directly to the source, we hoped to get them back.

We did the same thing with our customers, restoring the award-winning frequent flyer program that had been dismantled in another cost-cutting effort. I'll go into much more detail about Fly to Win in Chapter 3.

Fund the Future: The Financial Plan

We called the financial plan Fund the Future—and laughed. "If there ain't no funds, there ain't gonna *be* no future," we said, and poured another drink. We looked at the airplanes we were flying, the money we owed on them. We looked at all the money we owed as part of the 1993 Chapter 11 proceedings. We looked at the failure of the Continental Lite experiment. As I said, the amount by which the company was failing to make a profit wasn't that huge a percentage of our annual revenues, so the changes that we had to make to nudge Continental into the black weren't that hard to figure out, though they were pretty hard to actually do. Fortunately, we were just making the plan, so we didn't have to do them yet.

One of the scariest things about any financial plan we could cook up, though, was that we had terrible systems, so we had very poor information about how much money we were making or losing on a daily basis. Our cash and revenue forecasting systems were from the Stone Age compared with those at other businesses of our size. We factored in the cost of updating and improving those programs and then made forecasts of how much we would save by knowing what was going on in a realistic way.

By planning to renegotiate some leases, postpone some payments, refinance some of our larger debts, and make changes to our pricing structure, Greg and I were able to come up with a plan that, on paper, forecast a $45 million profit in 1995. For a company that hadn't been profitable in 10 years, not too shabby. I'll tell you a lot more about this in Chapter 4, but at the moment I just want you to know that we had a plan, and on paper at least, the plan made sense.

Market and finances—that's where most reorganizations stop. But Greg and I kept going. The problems we were having marketing and financing our product were basically the result of a company with unhappy employees creating a lousy product. So the next step, the key step, was to keep going and come up with plans to improve the product—to make it a product we would be proud of—and to change the culture at Continental so employees would enjoy coming to work every day.

Make Reliability a Reality: The Product Plan

We devised part three of the plan and called it Make Reliability a Reality. All the financial plans and marketing plans in the world weren't going to be successful until we had a *product* we were proud to sell. So we planned to turn our product into something we were proud of. And the only way we could do that was to get back to the basics, doing the things that people expect from an airline . . . which is, of course, getting them where they want to go, on time, safely, and with their baggage.

And the only way we were going to provide that service was by making our employees *want* to provide it.

I follow a simple dictum in working with employees: What you measure and reward is what you get. I'll go into more detail on that in Chapters 5 and 12, but that's what guided Greg and me in our meetings. We wanted our airline to be on time, with baggage, so we decided to measure that and reward employees with a $65 bonus each month that they were in the top half of airlines in the percentage of flights arriving on time. This doesn't seem like a huge thing—a little performance bonus for doing well. And in truth, it is a pretty minor thing. But I have to tell you, it's one of the programs we undertook that received the most press and the most attention, both inside and outside the company. People say that $65 isn't a lot of money, but I'll tell you what—if Donald Trump is walking down the street and he sees three twenties and a five on the sidewalk, he probably bends down and picks them up.

But, as ever, we had to worry about whether the employees would even believe us when we told them how we measured them. They had been lied to so much by previous managements that we would have been irresponsible to imagine they would accept any measurement we chose.

So we let the U.S. government do our work. We put in our plan a measurement of on-time percentage taken by the Department of Transportation. The employees would trust the measurement done by the government, and we wouldn't be able to wriggle out of paying them a bonus, which is what they were certainly going to expect us to do. (I'll fill you in on the complete details of Make Reliability a Reality in Chapter 5.)

So we identified our goal—reliability—and put it in our plan.

Working Together: The People Plan

Finally, I borrowed a term from my old boss, Phil Condit, who had led the 777 program when I worked at The Boeing Company. We designed a separate portion of the Go Forward Plan that dealt with the most important part of the turnaround we wanted to make: the Continental corporate culture. The environment was so bad that regardless of marketing strategies, financial plans, and reliability incentives, there weren't going to be any improvements in Continental's operations until we stopped treating people the way we had been treating them and got them to start working together. You just can't be successful in any kind of business without teamwork. A football team can't be successful if it doesn't work together; a family can't be successful if the people are sniping at each other. No group can be successful when the team members work against each other instead of together. If you have winners and losers *inside* the organization, you can't focus on beating the competition *outside* the organization. You have to beat the outside competition and reward your people for that success.

So part of our plan—and it was vague at this point, even though over the long term it was by far the most important part of the plan—was to make it a corporate goal to change how people treated each other: to find ways to measure and reward cooperation rather than infighting, to encourage and reward trust and confidence. That was the only real solution to our problems in the long run. Chapter 6 will detail how we made Working Together our priority.

Greg and I hashed this out over several meetings. We ran our ideas by the chairman of the board, by coworkers we trusted, by friends and family. And when the board meeting came, I figured I was as ready as I was ever going to be.

Taking It to the Board

We went to the board meeting. I stood in front of that board and told them about our plan, about how Greg and I had come up with a way to take a company that hadn't made a damned nickel in a decade and get it to turn a profit in our first year, about the change in marketing, about working together and making the company reliable, about turning out a good product. The board didn't have much choice but to like the Go Forward Plan. The company was in serious trouble, and a return to basics seemed to be the only way out. The appropriate people went over it, and then the chairman asked me to excuse myself from the meeting so the board could discuss the exit of my predecessor. I excused myself.

An hour or so later he came to get me.

"Gordon," he said. "We've decided we're not going to name a chief executive. We're going to have an 'office of the chairman,' and you'll still be president."

I consider it a great testimonial to skull design that my head did not at that moment explode.

I said, "That's a mistake. That's no way to run a company. I won't accept that. I want to talk to the board." He agreed. I marched into the boardroom.

I didn't take a lot of their time. I just told them: "You know that $45 million profit? You know that new company we're talking about? You know the solution to all those problems? Well, you're not going to get any of it. Without a leader, we're sunk. Without someone running point on this play, we can forget the whole thing.

"None of this happens unless you pick a person to be chief executive of this company. None of that comes true unless we change how this company runs—starting today.

"And that takes a leader." I looked around. I asked out loud: "Is anyone here prepared to step forward and lead this company?"

Squirming, but no hands.

I turned to David Bonderman, and I said, "David, can you come here full time and be the leader of Continental Airlines?"

He said he couldn't do that.

So I said, "Well, you'd better get somebody in the next two weeks, because that's about how long we've got. This place is going nowhere fast, and in about two weeks it's going to come apart at the seams. You can pick me—you may not think I'm the guy, but I am the guy.

"But if not, you'd better pick somebody else fast. I'm the chief operating officer, and I'll stand there and ring all the buzzers and bells and bring the engine ahead two-thirds or whatever you tell me to do, but you pick the direction. If you don't like my direction, pick one of your own. But somebody had better run this company, because it is not going to last long without direction. You don't believe me? We've got two Bain and Company partners here. They specialize in turnarounds. Ask them what their experience has been in turnarounds where there is no chief executive."

Board members were not convinced. One brought up other companies that had engineered slow turnarounds over long periods with committees at the helm—for example, Sears and IBM.

I said, "This is not Sears or IBM, where they have a huge amount of corporate momentum to carry them forward while they think things through. This is a failing company that needs a strong leader. And no 'office of something' ever led anybody. Some individual stands up and says 'I'm the guy, here's where we're going.' "

The chairman asked me to excuse myself from the room. I went and had a seat outside. I had said my piece. Now it was up to them.

And I was at peace. Because, as I said, step number one in problem solving is figuring out who's got the problem. If they didn't listen to me and decided to let Continental slip into the abyss, I had done all I could do. I wasn't the guy who fired the CEO without a replacement. I didn't own a company on the brink of disaster and have nobody in mind to fix it. That was *them*. I had a contract, a nice cash bonus in the bank from not jumping to United, and peace of mind. If they wanted me to remain chief operating officer and wait for my boss to tell me what to do, I'd be willing to do that for the next month or two or however long it took the company to collapse. But I had done my best.

They may have thought I had leveraged them. But in fact, they had leveraged themselves. A decade of chaos will do that. Companies fail because they get themselves into positions where they can't get leaders, and if they do get leaders there's so much infighting that somebody is always sniping against whoever's trying to emerge.

I sat there another hour and a half. Then the chairman came out and said, "Okay Gordon, you're it. You're the guy. We picked you."

I didn't let it damage my ego that I wasn't captain by acclamation, that I was a kind of leveraged captain. I was the captain. I was in the left seat. It was my airplane, and it was going to fly or not on my leg. I had my chance.

The board members all shook my hand and flew home. I had only one minor thing left to do: I had to figure out how to actually get this aircraft in the air.

The Key: Actual Change

Okay, I had convinced the board that I needed to be in charge, and they handed me the controls. I'm the guy who makes the final decisions. I'm the captain. I'm the pilot. I'm steering. As pilots say about a flight segment, this is my leg.

At Continental, however, being installed in the left seat wasn't necessarily a guarantee of success. In fact, if the past was any indication, it was closer to a guarantee of failure. Sure, I had convinced the board. But the employees? They were another story.

Here I was, the tenth guy in charge in a decade, and the nine previous guys had misinformed them, taken money from them, blamed the company's problems on them, and done just about everything wrong a management team can do to a group of employees. They had no reason to believe I was going to do any better job than the previous nine, and in fact they had plenty of pretty good reasons to believe I wouldn't. After all, most employees are smart. They can see trends just like anybody else. Continental had been through 10 leaders in the previous 10 years, and as they saw it the damn plane just never seemed to go straight no matter who was flying it. The employees of Continental have to be excused for figuring I wasn't going to be much different. In fact, I'd have been worried about any employee who didn't look at me with some degree of suspicion. You want employees who learn, employees who can take what's happened before and adjust their behavior to adapt. Continental had good employees—they had adapted pretty well to Continental as a place where management changed with the seasons.

And if the people in charge of their airline had been hiring people who didn't find a way to heal their broken company, there was no reason to believe number 10 was suddenly going to be magic.

Rule one is, you have to accept that. Employees of a chronically broken company are kind of like abused children, and any new management team has to view itself like a new adoptive parent.

You might have the best intentions in the world. You may be the exact person to stabilize the lives of these children and supply them with three meals a day, loving-kindness, a college education, and a Shetland pony, but when they first meet you they're not going to trust you. Their experience with adults is all bad, and just by being an adult you get their mistrust and disrespect. They figure you're gonna whack them around and yell at them and do all kinds of terrible things to them, just like the others they've known. And they're right to feel that way. It makes sense.

I had to figure on this. I had to figure they weren't going to rally around my ideas without some good reason to trust that I was going to be different.

So I made showing them I was different my first priority.

Making an Airplane out of Tinkertoys

I got a great lesson in how to strongly take charge and start making changes when I was a lieutenant in the Navy. I was sent to Wright Patterson Air Force Base in Ohio for a leadership management course. There were about 20 of us in the course, divided into groups of four. They put three groups, including mine, at the front of a conference room and made the others into an audience.

In front of each group, they dumped a big box of Tinkertoys—probably 500 or 600 Tinkertoys to a box. Then, on a table in the middle of the room, they brought out this incredibly elaborate Tinkertoy model of an airplane. It was fabulous—all kinds of gewgaws and bells and whistles. It was almost like a Salvador Dalí conception of an airplane.

The moderator said, "Okay guys, there's three teams. First team that replicates this model wins." Then they sat back to watch.

One of the guys I was with said, "Okay, how do we get started? I know, let's draw that model out on a plan, and then we'll follow our plan. We'll know exactly how to do it after we make a plan."

The other guy said, "Wait, I think we ought to see if we can segregate all the pieces first and then we'll get the plan. When we know where the inventory is and all the stuff, we'll know the plan, and we'll really catch up and beat the other guys when it comes to putting it all together in the manufacturing stage."

I said, "How about this: You take the front third, you take the middle third, and I'll take the back third, and let's just start making what we think is the airplane. The fourth guy will start segregating the pieces, and we'll solve our problems as we come to them." The other three thought that sounded good, so we started building an airplane. All the other teams were still discussing what they might do and how they might do it. Our team was beginning to make the airplane.

The moderator stopped us right there. This, he said, was a perfect example of how to get started: Have somebody step up with a workable starting plan and then *get started*. That's how you get your arms around something that big. You break it down into manageable pieces and you start a process as a team. You divide up responsibilities and just start working.

There's an old question: How do you eat an elephant? The answer is, one bite at a time, and the sooner you start, the faster it gets eaten.

But at Continental, we had a lot of elephant to eat and plenty of places we could have started. People in the military say that it's good to be able to take the hill, but it helps to know which hill to take.

So, where were we going to start?

Well, I have to tell you that knowing how to fly airplanes myself (I'm type rated on the Boeing 757 as well as other airplanes) helps me explain a lot of things to a lot of people in this business. And understanding your business helps you to decide which hills to take, as it were.

Getting Everybody's Attention

Direction has to come from somewhere, and it's got to be from the top. That's why I made my little speech to the board in November. I'm the airline's most visible employee, and its most powerful. When something goes right—or wrong—the employees and the customers know exactly where to look for an explanation. There's no committee or office or faceless gang making decisions. When we had to lay off workers in Los Angeles, I was the guy who stood up and explained it and took the heat; if we had gone bankrupt, it would have been me on TV trying to explain to reporters what went wrong. And when we won the Airline of the Year award, I was the one who got my picture taken. I told everybody who would listen that this was a team effort and that the Continental employees were the ones who deserved the credit, but it was my picture in the *New York Times,* not theirs. So I'm the chief, and I don't try to pretend I'm not. As I said, the first thing I did was kick open those doors to the executive suite. I wanted everybody to know: The old chief executive is gone. Gordon and his new team are in charge now, and things are going to be different.

Come Up and See Me Sometime

Getting those doors open wasn't quite enough, though. We had to entice employees into that suite, where they had been unwelcome for so long. So we instituted open houses. On the last working day of the month, we would invite any employees who wanted to explore the twentieth floor of our headquarters to come by, have a tour, and visit with me. We had food and drinks for them, and it was amazing to see them come by. They would timidly put a foot through that once-locked doorway as though a laser might slice it off.

I gave tours, chatted with them, and did everything possible to dispel the aura of fear and terror that those offices had held. They could talk to all members of upper management and ask questions: "Is this $65 bonus for real?" "Do you really think you can fix this company?" They peered around corners and got an idea of what things looked like up there. They could sit in my chair. I even had a little joke. I'd take a group of employees into my office, open up the closet, and say, "You see? Frank's not here." Frank Lorenzo had left Continental years before; the legacy of cost cutting and infighting of that era was finally gone, and I wanted them to know it.

Those open houses took a giant step toward showing employees that things were actually changing at Continental. (These open houses, by the way, are still going on, in a larger and different format, and have been every month for more than three years now.) For a decade, the employees had been kept out of the top offices— now they were being invited in. Things were changing.

Make Yourself Comfortable

Another thing we did immediately, which may seem minor, was to institute casual days. One great way to lessen the strife between managers and employees is to remove some of the differences between them. If one of the key points is making everybody see that they're on the same team, breaking down any barrier helps. So right off the bat I instituted casual-dress Fridays for everybody except those directly dealing with customers. I wanted to remove the idea that just because somebody puts on a tie or wears a suit and becomes a manager he or she automatically becomes a jerk. At least one day a week, the managers would be harder to spot, if nothing else, and people would be less inclined to direct hostility based solely on clothing. Managers would seem more approachable and less scary.

Plus, of course, giving people the chance to be a little more casual and relaxed never hurt morale. We expanded casual days by turning Houston's incredibly hot summers into an entire season of casual dress, and it's only helped. I know I'm a lot more comfortable in a golf shirt than in a dress shirt and tie.

True, I had to stand up on my hind legs and make a little noise about casual days. Some managers decided that their departments would stick with the old dress-up rules. (One of the things you always find in change is that some people kind of like things the way they are and don't want to make *any* change, even the smallest.) Well, I explained to them that if they really wanted to keep dressing up, nobody was going to stop them—casual days never meant you *had* to dress casually. But as far as giving their employees the option, that was not up for discussion. This was a corporate change, not a departmental change. They didn't have a choice: Their employees were going to be allowed the option to dress down on Fridays, and if I heard there was a problem they weren't going to like it.

After a very short while, I stopped hearing about any problems.

Just like the employees, managers were getting the lesson. Things were different.

Remember that I said that this all starts from the top down? I knew that the way I acted, the way I treated the people who reported directly to me, was going to set the tone that would filter down to every employee at Continental. So that's where I started. I demonstrated to them that things were going to be different in the simplest way imaginable: I sat in a different chair during the managers meetings. During the previous regime, and during every regime before that for more than a decade, the chief executive sat at the head of a long table. His closest cronies sat by his side, and on down at the other end of the table sat the people who had the most to fear for their jobs.

At the first managers meeting we had after I took over, I sat down at the middle of the table. Part of the reason was simple necessity: I don't hear so well, so it's better for me to be at the middle of the table. That way nobody is too far from me. But more important, if you want a place to have a collegial atmosphere, you have to do something to make it collegial. Mixing up the seating arrangement is one easy, tiny thing to do.

In addition, we made a simple rule that meetings would start and end on schedule. On time. People were encouraged to stand up and leave a meeting that ran overtime. Like our product, we were going to be reliable and predictable.

The result of those incredibly simple actions was to shake people up. Sure, I ran the meeting the way I run a meeting rather than the way my predecessor would have, but we telegraphed a straightforward message to every manager before they even sat down: Things are *different*. Everybody had to think about where they were going to sit rather than just sit where they expected to sit. And they got the message: Whether it's sitting in different spots in the meeting room, wearing different clothes, or walking through the doors without having an armed escort, things are different.

I told managers to follow up in their own departments. Do something different—*anything* different. And be on time. Change the time of a regular meeting; change the furniture in a break room; buy pizza. In some way, they needed to telegraph to their employees that things had changed.

And Stop Smoking

I did a few other quick but high-profile things, too. For one thing, I made all Continental buildings nonsmoking buildings, and I made all our North and South American flights nonsmoking flights. I thought we ought to be a nonsmoking airline, so we became a nonsmoking airline, and that was it. That meant no smoking anywhere in company offices worldwide. Not just our airplanes, but everywhere.

Of course, a lot of people didn't believe this was smart. The people in the marketing department said we'd lose business on our flights to Costa Rica and the Mexico beaches. But I hung tough: "I know what I want, and I don't want any smoking in our company or on our planes. We are the major airline flying those routes, and we won't lose our customers." We eliminated smoking, and we didn't lose our customers.

When we extended the edict to Europe and ultimately worldwide, it was the same thing—a lot of marketing people writhing around on the carpet, gnashing their teeth, sure we were going to lose a lot of money on flights to France and Spain.

We didn't lose a nickel.

I suppose if my no-smoking rule had caused the bottom to fall out of our European markets, I'd have had to admit I was wrong—and I would have. Not admitting mistakes is what causes organizations to get sick.

But it turned out I wasn't wrong. And more important, I was letting people know that things were changing, and I was willing to *do* something and take the consequences. That inspires trust, and when employees trust you, you have a powerful workforce.

Actually Doing Something

I'm an executive. That means I execute—I *do* stuff. I don't just talk, I don't sit around and make pronouncements, I get things done. Greg does, too, and that's what we expect from all our offi-cers. That's another thing that seems pretty simple, but nothing could be more important.

Good ideas are everywhere—the average person on a street cor-ner has more good ideas than he or she knows what to do with, and new ones arrive every 15 minutes. Same with me, same with you, same with every person who works at or runs every business in the world. A couple of the ideas that helped turn Continental around, in fact, were already bubbling around Continental before I got there. The trick is to translate a good idea into action.

Think of a football team. Everybody knows the goal: Get the ball across the goal line. The key is figuring out what 11 different guys need to do to make that happen—what plays to call, what to practice, what will work. And then, of course, to motivate your team to actually go out there and do it.

Once I had the employees' attention—by just plain doing a few things myself, however minor—the immediate goal was to get them involved in doing things themselves that would make demonstrable changes as fast as possible. Once they saw that they could actually help change the place where they worked, making more (and more difficult) changes would be that much easier.

Burning the Book

Getting through to employees who don't trust you takes a long time, and we kept doing things to show them their company had changed, changed in every particular. One of the best ways we showed this was by literally burning the manual that described the particulars of their jobs. Every company probably ought to burn their employee manual every now and then—it is merely a repos-itory of rules that fit certain situations, and those rules eventually spread far beyond their applicability and become calcified into dumb rote.

Our employee manual was a lot worse than that. Symptomatic of an organization in which nobody trusted anybody, we had rules—specific rules—for everything from what color pencil had to be used on boarding passes to what kind of meals delayed pas-sengers were supposed to be given to what kind of fold ought to be put in a sick-day form. Even worse, it spelled out job responsibilities to such a fine degree that employees were utterly bound by arcane rules and demands, and the penalties for disobeying the rules were severe. If a person whose plane was canceled had an unrestricted full-fare ticket, that person might get a hotel room; an adjoining passenger with a less expensive ticket might get a meal voucher and a pat on the arm. It didn't matter if this policy started a war at the airport. The gate agent was not allowed to solve a problem that didn't make sense, so he or she just had to take the abuse the passengers gave and try to smile. The smiling, needless to say, had pretty much stopped.

Well, nobody likes to work like that. Nobody likes to be treated like a robot, like a little kid who can't solve a problem and make a contribution.

Very soon after I kicked open the doors to the executive suite, we took a bunch of employees and a bunch of those manuals out to the parking lot and had the employees set fire to the manuals. I have to tell you, they didn't mind doing it. And we sent word into the field that henceforth we wanted our employees to use their judgment, not follow some rigid manual. When faced with an atypical situation, employees were instructed to do what was right for the customer and right for the company. Not just blindly make the customer happy at our expense, not blindly follow procedures and needlessly upset the customers, but balance the two interests and solve the problem using good judgment.

After that we created a task team of employees to go over the entire manual and come up with guidelines that would help them—not give them rules down to the nth degree, but help them. If you start writing rules to cover every tiny eventuality, you kill your employees' creativity, their ability to solve problems. If every time they start to address a problem they think, "Jeez, if I do this the wrong way Houston's gonna be calling me and reaming me out," they stop thinking. They figure, well, let Houston tell me what to do in that case.

But we're doing the opposite. We're saying, use these guidelines, think things through, and unless you do something completely out of bounds, you don't have to worry about hearing from Houston. Houston wants you to do your job. Houston wants to leave you alone unless you need help. And believe it or not, if you need help, Houston wants to help you.

Yes, things were looking different.

Shake a Tail Feather

One more example of making sure things looked different was something we undertook a little further into our turnaround, once it looked like we were probably going to manage to stay in business a few more months and could actually look further ahead than tomorrow's cash receipts.

We got our planes painted.

To understand the power of this action, you need to know a little about the history of Continental. Before the explosive deregulation era of the late 1970s and 1980s, Continental, "The proud bird with the golden tail," was one of the country's most respected airlines. During deregulation, however, the airline was part of the merger mania that gripped the industry, and Continental was one of the many airlines bought by Frank Lorenzo's Texas International Airlines, which also bought People Express, New York Air, and Frontier Airlines, merging them all under the name Continental.

Continental had also tried to create a new image with a completely new paint scheme but had repainted less than half the fleet because of cost-cutting pressure. You could look out the window at a Continental terminal and see any number of different-looking kinds of airplanes pull up. When I took over, the only thing consistent in our paint schemes was that they were all peeling.

Once we had taken just a few steps back from the precipice of bankruptcy, I issued an order: Every single one of our planes was going to have a new paint job by July 1. Every single one. There were going to be no exceptions.

In my opinion, if you want people to know things have changed around your house, you can knock down the house and completely rebuild it, or you can give it a new paint job. The new paint job is a lot easier, and it works just as well. I felt that our planes looking professional and identical would send a message to employees, customers, and competitors alike that we were running a better operation around here. It was a statement the new management team felt we had to make. We weren't going to be the residues of five different airlines any more—we were going to be one airline, and a damn good one. We would paint our planes to reflect that.

The people in operations said it just wasn't possible. They were starting to implement changes of their own. They were trying to get control of all kinds of processes that had been out of control for a decade, and getting some 200 planes painted was something they just couldn't do.

I did something I rarely do: I made a threat.

I said, "Yes you can, and you know why?"

They wanted to know why.

I said, "Because I have a Beretta at home with a 15-round magazine, and if you don't get those airplanes painted by July 1 I'm going to come in here and empty the clip. You're wonderful people and I love you, but you're going to get those airplanes painted or I'm going to shoot every last one of you."

Well, they got the last airplane painted on June 30, and the entire industry—including all of our own employees—could see we were running a different ship. Mind you, I don't recommend threatening to shoot your employees—it won't work more than once or twice, and if you have to do it more than that you're probably not doing a very good job.

But I think they got the point. Things were going to be different, and everybody was going to know it. I wasn't messing around.

Spreading the Word

As we got those projects under way, the upper management team spread the word. We made sure every employee in the organization understood that the Go Forward Plan was our blueprint—and why. Greg Brenneman and I and other top-level managers spread the word on the Go Forward Plan throughout the company. In meetings at virtually every site in the company we introduced employees to the plan, explaining how it addressed not just some but all of Continental's problems.

They were already hearing about some of it. Certainly they were hearing about the $65 on-time pay bonus. They had heard about the new open-door policy regarding the executive suite. They had heard about the burning of the employee manual. They knew things were supposed to be different, but they needed more information.

So we went out and told them.

Many of these meetings started out pretty rough. People didn't trust us, and you couldn't blame them. To the obvious question— What makes you different and why should we trust you?—I had a pretty simple question in response: What are your options? Where's it going to get you by resisting? One definition of insanity is doing the same thing over and over in exactly the same way and expecting different results. The employees could have resisted, figuring that somehow maybe things would get better if they just kept out of the way and let the new regime run its course. But that's what they had been doing for a decade, and things never got any better. We had gone to a great deal of trouble to show them that this time things were *really* different. We could only emphasize that giving us a shot couldn't hurt them, and it could help them a lot—by earning them $65 monthly in on-time bonuses, by improving where they worked generally . . . by saving their company.

We tried, during those meetings, to accept their skepticism. It only made sense. They used to attend employee meetings in droves, because they never knew what was happening and that was the only way to get information. Now that my gang was in charge, employees were showing up and giving us at least half an ear. We tried to reward them for that.

But that didn't mean we let them trash us. We'd tell them about the Go Forward Plan. We'd patiently answer their questions. And if they wanted to say, "Well, you're just like all the others, you won't last long, I don't believe it," we'd listen. We couldn't really blame them. We'd make our pitch and hope to reach as many as we could. To be honest, employees who are too embittered and angry to listen—even with just cause—would probably be better off someplace else, and we'd probably be better off not trying to make them happy. Sometimes a company and an employee just don't mesh.

But the vast majority of employees were just so happy to have someone telling them the truth that they were willing to come along with us, at least to give us a try.

And we did tell the truth. We told them that the wage snapbacks they had been promised as part of the bankruptcy proceedings would have to be put off. We told them why, and we told them straightforwardly. We told them there would probably be some lay-offs. We told them we would have to close down a maintenance facility in Los Angeles and probably a hub in Greensboro. (I'll tell you all about it in the next chapter.) But we also shared what things would look like once our plans took effect. And most of them were willing to give us a shot. As I said, what were their options?

But I only went so far. We were having a meeting one day in Newark, and it was a bad time. Newark was one of the more difficult places—our people went to work every day expecting to get yelled at by passengers. (And, meaning no disrespect, New Yorkers do a pretty good job of yelling at people once they get started.) These employees had put up with about as much as anybody had, so they weren't exactly surly, I'd say, but they weren't cheerful, either. I was down in the pilot crew room, talking informally with 20 or 30 pilots gathered there. A pilot stood up, and he was full of objections. He'd heard it all before, and he just wasn't going to buy it. He wanted to be paid more, he didn't like this, he wanted that. I couldn't blame him, but just the same, I couldn't give him what he wanted or fix the past injustices he'd suffered.

I explained. That was all rearview mirror stuff he was talking about, I told him. I can't go backward and fix what was done before I was here, but I'm going to do everything I can to make things right, to make things better as we go forward. But I'm concentrating on what I can see out the front of the plane. There's no rearview mirror in the cockpit of most airplanes. I'd rather look forward. I told him again about the Go Forward Plan and what it would do for the company.

He still wasn't buying it. He said, "You're the tenth guy I've seen, and you sound good, but let me tell you, this goddamn place is broken. There ain't nobody gonna fix it, including you. So it doesn't matter what you say, this place is going to fail."

I shook my head. I said, "I don't know about you, but I don't know of any self-respecting pilot, regardless of what predicament the airplane is in—it's on fire, it's upside down, it's spinning around, whatever—who stops trying to fly the airplane before it hits the ground. You don't ever give up and say, screw it, it's over, I can't do anything. That's a decision made only by the ground, when you smash into it. Until then you keep working.

"When I get on an airplane, I always say hello in the cockpit. I look at the captain. If I don't like the way the captain looks or something else doesn't feel safe, I can always get off the plane, since we haven't yet left the gate."

I told the pilot, "Listen, I'm the captain for this company now. This is what we're going to do. I'm flying, it's my leg. If you don't like the way I'm working, the jetway is still attached. You can step off if you want to. But I'm going to fly this company where it's going."

You see? I can understand his frustration. I can understand a lot of questions and uncertainty. But just standing around saying we're going down, I won't listen to that. So if that's how the guy feels, maybe he'd better get off the plane.

He didn't. He sat down, and we went on. And I think he knew who was flying the plane.

Leading the Way

And so did everybody else after a short while.

That's what I was doing: helping lead the way. We deeply believed that our only hope, as we had told the board, lay in somebody visible, somebody trustworthy, somebody people could believe in.

My definition of a leader is pretty simple. The leader is the person who looks at the big picture and says, "Okay, everybody, go *west!*"

Now west is precisely a compass heading of 270 degrees, but anywhere from about 240 to 300 degrees is heading generally west. So if I say go west, and one person is heading out at 295 degrees, that's okay with me. He or she is kind of headed in the right direction.

Maybe you're down here at 245 degrees, which is southwest. That's okay with me, too. I don't want to precisely determine how you interpret it when I say, hey, let's go west. You see things a certain way, and what's happening in your department and what's happening to you today may affect what has to happen when I say go west.

On the other hand, the guy who's going 090 degrees, which is due east, is a problem. You have to catch him and readjust his thinking so he's going the right way. If he won't be readjusted, I say no way, buster: You either head west or get out of here. Maybe he needs to go to a company that's headed east, where he'll fit in, but he's not going to work out here unless he can go west with the rest of us.

I'm not saying everybody has to be marching in lockstep—in fact, that's exactly what we *don't* want. We want people doing their jobs with a minimum of interference from their bosses. That's why we burned the employee manual. But that doesn't mean you're not the leader.

In fact, that's what leadership is. Your real job as boss—my real job as chief executive—is to *let* people do their jobs. It's to assemble the right team, set the big-picture direction, communicate that, and then *get out of the way*. If employees have a problem or if something is really bothering them, you help them with that. You say, "Okay, you go back to work and I'll get this straightened out for you." That's what bosses are for. A boss's job—a leader's job— is to facilitate, not to control. You have to trust people to do their jobs. That's the strongest leadership there is.

Trusting your employees.

As I said, things were finally looking different at Continental.

Fly to Win,

or You Can Make a Pizza So Cheap Nobody Wants to Eat It

Think of a patient in an emergency room. What does the emergency team do when they first get a patient? Same two things, every time: Check the breathing, check the pulse. Nothing else is going to mean much if the breathing and the pulse aren't there. Maybe you have just the thing for a rash on the leg; maybe you have a great new experimental cure for lung cancer; maybe you've even found a cure for AIDS. But, whatever the problem, if there's no respiration or pulse—or if the patient is bleeding to death—all the miracle cures in the world aren't going to help. So you have to focus in like a laser on the things that, if not dealt with immediately, will put you out of business, will kill the patient before the long-term therapies can kick in.

We were that patient. Our pulse was money, and I'll tell you all about how we stanched the bleeding and gave Continental a heart massage in the next chapter.

Our breathing was our product, and it was lousy. That was the other thing we needed to start fixing immediately.

We could see from the start that it wasn't going to be easy. We had problems with *where* we flew, we had problems with *what* we flew, we had problems with *how* we flew . . . and we had problems with who was flying.

Fly to Win is about our market: determining our target market, making our product fit that market in price and position, finding the amenities our customers want and will pay for, and making it easy for our customers to get our product.

Stop Doing Things That Lose Money

It was easy to get lost trying to scramble around and decide what had to be done first. So we started having meetings, me and a lot of the people I had hired to get us out of this mess. We'd talk about this, we'd talk about that, and then in one meeting, Greg Brenneman finally said, "Well, why don't we just stop doing things that lose money?"

You know, it was a damn good idea. It was a remarkably good idea. And when people ask me to outline the first step in recovering from the kind of disaster area we had become, that's what I tell them. It's what I suggest they do if they find themselves in a similar spot: Stop doing things that lose money.

Take a moment to consider why your company is in business in the first place. Yes, certainly because you love the business of flying airplanes or making pizzas or fixing watches or selling shoes or whatever it is you're doing. But if you're in business, you're in it to make a profit. You've got to be; otherwise you're going out of business.

Get the Money

The first step in making a profit is to stop doing the things that are specifically causing you *not* to make a profit. Stop doing the things that *lose* money. That is, stop selling the stuff that nobody wants to buy at a price that will generate a fair profit. It seems simple, yet that clear-cut statement got us all to stop and look at what we were doing.

As for what we were doing that was losing money, well, we had a lot of choices. We had been losing money for a decade and a half, and just about everything we did wasn't working.

Eighteen percent of our flying was cash negative. Do you get that? That means you could put the parking brake on, evacuate the airplane, and lose less money than you would by flying the damn thing.

To stop losing money, one of the things we had to do was stop flying that 18 percent of our routes. Which meant we had to take a good hard look at where we flew, how often we flew, and how we flew. Which immediately brought up Continental Lite, our low-cost airline within an airline that had become, sadly, a colossal failure.

Don't Be Telling People What They Want to Buy

In the early 1990s, Continental, with its profound focus on cost saving, still wasn't making a profit, and it still wasn't a successful airline. Companies like Southwest were doing a better job of providing cheap fares to places people wanted to fly.

So the people running the Continental got the idea to turn a third of our operation into an all-cheap-seat airline. That is, if Southwest could run a low-cost airline and make money, then maybe we needed to start our own low-cost airline. That's what we did.

We invented a product called Continental Lite, and we defined it.

Continental Lite, we said, would have "Continental Lite" written on the side of the airplane to identify it. A good start.

To keep the costs per available seat mile low, we'll take out the 12 first-class seats and replace them with 18 coach seats. That way we'll get six extra seats. Divide that by the cost, which remained the same, and we'll reduce our average seat cost per mile commensurately.

That's good.

We'll increase airplane use by flying more each day, and we won't spend a lot of time on the ground, so we'll start out real early in the morning and we'll finish up real late at night. If the quick turnaround means the plane might not be as clean as it ought to be, well, the flight will be cheap, so who's going to care?

So far so good. We'll be flying a lot more miles, with a greater number of seats, at the same cost for the airplane.

But according to our projections, we needed still more cost reductions for CAL Lite to turn a profit. So we looked at the food budget. We figured that we could save $30 million by not serving food on flights of less than 2½ hours.

Congratulations! We had our airline. Continental Lite would be an airline of flights of less than 2½ hours; it would have all coach seats; it would have no food; and it would say Continental Lite on the side of the airplane.

It was a great definition. Continental deployed 100 airplanes across the United States with that configuration of seats, that paint job, and empty galleys and waited for the money to roll in.

Oops

There was only one problem: People said, "I don't want to buy that. That is not what I want."

It doesn't take much to see why not. Take a look at CAL Lite from the perspective of the customer flying, say, from Houston to Jacksonville. Now remember, CAL Lite flies all day long with little time on the ground, and it starts real early to take advantage of that. So to grab a 7 A.M. flight to Jacksonville, the passenger's got to get up at 5 and rush to the airport to catch a flight. It takes off at 7, lasts 2½ hours, and arrives at 10:30 in the morning Jacksonville time.

But the passenger hasn't had a thing to eat.

And he's forgotten that it says Continental Lite on the side of the airplane because his stomach can't read the sign. He's annoyed because he's hungry and he doesn't feel well. And he doesn't feel very happy as he's getting off of our airplane, which, of course, he identifies with Continental. And because he's annoyed, he's short with the flight attendant, who begins to identify annoyed passengers with Continental Lite, which might in turn make the flight attendant less than cheerful toward the next passenger.

And the following week, that passenger's boss is sending him to Los Angeles. His company is paying for the ticket, but this person is not going to pick up the phone and call Continental for their full-service flight. He's going to go on somebody else's airplane, because he remembers how he felt the last time he flew Continental. Although we have two separate products—full service and bare bones—the passenger remembers only that when he flew Continental he didn't feel good about it.

That's what I'm talking about when I say you can't tell people what they're supposed to buy.

Continental Lite is the kind of product you get when you use backward thinking, when you define your products by what would be really nice to sell. It would have solved a great problem for Continental Airlines if we could have run those 100 airplanes with their coach seats and no food and 2½-hour flights. It would have given us a nice revenue stream and a way to compete in a market we were having trouble competing in.

The problem was, no matter how great it would have been if we could sell that product, it still wasn't a product people wanted to buy.

By chasing away customers, we lost more money than we made. That's the kind of backward thinking we got by letting the accountants tell us what we needed to sell. We created products according to our needs and tried to tell customers to buy them.

But customers are very smart. And they said to us, "No, no, no. *We'll* tell *you* what we want, and then you provide it at a competitive price."

Or I'm sure they *would* have told us that if we had been the type of airline that listened to its customers. Given no other options, they did what customers always do: They voted with their feet. Or in the case of airlines, their fannies. And they put those fannies in the seats of other airlines.

The problem, as I've said, was that Continental believed there was one way and one way alone to win, and that was to decrease costs. Everything was measured in terms of cost per available seat mile (the standard measure of costs in the industry), so that's what people did—they reduced costs.

How Running an Airline Is Like Making a Pizza

Say you're running a pizza place, and your boss says, "The only way we're going to be a successful pizza place and get customers and make money and win is to make a cheaper pizza." What are you going to do?

If you want to win, if you want to be rewarded by your boss, you're going to keep trying to make a cheaper pizza. You're going to make thinner and thinner crusts to save on flour. You're going to use less and less sauce to save on tomatoes. You'll buy canned rather than fresh vegetables, frozen rather than fresh meat. Sooner or later somebody's going to get the bright idea to take half the cheese off, or all the cheese off, or make the pizza out of cardboard.

Well, you can make a pizza so cheap nobody wants to eat it.

And you can make an airline so cheap nobody wants to fly it. Trust me on this—we did it. So, you're going to be making these incredibly cheap pizzas, and the people in the cost department, the people in the supply department, are going to be happy and high-fiving each other: They'll be saying, We're winning back here! And meanwhile, up front, where the orders have dried up and the customers are complaining and no pizzas are selling, you're not winning at all.

In the end it's like a canoe—the back end can't be winning while the front end is sinking. If any part of the canoe is sinking, nobody cares how good the rest of the canoe is doing, because the whole thing is going to sink.

Figuring Out What People *Do* Want to Buy

We had learned the hard way that just having the cheapest possible fares wasn't making us win. It wasn't making us a very good airline. In fact, it was making us lousy, and people didn't want to buy what we offered.

We started looking at our operation from the perspective of what people might actually want. Not surprisingly, we started to see things in a different way.

Our first moves were pretty simple. We realized that all those low-cost fares were doing worse mischief than just pushing down our prices. They were flooding the market with seats, thereby *keeping* the prices down. We were flying countless flights a day between cities that had very little need for intercity transportation. That is, we were competing with ourselves to provide a service people didn't want in order to take them where they didn't want to go.

Fly Where People Want to Go

We quickly changed course. We made it a rule to fly to places people wanted to go. Here are a couple examples.

We used to fly about six flights a day between Greensboro, North Carolina, where we had a hub, and Greenville, South Carolina. We looked at that run and I joked, "Whose girlfriend lives in Greenville?" Neither of those cities is big enough to generate that kind of traffic, yet we were flying between them constantly. We immediately cut back on those flights.

It was easy to understand how it had happened—some business school grad had probably figured that the way to increase market share was to make it easy for people to fly and give them a lot of flights per day. We'd choose some market that looked underserved, flood it with flights, and wait for the cash to start pouring in. The problem was, of course, those markets weren't underserved—they were markets in which people didn't need more service. Nonetheless, we'd be a big player in a tiny market, and we'd have the market share somebody thought was important: We'd have 90 percent of the Greensboro-to-Greenville market. We'd be losing money, but that didn't matter because our business school grad was worried about market share.

The thing is, the answer isn't market share—the answer is finding a way to make a *profit*.

Here's another example. In Florida, we found some shocking things going on. We had $49 introductory rates on intra-Florida fares. Well, those rates were six months old. Also, we had started another low-cost strategy, the Add-a-Penny-Add-a-Pal fare, to compete with Southwest's Friends Fly Free fares, which essentially allowed passengers to fly anywhere within the state of Florida for $24.50.

Well, I said, that's just crazy. That's less than a cab fare to La Guardia from midtown Manhattan. A lot of these fares were introductory offers, and I finally said, "By this point, haven't we been introduced long enough? We have to cut this stuff out."

And it was *everywhere*. We were flying between Kansas City and Omaha, for crying out loud. What on earth were we, a carrier with hubs in Houston, Newark, and Cleveland (and at that point still

Greensboro, North Carolina), doing flying between Kansas City and Omaha? That's somebody else's turf. Nobody knew us there; if there were 70 passengers looking to fly between those cities, 65 of them were on some other plane. Why were we trying to compete for those few passengers? Why waste a lot of resources trying to pry passengers off someone else's planes and onto ours?

So we pulled out of that market. We still flew to Kansas City and Omaha, but we flew there from Houston, where we had a hub and could compete, where people knew us.

Why were we there in the first place? Probably the old testosterone factor—the airline business has always been run by guys with big egos, and they compete to have the most flights, the most airplanes, the biggest market share. The problem with that philosophy is you can win all those little games and still come out losing money. We were doing that in a big way.

We found situations like that throughout our system. Too many flights to places nobody needed to go and prices too low to make a profit on the passengers we had.

So we cut that out. We had hired Bonnie Reitz to head our sales and distribution department and David Siegel in our scheduling department, and they started working together with Ben Baldanza, whom we had hired to work on pricing, and together they started figuring things out.

David Siegel, who worked in scheduling, said there were a good 15 percent too many seats out there. We had to determine how to reduce them. We discovered, not surprisingly, that about a third of our short-haul system, mostly the Continental Lite portion, accounted for about 70 percent of our losses. So those flights were the first to go. Between January and March of 1995, we dropped our Continental Lite flights from more than 500 per day to fewer than 100.

We stopped running a lot of those Greensboro-to-Greenville-type flights and started concentrating on the flights that would turn a profit, which were mainly flights out of our hubs: Houston, Cleveland, and Newark. We had learned for a second time one of the main lessons of the airline industry: that the best way to run an airline is with hubs that can centralize your passenger traffic, increase their options for transfers, and allow you to become a major player in a specific market.

It's a pretty simple affair, really. Once we were getting out of the point-to-point business, choosing cities to serve became much easier. Take a place like Raleigh-Durham, for example. We did a little market research and found that the New York area was a key destination for that region. Well, with our Newark hub, it made perfect sense to serve Raleigh-Durham. Besides, when passengers are in Newark, they can be connecting to other flights on the eastern seaboard or to international flights with our overseas service.

Once we were serving the market to Newark, we did further research and found that the market would support flights to Cleveland and Houston (our other hubs) as well. And from those hubs, passengers could easily connect to Continental flights to other cities they wanted to go to, at reasonable fares and in reasonable times. We weren't flying from Raleigh to Kansas City or Orlando or Cincinnati, or some other city that looked like it might be good for us if people flew to. We were taking people from Raleigh-Durham to our hubs, where they wanted to go in the first place, and from where they could conveniently go other places if they wished.

With fewer seats out there, we were able to see where our prices were unnecessarily low, and we raised those prices. Suddenly, we were flying fewer planes, but making more money.

That was definitely the right direction.

Get People Working Together

A big part of every portion of our Go Forward Plan was getting people to work together—the entire final portion of the plan is called Working Together, and it's probably the most important part. We'll discuss it in detail in Chapter 6. Meanwhile, here's an example of an everyday manner in which our employees work together.

At the *old* Continental, strife was our normal way of doing things. We'd have someone like David Siegel come in and figure out how we could improve our scheduling, but the scheduling and market planning people would write a new schedule and then

basically throw it over the wall to the operations and airport people—and run. Maybe we'd have a nice new schedule with perfect
connecting banks in our hubs and flights serving cities that market research showed people wanted to fly to. Everything would
look great—only we didn't have the planes or resources to fly it.

Maybe we could fly it if we never had a plane break down. Or
we could fly it if we didn't perform routine maintenance on our
planes, or if we maintained some planes in Houston and some in,
say, Seattle. Solving any problem always caused two more, because
nobody was talking to anybody and turf wars destroyed any
progress the company might have made. There were sort of separate little silos here—the marketing silo, the operations silo, the
scheduling silo, the finance silo—and people at best tossed ideas
over each other's ramparts.

More often they shot at each other.

Well, not under the Go Forward Plan. David Siegel started
improving the scheduling and planning, but from the first meeting
he'd involve C. D. McLean and his operations people. That way he
could get crucial input as he was scheduling: Where is it best to
overnight pilots? Where is it best to leave planes overnight? Where
is a maintenance facility that can efficiently and reliably get a
plane ready to go out the next morning or do a 3,000-hour check?
Is the flying time between cities different at different times of day?
In different directions?

Once the operations people were brought into the scheduling
process, remarkable improvements started to occur. Instead of the
planners scheduling an airplane for an 8-hour layover and letting
the operations people figure out how to accomplish a 12-hour
maintenance check in that time, operations and planning people
worked together. Planners worked with the maintenance people,
the airport people, the pilots, and the flight attendants.

For example, before I got here, we somehow warehoused parts for
our A300 airplanes at our maintenance base in Greensboro, North
Carolina. Good idea—plenty of space for them there, all kinds of
good reasons for them to be there according to the operations people
whose job it is to figure out where our airplane parts go. Only here's
something our schedulers could have told them, if they had been in
the habit of communicating: *We didn't fly A300s to Greensboro.*

How smart is that? It meant we were always shipping parts to an airplane in a distant city.

Once we got people to sit down and work together, of course, they loved it. Everybody benefited, and they had to do jobs only once, instead of over and over as they kept tossing plans back and forth over each other's battlements. It meant that we could make a schedule together that worked for everybody—not one that worked well for the scheduling people but not necessarily everybody else. Everybody had a hand in the schedule, so naturally we started adhering to it.

To an airline, the schedule is its business plan. Predictably, once we had the people who actually operated the business working with the people making the business plan, things started working better.

Not only were we starting to fly to places people wanted to go, we were getting the hang of flying according to a schedule that had the support of the people who would actually have to run it— beyond accomplishing some financial goal that looked good on paper to somebody in some scheduling office.

Pretty nifty, huh?

Fly Full Planes, Not Empty Planes

Another fairly simple thing we did was to recognize that we just had too many seats up there in the sky. My predecessors in management had recognized this, and they had begun talking about it, but the company was too dysfunctional for them to actually do anything about it. Well, with the help of the new people we had hired in the scheduling and pricing arenas, we figured out some rather simple yet extremely helpful ways to change that.

We had already begun, as I said, to cut down drastically on the number of Continental Lite destinations. But in the airline business as in every other business, everything's related—solving one problem presents another. In this case, it exacerbated our overstock of seats. In the airline business we measure everything in available seat miles (ASM)—revenue per available seat mile (RASM), cost per available seat mile (CASM), and so forth. Well, we started cutting down our miles, but we still had an awful lot of available seats that we didn't know what to do with, and as the number of cities we served decreased, the number of extra seats grew.

We needed to get rid of some planes.

It didn't take a genius to look at our inventory and see what to do. We were running more different kinds of airplanes than you can imagine—747s, DC-10s, MD-80s, DC-9s, 727-200s, 737-100s, 737-200s, 737-300s, 737-500s, and these huge airplanes called A300s (the ones with the spare parts in Greensboro). They were big. They were expensive. We paid a lot of money in leases for them. And we didn't get much revenue from them.

In fact, to be honest, David Siegel, who I had moved to head of scheduling in 1994 to help us out of our morass of scheduling and route planning, figured out that we could fly those A300s and lose less money on certain flights (transcontinental flights, say), but we couldn't fly them and actually make money anywhere. Our lease payments were too high, and they just weren't economical airplanes for us to fly.

They required special maintenance procedures; they were different than any other planes we had (made by Airbus, not Boeing or Douglas); and they just weren't working out. We simply couldn't make money with A300s.

We had to get rid of them.

Getting rid of the A300s would not only reduce our inventory, it would remove the necessity of having special facilities, people, and procedures to manage that separate fleet.

Of course, you can't just take a leased airplane, give it back to the lessor, tell them you changed your mind, and walk away. We had to do a lot of work with the lessors of our A300s, and I'll tell you about that in Chapter 4, "Fund the Future." The way we handled this problem showed our employees and our business partners that Continental had drastically changed.

But for the moment, it's important only to understand that we removed an entire type of airplane from our fleet in 1995.

And removing A300s from the top of our fleet (they were some of the biggest planes) allowed our fleet to readjust itself to our new schedule as neatly as the blocks drop in a Jacob's Ladder a child plays with.

Because we took the biggest planes, which were running half full in the first place, out of circulation, our next-biggest planes were suddenly running much closer to full, and thus generated a better margin.

The routes formerly flown by A300s could now be served by smaller planes, and on down the line. By cutting the fat off the top, we sort of right-sized our entire fleet at one blow. And at the bottom of the ladder, where the numbers were smallest, that's where we wanted to quit flying anyway, so we eliminated the flights as well as the planes. These were the Greensboro-to-Greenville flights.

So one more thing suddenly fit right. We got rid of the big planes, but we kept most of the money they had been generating.

Now things looked a little better from a planning, scheduling, and operations perspective: Everybody was working together to sign off on plans. We were flying planes to places people wanted to go, making schedules that allowed maintenance to be performed sensibly, pouring our resources into strengthening our hubs, and removing from our fleet planes that were too big and had special maintenance requirements.

And not only that—we were finding ways to stop competing with ourselves. But the changes we were making under Fly to Win were not just operational. Flying less was helping, and charging more when appropriate was helping, but we had other problems.

Winning Means Saying You're Sorry

One of the things I had done even before finally getting my 10-day chairmanship was to hire Bonnie Reitz, who was working with System One, a subsidiary company for our computer reservation system, which travel agents use to book flights. We brought her in as our senior vice president of sales and distribution. A longtime professional in the travel industry, Bonnie was just the person we needed to help us.

Bonnie could give us something we sorely lacked: *credibility.* With our emphasis on cost cutting and money saving, we had done almost everything you could imagine to bring our house crashing down onto our heads.

For one thing, about 80 percent of passenger reservations in this country are made by travel agents. In our quest to save every dollar possible, Continental had reduced commissions to travel agents, gutted our frequent flyer benefits, and taken away things agents could use as selling tools: first-class seats, upgrades, meals, and other services. By generally being a wretched company to deal with, we had annoyed more than just our passengers. We had alienated just about every travel agent in the United States.

Remember that average business traveler I told you about, the hungry passenger on Continental Lite who hated flying with us? Well, that person represents an entire class of the highest-paying passengers in the airline business. And we were chasing all of them away.

Here's the scenario: We've alienated the entire distribution network for our business. We've done all we can to chase away our highest-paying customers. We're trying to make our way by selling tickets to the lowest-paying customers—occasional travelers and vacationers—by selling them the cheapest seats possible. Then, if we're real lucky and don't completely screw up their flight, two years from now, when they're ready to take another long trip, maybe we'll get them again!

Well, as Bonnie said right off the bat, the idea of saving your way to profitability is ludicrous. She knew intuitively that we had to make our product into something people wanted and that we had to sell it in the traditional way.

She also knew we weren't going anywhere without travel agents or business passengers. So, hat in hand, we started apologizing to anybody who would listen. We went to the top people in the travel world—the Rosenbluths, the American Expresses, the Carlson-Wagonlits—and told them we knew we had chased them away, and we wanted them back.

We didn't send them letters or coupons for free drinks. We went to their offices. I went. Bonnie went. All corporate officers went. All of the chief people in our marketing and distribution areas went. We plainly and sincerely apologized. We told them we were going to do better. And we told them we wanted their business back.

And you know what? People love it when you apologize. They adore it. You can apologize 24 hours a day, and they'll listen nicely, and they'll pat you on the back, and they'll thank you for dropping by—and then they'll pick up the phone and put their travelers on other airlines who don't have to apologize.

So, along with the apologies, we told them something else: We planned to *earn* back their business. We would make it worth their while. One of our catchphrases at Continental is, "What you measure and what you reward is what you get." So we went to agencies and developed packages *with* them—ways to measure what we were accomplishing together and ways to reward them for working with us again.

We didn't say, "Gosh, we're sorry we've been crummy for a decade. Now forget it and come back." We said, "How can we win *with* you? How can your coming back to Continental make *you* more money?"

This meant we had to do things above and beyond the usual, and we did. Bonnie was willing to learn how to do things in a new way, willing to think differently than she was used to. She demonstrated this once early in her marriage, she told us, when cooking a roast. She had learned to cook a roast from her mother, who always cut the end of the roast off, put the rest of the roast in a pan, and put it in the oven. When she got married and went to cook a roast, her husband watched her carve off part of the roast and asked her what she was doing.

Bonnie's smart—she realized she didn't know, so she called her mom and asked why she always cut off the end of the roast. Well, it turned out that her mom had a small oven, so she had a small roast pan, and often the whole roast wouldn't fit. Cutting off the end of the roast was something her mom had done to adapt to her particular situation, and it no longer made sense. So we examined our relationships with travel agencies and figured out we were cutting the ends of our roasts off because that made sense in the old, cost-cutting environment.

And we started giving travel agencies the whole roast.

We worked out deals to work with their biggest clients: the Fortune 500 companies that did the most traveling. What did those customers need that we could provide? And when they told us—more first-class seats, particular destinations, discounts for certain volumes—we found ways to provide that. We set up programs whereby if the travel agencies sold a certain volume of tickets or accomplished other goals, they not only got a reasonable commission, they got an incentive above and beyond what we (or other airlines) would normally pay. From giving them less than anyone else, we were moving toward giving them more than anyone else.

It may seem like an unusual move for an airline that was in terrible financial trouble to be handing out money in the form of incentives to travel agents, but it made a lot of sense. We were losing money. If we could get travel agents to help us make money, it only made sense for us to share some of that with them. As you'll see in Chapter 4, it wasn't so much a question of whether we could afford to do it, but that we couldn't afford *not* to do it. Our wretched financial state was proof of what had been happening as we tried not to.

To no one's surprise, once we started treating travel agencies like our partners instead of our competitors, once we started working with them instead of against them, they started taking chances with us.

Of course, taking chances is what they were doing. They were trying to put their customers on planes that, over the preceding decade, the customers had clearly come to distrust. We wanted to move our business, as Greg Brenneman likes to say, from the backpack-and-flip-flop crowd to coats and ties—or at least from Kmart backpacks to Patagonia backpacks. Those aren't customers that traditionally like to take chances with their comfort.

So we made it a win-win situation for the travel agencies. We brought in the corporations they serve and made it a win-win-win situation. But there was one more winner we needed: the customers.

So we threw a party.

Come On to My House

In fact, I threw the party. Anyhow, the party was at my house. We threw the party to announce that we were going to give back to our customers something we had recently taken away from them. We reached out to our best customers, our most frequent flyers, and tried to make up for something we had recently done.

Throughout all the years of Continental's dwindling productivity, declining service, and insane cost cutting, our frequent flyer program, OnePass, had consistently retained its high rankings. We had the best upgrades, the best mileage partners, the best ancillary benefits. Year after year it won *Inside Flyer* magazine's Freddie Award.

So naturally the people who had been running our airline decided it needed fixing.

In the last years of my predecessors, the accountants and lawyers got just about everything, so it was not surprising they got those frequent flyer benefits, too. "We're giving away our best product," they said, "and let's cut it out." So we did. We changed our rules about upgrades; we changed the rules about earning miles. (Most of our flights were removing the first-class seats anyhow, so you *couldn't* upgrade.)

We got thousands of letters. Thousands. Saying, "You idiots, you took away the stuff I really liked—signed, an ex-customer."

But the lawyers and accountants were running their computer programs and getting the kind of nice-looking graphs that got them excited, the kind of cost-benefit analyses that they thought made a good airline, so they ignored the letters. They didn't notice that in pursuing their little formulas they were wrecking our product—or at least one of the few things about it that anybody still liked.

I noticed.

I said, why don't we just put it back? Why not admit we were wrong, send a letter to everybody apologizing, and tell them we're going to make it like it was? Our international senior vice president Barry Simon agreed. Bonnie agreed. Greg Brenneman agreed. All the people I was paying a lot of money to be smart agreed. So we did it.

And we focused on the actual customers. We sent letters not just to the CEOs but to the middle managers and the sales reps. The people who actually *did* the flying.

We told them we were wrong and that we were going to fix things. And to prove it, we invited them over to my house one evening. We sent out invitations to 100 of our best, most frequent flyers, and we asked them to bring their spouses. When they got there we had cocktails and tables full of food. We gave them a little leather ticket case as a gift, and we flat out apologized.

I was there. Greg Brenneman was there. Bonnie Reitz and her team were there. Our corporate communications vice president

Ned Walker was there. And we all circulated, mostly thanking people for coming. We were dressed nicely, we were in my house, which is in a nice Houston neighborhood, waiters were circulating with hors d'oeuvres, and it was a very pleasant evening.

Then we asked for their attention and I made a little speech.

I said that they had told us what was wrong with our service and we had heard them, and we were going to restore it to exactly the way it was when they liked it. I didn't say that we had fiddled with it and somehow made it better. I just said we screwed up and we were sorry. And I told them a little bit about all the changes we were making, and we hoped they'd come back and stay with us and let us know how we were doing, because we listened now. People were pretty pleased—and pretty amazed. How often does the CEO of a company invite you to his house just to say he was wrong?

Of course, it wasn't just one party. We apologized all over the place. Every one of our top executives (from vice presidents and directors all the way up to me) got a list of customers to call and apologize to. We called, we apologized, we explained where we were headed. We asked for suggestions.

We went to the Greater Houston Partnership, a Chamber of Commerce and development organization of business leaders. They had stuck with us more or less because they had to. We're the hometown team, and we have the most local nonstop flights.

We told them the same thing we told our other customers and our travel agents and corporate partners: that from now on we wanted to *earn* their business, not just have it because they really didn't have much choice.

We did the same thing with the organizations helping Cleveland improve its city. We sat down with them and listened to them. We listened to people like Mayor Michael White of Cleveland tell us that our airline was lousy. We agreed. We told him we planned to fix it.

We just told them: "We're flying to win now. We want you back, and we're going to do what it takes. We want you to fly with us because you win when you do." We went to hundreds of customers; we made thousands of phone calls. Like I said, we were determined to get the word out that this wasn't the same old place. And you know what? This stuff works.

The best example I can recall was when I went to visit Marc Shapiro, then chief executive officer of Texas Commerce Bank. They had about $2.5 million of travel every year. We had about $2 million of it, and Southwest—whose chief executive officer is on the board of TCB—gets the other half million.

It was pretty clear that we had nothing to ask from TCB. But I went over there and basically said, "Thank you for your business, we appreciate it, and we're going to get better and make you glad you're flying with us."

Marc Shapiro said to me, "Gordon, I've been here maybe 8 years, but you're the first person who's ever come to this office just to thank me for my business, not to ask me for anything. Just to make me feel appreciated."

I said, "Marc, maybe that's why we haven't been doing so well."

The Key to the Universe: Value-Added Cost

If you look at it with the widest possible view, Fly to Win is, in the end, about selling something people want to buy. That's our philosophy: Stop doing things that lose money. Fly where people want to go. Work with customers and distributors to find out what *they* want, and provide that service. And run the kind of company that can compete.

It's as simple as that. Fly to Win is the market portion of our business plan, and a pretty simple market plan is just that: Sell what people want to buy.

- We stopped flying point-to-point routes to marginal markets because those routes weren't what people wanted to buy from us. Instead, we concentrated on our hubs, because there we could provide service people *did* want to buy.

- We restored our OnePass system because people wanted to buy it.

- We put first-class seats and food back in our planes because that's what people wanted to buy.

- We started flying to places people wanted to fly.

- We begged forgiveness from travel agents because without them we really couldn't sell our product.

- We begged forgiveness from our customers, because we had treated them in a way that made them, with good reason, not want to buy our product.

Again, it all comes down to making something that people want to buy.

The Definition of Better

Another way to say this is to define success the way your customers do. Say you're running an airline. Do you think success is market share, number of flights, the best technology, the most impressive-looking route map? Maybe.

But chances are your customers define it by clean, safe, reliable flights, at reasonable prices, with the amenities they want. Lose track of that and you've lost track of everything.

We had indeed lost track—and refocusing on it is the key to Fly to Win. We now define success the way our customers do. When dealing with suppliers or distributors, as with travel agents, you have to include them in your definition of success.

The biggest change we made at Continental was to apply that simple criterion not just to our marketing plan but to *every segment of our operation*. And we still do today.

To do this, we apply an extremely important, but extremely basic, idea: value-added cost.

The simple description of value-added cost is that it increases your cost by adding value—that is, adding something your customer wants to buy. Say I'm delivering the newspaper to your house every morning. One day I get the bright idea that if I drive a better car, I can get the papers to your house earlier. So I buy the new car, increase the cost of your paper by a nickel in order to pay for it, and start getting the papers to your house at 5 instead of 6 in the morning.

Whether that's a value-added cost depends on whether you *want* me to be delivering your paper at 5 instead of 6. If you rush out of the house to get to work by 6, then you're probably delighted with my new service and don't mind the extra nickel. But if you don't get up until 6:30 anyway, you probably think the new charge is a waste of money, and my new supercharged car may even disturb your sleep when it roars by at 5 A.M.

The Row-Five Test

Here's a great example I ran across when I worked for The Boeing Company in Seattle, an outstanding company known for excellent planes and first-rate technology. They have the best engineers in the world designing the best planes in the world, and naturally they want everything to be first rate.

When I worked there, one of my responsibilities was managing a division designing a new airplane, the 737X. I once got into a short debate with some engineers who wanted to improve the design of the start control panel on a 737. They wanted to make a "better" panel with a better switch technology and fewer functions. To make it work, the pilot and copilot would have to punch only two buttons instead of the eight on the current model.

Well, that's great. But it was going to cost more. I didn't think it was worth it, and they couldn't understand how I could think such a thing. How could I not want to improve the technology? After all, two operations before start-up was obviously better than eight.

So I said, "Look, Herb Kelleher of Southwest Airlines already has 200 of these airplanes. They need spare parts. He has all his pilots trained on the current model. For him to make a change, that's going to require retraining pilots and mechanics and additional spares inventory at all the cities Southwest serves. The question is, is he going to think that change is worth the extra cost?

"I think to decide that, he's going to walk down to the back of his airplane, to the passenger in row five, and he's going to say, 'Would you give me 50 cents more for your ticket to Amarillo today because we have a better start control panel?'

"That passenger might say, 'Well, the engines started okay. And they're both running now. And it takes only a couple more seconds to use the old panel, and it's always worked. And it's not an emergency procedure. So to be honest, no. It's not worth another 50 cents to me.' "

They got the idea. From then on, every time engineering would come to me with some kind of new technology they wanted to put into a plane we were building to customer specifications, I'd always ask, "Does it pass the row-five test?"

Sometimes that helped us keep Boeing on track as a company. We were once getting whipped in the press because our competitor, Airbus, touted that it had a whole bunch of advanced technology in its new planes: fly by wire, advanced controls, all kinds of automated features. There was no yoke in an Airbus airplane. It was controlled by a little joystick electronically, like an F-16 fighter. Instead of hydraulics and cables, it's all electronic. A lot of people thought we needed to keep up with them and put that system in the new 737, even though the old model had been working perfectly for 20 years and had a manual-reversion control for backup in cases the hydraulic system failed.

So I said, "Let's walk back to row five. And let's ask our traveler whether he'd be willing to hand over 50 cents so the pilot could fly with a little joystick instead of a yoke and have electronic backups instead of manual cable backups."

And we figured the passenger was a lot more likely to say, "I think you ought to give *me* 50 more cents, because I kind of liked the cable backup—it's a physical thing, not just some fuse or circuit breaker."

The engineers worried that we were losing the technological battle. Boeing was famous for having the technology to put people on the moon.

I said, "You know what? This battle is not about technology. The passenger in row five is not *going* to the moon.

"He's just going to Amarillo."

This is about customer value. This is the row-five test.

Our planes flew just fine with the controls that had worked for 20 years, and we didn't need to ask customers for more money.

That's the row-five test.

You can look at it from any angle. Is a Cadillac a "better" car than a Chevy? Of course it is—better automation, bigger engine, all kinds of better stuff. But do they sell more Chevys or more Cadillacs? Hmm. So now you tell me, according to the row-five test, for a whole lot of people the Chevy is the better car.

Not that you shouldn't sell Cadillacs. But you should sell Cadillacs to the people who want them and Chevys to the people who want them. Don't glitz up your Chevy with a lot of stuff that's going to make it cost as much as a Cadillac if you're marketing to people who just want to be able to drive to work and back and not blow up or fall apart.

Consider jewelry. Is an 18-karat ring better than a 14-karat ring? Obviously. Of course. And then young Larry, who's getting married and whose fiancée insists on a ring even though it's only symbolic, comes into your store to buy a ring. You say, "Here's a lovely $300, 18-karat ring." Larry says, "I've only got $150." Do you say well, "Sorry, Lar, but an 18-karat ring is better, and we only sell better jewelry," and watch Larry walk out the door? Or do you get out the tray of 14-karat rings, knowing that, for Larry, the definition of *better* is a 14-karat ring?

See? It depends on how you define better.

If you want mostly customers who are looking for better-quality rings, then you're not going to have a whole lot for the Larrys of the world. And maybe that's fine for you. But the point is, you'd better figure out what your customers—the customers you want— value. Because that's what they'll buy. Anything else is a waste of their money, and they'll figure that out in a hurry.

Finally, if Your Floor Is So Clean You Can Eat off It, You May Be Paying Too Much Attention to Your Floors

So that's Fly to Win. We've stopped doing things that lose money. We fly to places our customers want to go. We got rid of Continental Lite because nobody wanted it, and we replaced it with more service from our hubs, which people did want.

We worked hard to rebuild our relationships with our distributors (travel agents) and with our customers (frequent flyers). And we focus every single day on the most basic trick in the world: valuing what our *customer* values and providing it. We now understand the concept of value-added service.

We had to define success the way our customers did. It wasn't cheapness, we had learned. It wasn't the biggest planes with the best technology going to the most exotic locations.

It was clean, safe, reliable service from hubs we could manage in planes we could fly to places they wanted to go, with amenities like first-class seats and food and frequent flyer miles—things that made their traveling experience better. They had been telling us how to win for a decade, and when we finally started listening and flying that way, we started winning.

Keeping on the Winning Path

We felt great about regaining the respect and cooperation of the travel agent community, and we were glad we were winning our customers back by returning to the things they wanted from us.

The key thereafter has been to keep going in that direction. It's great to solve a huge problem and redefine the direction of a company. A much harder task has been to keep moving in that direction. But we have.

We've installed new reservation systems to make it easier for travel agents to work with us. We hired the best people in technology, like our chief information officer, Janet Wejman, and as a result we've become an industry leader in electronic ticketing, with E-Ticket terminals in airports around the country now. We developed our hubs by having our senior vice president of airport services, Mark Erwin, find the service elements those customers said they were willing to pay for. We've kept on improving our destinations, by having our senior vice president of corporate development, David Grizzle, find new alliance partners to share routes with.

Again, our key remains: Focus on what the customer wants.

One of my favorite management lessons comes from my days as maintenance manager at Western Airlines. Airlines were, then as now, trying hard to manage costs, and one of the places we needed to cut costs was from the maintenance budget. Well, I went out to the maintenance hangar one day to look around and saw that we had a special class of employee whose entire job it was to clean up after mechanics.

I wasn't too impressed. I started out as a mechanic, and one thing I know is that a good mechanic cleans up after him- or herself. I told the mechanics then and there that they were going to have to get used to working without people cleaning up after them and to clean up their own work areas each shift.

They were frantic. "But Gordon!" one said to me during a walk-through. "That's one of the things we've always been known for! Because people clean up after our mechanics, it's always spick-and-span back here. Why, our floors have been so clean you could eat off of them!"

I paused briefly.

"Well," I said. "Get paper plates."

You see? It's just like the fancy start control panel or the Cadillac or the 18-karat jewelry. The customers don't care how clean the floor is in the shop. They want the shop clean and safe for work, but they don't want to pay for anybody eating off the floors.

Focus on what the customer values. Add cost only when it adds value.

That's acting like a real airline.

I've always liked that phrase, "acting like a real airline." It's what we said when I took over in 1994: "It's time to act like a real airline." It's the phrase that appeared on the cover of our 1994 annual report, which told shareholders about the Go Forward Plan. That annual report also told them about what I hoped were our last annual losses for a long, long time.

We addressed our losses—or I should say, our financial catastrophe—in the Fund the Future portion of the Go Forward Plan, which I'll tell you about in Chapter 4.

Fund the Future, or If There Ain't No Funds, There Ain't Gonna Be No Future

t the beginning of this book, I said the only place we could fly
you with any degree of certainty was nowhere. I now admit
that I was exaggerating: There actually was one place Continental Airlines could get you besides nowhere.

Bankruptcy court.

In the decade before I joined Continental, the airline had gone into bankruptcy twice, in 1983 and 1990. We couldn't get to a lot of places, but we were racking up the frequent flyer miles on tours of the American bankruptcy court system. And when I took over, we were mighty close to going down for the third time, which would have been fatal. As John Casey of Braniff used to say when I worked there as Braniff made its way toward bankruptcy, it wasn't the end of the world, but we could see it from where we were. Plus we had a confirmed landing slot and people waiting for us at the gate.

Things didn't look too good.

No, I mean they *really* looked bad. Much worse than I imagined when I fought so hard to become chief executive of Continental Airlines. In fact, one day in December, 1994, not long after I had finally taken over as chief executive, Greg Brenneman was looking over our financial numbers—and looking them over a little more carefully than they had been looked over in many, many years. I was in charge, and he finally had access to all our numbers and all the financial information. Greg found something he thought was worth mentioning, and he came into my office.

"Gordon," he said, "Did you happen to know that unless something drastically changes immediately, we're going to run out of money in January?" The cash and cost forecasting systems we had been using were sloppy and not detailed. So Greg started double-checking things manually, literally crunching columns of numbers to finally see just where we stood. As he began running detailed estimates of what we had to spend and what we would likely make in the coming weeks, he saw that we were in much worse shape than we had imagined. He wasn't saying we just needed to shuffle numbers somehow. He wasn't saying we could slow-pay creditors or do a little dodging and feinting to buy some breathing room.

We were going to go broke. We weren't going to make payroll. We weren't going to be able to pay our bills. If we didn't do something soon, we were going to be in the kind of situation where you either give up and start bankruptcy proceedings or get creative and end up in prison.

I hadn't known that, and I thanked him for telling me. It wasn't a situation where we started shrieking and rolling around on the carpet; we had known things were bad. Now we knew things were as bad as they could get. I didn't like it, but I was certainly happier knowing it than not knowing it. It meant that our emergency financial plans were going to have to begin moving at an even faster rate.

Greg suggested two alternatives. We could enter a third bankruptcy, from which no company our size had ever emerged. Or we could start quiet renegotiations with our large creditors. Some choice.

We knew we had to keep the negotiations quiet, because if the press caught word we were almost bankrupt, our customers would back away from us. If that happened, we estimated it would cost us between $100 and $200 million in revenue, which would bankrupt us for sure.

As I said before, product is the breathing function of our company. Cash is its blood. And we were bleeding everywhere it was possible to bleed. We knew we needed a tourniquet (or several), and it was tempting at times to apply the tourniquet to the patient's neck and be done with it.

But as I said before, I'm trained as a pilot. And a pilot doesn't just give up a plane, no matter how bad the situation is. I could have jumped to another company. For that matter, I could have retired. But Continental was in trouble, and I was at the controls.

I surrounded myself with the best people I could find, starting with Greg Brenneman. And we got to work.

How to Stop a Spinning Plane

When I talk about the Go Forward Plan, I remind people that we had to work on all four parts of the plan to succeed.

But there's no doubt that we had to focus on some parts a little harder at first. To explain this, the airplane itself provides a great metaphor. I demonstrated this to one of the better writers who came up to do a story about our success in the last couple of years. People tend to be intrigued by the fact that not only do I run an airline but I can actually fly the planes, so I took this writer down to one of our simulators. We got into the simulator and virtually flew around in a Boeing 757. I showed him all the different gauges, all the different ways by which the pilot knows how the plane is flying, where it's flying, what it's doing, and what its prospects are—which pedals operated the rudder, how the throttle worked, what happened if you pushed the nose down, what happened if you pulled the nose up.

I even demonstrated to him how the cockpit is equipped with all kinds of spoken-voice emergency messages. The plane will actually yell, "Too low . . . terrain! terrain!" at the pilot if it gets too low. It will shake the throttle and buzz if it slows toward stall speed. That is, the airplane will do everything it can to tell the pilot everything he might need to know if it's in trouble.

So then I forced the simulated flight into trouble. I slowed down the plane so much that it started to stall. Then I pushed in hard on the right rudder, jerked the nose up sharply to accelerate the stall, and flipped the airplane into a spin. It started falling and spinning as it did.

So all these dials and lights and verbal warnings are going off. The altimeter is unwinding, showing how fast we're dropping altitude; the lights start flashing; the plane itself is yelling; every light, buzzer, and dial in the cockpit is going crazy. With the plane in the worst possible position, we are besieged by information. Then I turned to the poor guy doing the story and said, "Well, now what?"

It was probably unfair, because he didn't know the first thing about what to do. He might have been able to jump to the right conclusion if the plane were veering right or left or climbing or diving too fast. But with all that stuff going wrong at one time, you'd have to be a trained pilot to know what to do first.

So I showed him.

They teach you in primary flying training that when you're spinning, no matter what else is going on, first stop the spin: That's priority one. You do it by pushing the opposite rudder. If you're spinning to the right, you push in and hold the left rudder. I did that, and suddenly the plane was no longer spinning around in circles.

To break the stall, you push the yoke and throttles forward to get some airspeed. Then, very gently, when the spin has stopped, release the rudder, relax the forward pressure on the yoke so as not to accelerate the airplane too fast and overload it (that is, give it too much to handle and start the same problem all over again), and bit by bit level out your flight.

And there you are—flying level, in a straight line. After that, there's plenty of time to figure out what your proper altitude ought to be, what your heading ought to be, whether your landing gear is up or down, and on to what kind of food you might want to be serving. First, get your plane flying stable. Everything else is secondary.

The Morals of the Spinning Plane Story

I use that story to make two points.

First, there's just no substitute for knowing what you're working with. It should have been no surprise that all those high rollers running Continental couldn't fix the airline. They were deal makers, financial experts, business school wizards. When their plane was spinning around and flying upside down, they came up with stuff like, "We gotta cut costs and then the tickets will be so cheap that maybe people won't mind riding on a plane that's upside down and spinning around." Or maybe they'd decide that it was no good that the plane was upside down and spinning around, but what they needed was a whole new flight crew because it was this one's fault that the plane was spinning around.

Point number one: If your company is in trouble, the people who can best fix it are going to be those who know something about people and the business you're in, whether you're selling shoes, watches, pizzas, or airplane flights.

Point two is a little wider, but even more important: You have to figure out exactly what's wrong—and fast. It's easy to become mesmerized by those spinning dials, listening to those buzzers and voice messages hollering at you, trying to tell you what to do and what not to do. The problem is, if you're in crisis, you probably don't have that much time.

What to Actually Do

That upside-down and spinning airplane, that emergency room patient I talked about at the beginning of Chapter 3, was Continental Airlines when my management team finally got the controls. We had to figure out those few essential measures that would stabilize the patient. And it wasn't easy: We had very unhappy employees, a rotten product, no money on hand (and not much coming in), and a backbreaking debt structure. We flew the wrong planes to the wrong cities for the wrong prices, and they were usually late to boot. Every vital organ we checked uncovered more problems, severe ones. Every one seemed to be an emergency. All four parts of the Go Forward Plan needed our attention.

But we couldn't solve them all instantly. We had to cope with what had us spinning and flying upside down before we worried about altitude and heading. We had to stabalize our pulse and our breathing before curing the rashes and even the larger underlying causes of our illness.

Fortunately, I've worked around people and airplanes my entire life, and I hired and surrounded myself with people who were experienced and successful in management. We didn't have any-body who was going to look at our broken airline and think that the problem was the employees or their uniforms or the economy or the government. We had very experienced people who were ready to find the airline problems and solve them, and we didn't have much time.

It didn't take a genius to figure out what our pulse and our breathing were.

Our breathing was our *product*. (I told you what we did about that in Chapter 3.) But our pulse was *money*. It was almost gone, and without solving our problem we were going to bleed to death. Soon.

First, Stop the Bleeding

The first thing, of course, was to stem the nonstop hemorrhaging of cash that Continental had made its specialty in the previous decade. We had the most expensive maintenance operation in the business—and the worst maintenance record. Same thing finan-cially—we had the largest financial systems department of any air-line flying, but we had no idea what was happening to our money. We had terrible systems, and our daily cash reports were close to useless. The books for this airline, it seemed, were being kept on the back of an envelope with a dull pencil. We had no idea where our money was going or what we were getting in return, though looking around gave the short answer: It was going down the drain and getting us nothing.

In 1994 and part of 1995, before we finally got our cash estimate and accounting systems in place, we went through nearly $400 million. Part of it went toward bad decisions about Continental Lite and the like, but to be honest, we simply had no idea where most of it went. Our systems were so general that we just didn't know where our money was going.

Four hundred million dollars. We may as well have set fire to it.

As I said, money is a business's blood. It's fuel. It's the great go/no-go decision maker. No matter what else was going on, before we did anything else we were going to have to stop this hemor-rhaging of cash.

And interestingly, though the cash problem was certainly our most visible crisis, its management required the simplest—and most obvious—solution. What's more, it's been pointed out that the Chinese character for *crisis* is the combination of two other characters—those for *danger* and *opportunity*. We were certainly aware of the danger in our situation. What we found in addressing our financial crisis, though, was the same as we found in every other area of our company. Once we started addressing the danger, opportunities presented themselves all over the place.

A Word about the Courts

People have asked me, "What about bankruptcy court?" Well, bankruptcy court, though a necessary and important thing, is really just another deal. We went through bankruptcy twice, and both times we emerged with reorganized financial obligations, with new stockholders—and with the same crappy company. A bankruptcy court judge knows a lot less about how to run an air-line than even the worst airline management team, and although we'd come out on somewhat more stable financial ground, we still had the same infighting, the same bad service, the same poor scheduling, and the same lousy pricing that got us into bankruptcy court in the first place.

They say the definition of insanity is doing the same thing over and over in the same way and expecting different results. Well, try this on for size: When we emerged from bankruptcy in 1993, the company threw a big party—caviar, champagne, the whole works. "Whoopee! We're not broke! Let's celebrate."

Well, not broke for that moment. Because, as I said, the prob-lems remained. That's why, when he finally got his hands on our books to give them a complete and thorough going-over, Greg found that we were closing in our third bankruptcy. No, bankruptcy court will not save your business. It might restructure your balance sheet for a mile, but *you* have to save your business.

Stop Borrowing from Pawnshops

The first thing we had to do goes right back to Fly to Win: Stop doing things that lose money.

The key there, of course, was debt. Continental had about $2 billion of debt that was soaking it dry (similar to that of the U.S. government, which would be in pretty good financial shape if it weren't paying the freight on debts accrued during decades of excessive spending).

Our debt problem had several facets. One, naturally, was the size of it. After all these bankruptcies during which the court had tried to make sure every one of our creditors received at least something, we owed money, and plenty of it, to just about everybody.

The next problem was interest rates. A corporation is just like a family: It can have a good credit rating or a bad credit rating. After two bankruptcies, as you can imagine, our credit rating was about as bad as it could be with us remaining in business. So we had been borrowing money at terrible rates. We kidded that we were borrowing from pawnshops instead of banks. We were going to have to do something about that.

Same thing with our airplane leases. A lessor that thinks you're probably going to pay for your airplane on time is going to give you a certain rate on a plane; a company that wonders whether you're still going to be in business when you get the plane home is going to give you a less favorable rate. We had a lot of the latter.

And we didn't have much time to dally. As Greg found out when he examined the figures, we were going to be out of money in January of 1995.

When I say "out of money," I want you to understand what I mean. We were running $6 billion through our profit and loss over the course of the year, and our savings had dwindled to . . . well, to just about nothing. We could barely pay our daily bills, much less plan any kind of managed payments that would help us stabilize.

Our savings were down to a float of less than $40 million dollars, and we were running about 10 times that through our profit and loss each month. Which means, honestly, that two days of bad receipts in a row could have killed us. If we were off in our credit card receipts by $5 million for a few days—a significant but plausible fluctuation for a company whose daily receipts were in the $20 million range—we could have been out of business.

We did have some money put away for taxes, but if you start raiding those accounts you end up in minimum security prison, not in your nice twentieth-floor office. That wasn't where we wanted to go.

But we had to go somewhere, and quickly.

A Pleasant Meeting among Friends

In the last chapter, I told you we invited some of our best customers over to my house to apologize for our crummy service. We did the same thing here: We invited most of our major creditors to Houston for a little meeting. We sat down in our boardroom, right here on the twentieth floor outside my office. I shared our vision for the future, the Go Forward Plan, and all that. Then Greg explained the harsh realities of our cash flow. He reviewed our dire situation as thoroughly as he could. As he started to outline some of the changes we planned to stabilize us and increase our ability to meet our obligations in the long run, he didn't meet with very many friendly faces in the crowd.

And how could you blame these folks? These were the new investors, people from GE Capital and Air Canada, those who had put themselves at risk to save us. As I've said, Continental was a hodgepodge of several airlines—Continental, Frontier, People Express, and New York Air—that had merged during the explosive era of airline deregulation in the 1980s. The problems left over from all that buying and consolidation had landed Continental in bankruptcy court a couple times, and this final group of investors was a combination who had taken over Continental after the U.S. bankruptcy court had given us our second "Go and sin no more." They were themselves a mixture of diverse investor groups, a creditors' committee, and a few independents. We had dragged them to our boardroom, given them ice water and coffee, admitted we had somehow run through $400 million in a year, and now we wanted *more* of their help.

Not surprisingly, they started squawking. Greg tried for a while to be heard, but he finally shrugged his shoulders and stood up.

The yelling increased in volume, with most of the voices wanting to know where he was going. He gave them the story I often use: The first question in any problem, he said, was to determine whose problem it was.

He laid it out for them. He worked for a company that was at that moment worth barely $200 million in assets—planes, facilities, and so forth—and not much else. He could see the end of the world coming fast, and he had gone to the only people who could help and had made his case. His conscience was clear, he said.

They, on the other hand, were people who had millions of dollars invested in an airline that was in deep, deep trouble. If they didn't want to help save it, that was up to them. But at that point, it was their problem.

Suddenly Greg could make his suggestions. Suddenly, they listened. And to be honest, they did the only thing they could: They cooperated.

General Electric, our biggest creditor, took a huge step, stretching out most of its loans from three years to seven or eight. We received similar concessions from other creditors. They didn't have much choice, I'll admit, but I think they could look down the road and see, with the changes we were making under the Go Forward Plan, that they weren't just stretching out our demise. I think they believed, at least to a small extent, that we were really going to turn things around here. In any case, without much of an alternative, they were willing to take a chance.

I want to stress here that a big part of the reason they were willing to take a chance is because they could see that we were acting like a different company. Just coming to them and opening our books, explaining our problems, and having a sensible plan for the future demonstrated that we were doing things in a completely different way than we had before.

I'll repeat something that I cannot say too often: Every segment of the Go Forward Plan worked together and worked at the same time. Yes, renegotiating leases and debt structures falls under Fund the Future, but we were able to generate enough confidence to renegotiate those leases because we had a plan to fix the way we positioned our product (Fly to Win) and because creditors could see that our prospects looked at least marginally brighter. When we told them about how we planned to improve our product itself in the Make Reliability a Reality segment of the plan, they could see that we were finally addressing the real problems with our airline.

Most important, by coming to them in a spirit of honesty, by straightforwardly telling them what we could and couldn't do, by trying to help find a satisfactory solution, we were demonstrating the most important segment of the Plan—Working Together— which underlies every action we have taken since those first days.

We spoke to the lessors in the same way we talked to the travel agents and our customers, asking what we could do to better satisfy them and improve our relationship. We didn't announce that we were parking their airplanes and we'd see them in court. That was the way Continental *used* to do things. That was what we wanted to stop doing.

Remember, the Go Forward Plan was more than just a way through a financial crisis or an operational problem. It was a way of completely changing how Continental did business.

When it came time for us to sit down with our airplane lessors and explain to them our dire situation, we did everything we could to work with them to find solutions to our problems that would not only get us out from under leases we couldn't sustain but also make good our obligation to them.

No Fat Jockeys

To that end, we worked with the companies whose planes we were trying to return (the A300s, for example). As I said, we realized we could not make money with them. We were paying $200,000 a month for some of these planes, whereas our competitors were paying $140,000. That was our own fault—we earned the bad credit rating ourselves, after all—but we still couldn't make them pay off.

I liken that to a horse running with a 350-pound jockey. We were developing the right routes and marketing ourselves in a better manner, but we were still saddled with these high-interest leases left over from our years of mismanagement. We just couldn't win. We had to get out from under those leases and eliminate those planes.

We recruited a new general counsel, Jeff Smisek, the smartest and best attorney we could find. We packed him off to New York with the assignment to get us out of the leases and keep us out of bankruptcy court in the process. But instead of just dumping the planes on the lessors and folding our arms, we helped the lessors identify markets and lessees who could make money with those planes. We even worked with the new lessees, training them to fly and maintain those planes. We sent training teams and spare parts all over the globe to satisfy those lessors. That made working out the details of those ended leases a lot more pleasant—and a lot less litigious.

Better than that, we put our money where our mouth was. We got some lessors to accept convertible securities instead of money to let us out of our leases. Our stock was selling for $4.50 a share at the time, and they had the right to convert into stock when it got to $13, or we could pay them off. Once our stock started climbing as things began to turn around, we paid them off. In full.

A far cry from the former Continental attitude: "We don't want your planes anymore, see you in court" would have been the best they could have hoped for. As the years have gone by, every single one of the lessors and creditors from whom we had to beg new terms has continued to work with us.

When All Else Fails, Beg

It's worth taking another look at what we did. Nothing fancy, nothing fancy at all. We were going under with our current debt and lease structure, so we simply went to our creditors and lessors and accepted responsibility for our mistakes. More important, we gave them reason to believe things would be better in the future. Then we hoped for the best.

It worked. In 1995 we saved a good $25 million in lower interest payments on long-term debt. That's over 10 percent of our 1994 loss right there.

It wasn't anything that hadn't already been considered by my predecessors, but because we were changing the culture within the airline, we could actually implement changes. Jun Tsuruta, our senior vice president of purchasing and material services, found lots of ways to save money—he sold excess inventory and renegotiated contracts for maintenance. One, he renegotiated a 10-year contract for landing-gear maintenance that included the buyback of excess inventory we had on hand. The upshot was that not only did we have a better contract and less material sitting around, we got a check for $2 million. Once we started paying close attention, there were many ways we could help ourselves. We implemented lots of little things that saved a few million dollars here and there.

Take Larry Kellner, my new chief financial officer, for example. Shortly after I took over and lost all confidence in our financial projections, I asked our board chairman who the best chief financial officer in the country was. He said Larry Kellner, who was working at a bank in California. We flew him out here, told him our story, and convinced him—with salary and, most important, stock options that would give him the opportunity to do as well as our company did if he helped us save it—to join us.

Not long after he got started, he came into my office one day with an idea for a fuel hedge, by which, for a small amount of money, we could guarantee that our cost for crude oil (the source of jet fuel) would never rise above a certain amount. It looked to Larry like this was a pretty safe bet—kind of an insurance policy. If fuel prices went down, we'd just be out the price of the hedge. If they went up, our hedge would protect us from the effect of the higher price.

What it did was take a variable cost—fuel—and turn it into a known cost. It removed one more excuse for failure and made things one click more predictable.

We jumped on it, and the decision saved us another $3 million over the course of the year as fuel prices rose. So that's another $3 million saved, and one more reason for why things could go wrong that we had removed from the equation. This has continued to save us millions of dollars every year since then—tens of millions, in fact—but the most important point then was that it removed a variable from the equation at a time when we were drowning in variables. Anything we could stabilize helped us find the way out of our morass.

Things like that start to build on one another. By renegotiating a couple of leases, all of a sudden you have a little more cash on hand to, say, invest in some cash-flow systems that will give you better control of your money, and that saves you a little more, which makes you a better credit risk, which enables you to borrow money at a rate that makes a little more sense. Everything starts to improve. We were reversing the spiral—instead of heading down, we were heading up.

But not before our final, heart-stopping moment of terror.

When Greg figured out the kind of crisis we were in, we all took different companies to contact.

Mine was The Boeing Company, where I had worked over the preceding years. We had previously sent them about $70 million in deposits for new airplanes we needed. As it turned out, of course, we couldn't afford the airplanes. Not only that, we really couldn't afford the *deposit* on the airplanes. Which was too bad for us, because in that industry a deposit is nonrefundable. Your supplier uses that money to start working on the airplanes you ordered. If you change your mind, it's not like they have the cash laying around. Your deposit is credited to your bill when you actually buy your airplanes.

Keep in mind that Boeing was already allowing us to refinance leases at lower rates than in our original contract. But we were still looking at a hole in our finances, and we were approaching difficult choices.

As I said, we were working on that little $40 million float, and every day was a crisis. As leases were renegotiated, planes retired or released, and debts refinanced, things started to look a little brighter. But even though the long-term picture looked brighter, by mid-January we were still going to hit bottom. We had done about everything we could, and it still looked like we were going to fail.

I called Ron Woodard, president of Boeing. He took my call because we were close friends.

"Ron," I said, "I know you're not contractually obligated to return that money for our canceled orders. But dammit, you need to give us this money back. We need it in the worst way."

Ron kind of laughed, because he knew I wouldn't be asking if we weren't desperate. He said, "Gordon, I don't know how we can, because the financial people don't always want to do things like this." Then he thought about it for a while. He trusted me. He believed in the direction we were pushing Continental.

"I'll tell you what," he said. "We'll give you half of it back."

I said, "Okay, Ron, I'll certainly take that."

He said he'd send it to me.

I said, "Ron, you don't understand. I need you to *wire* it to me."

Ron laughed. And he wired us $29 million.

Amazingly, that was it. Our cash balance never dipped below that number again. In the first half of 1995 we actually made money, a result of all the changes we had made in every aspect of our operation. By the end of 1995 we had built up our cash balances by more than $350 million. We also retired $318 million of debt and capital lease obligations and increased our equity by $200 million.

We've kept moving in that direction. Our annual interest payments have gone down by almost half. In 1994, we paid $202 million in interest alone; in 1996, that was down to $117 million, and it gets better every year.

We're now financed by a mixture of enhanced equipment trust certificates and debt that is the envy of many in our industry and has resulted in regular upgrading of our credit ratings by companies like Moody's and Standard & Poor's, which further improves our ability to get the best available interest rates when it's time for us to invest in new planes or facilities.

Speaking of new planes, we've placed several major aircraft orders. As we did so, we continued to improve our aircraft mix and reduce the average age of our fleet. By the end of 1999, we expect to be running only five different types of aircraft in our core fleet, down from nine in 1995, thus saving millions in training and maintenance costs. We'll have the youngest—and thus the lowest-maintenance—fleet in the industry.

Currently, we've got some $1 billion in cash. A drop in the day's cash receipts—or even some other glitch 10 times that size—is a problem we can weather and correct. In early 1995, such problems could have put us out of business in the blink of an eye.

When I thank all my employees and fellow managers for helping us turn Continental around and save it, there's no question that two guys from Boeing, Ron Woodard and chairman and friend Phil Condit, get a huge portion of thanks, too—along with the managers, CFOs, and chief executives of dozens of companies who were willing to work with us during this crisis. We simply couldn't have done it without them.

It took a lot of working together, and a lot of people willing to see that the members of your team aren't just the people wearing the same color shirt. Your team also includes your customers and your suppliers if you're trying to run a first-rate business.

There's one other lesson here that is small enough to overlook, but you shouldn't: Don't be too proud to beg. Use *everything* at your disposal when you're trying to resolve a crisis. I simply reached out to the guy who could give me the most help, and damned if he didn't do it. Nobody likes to call a friend or a colleague and ask for money. But given a choice between pride and watching our airline fail, there wasn't really a choice. The worst that could have happened was Ron would have said no. The best that could have happened—which *did* happen—was that we had one more partner in our remarkable turnaround.

Financial Systems We Could Believe In

We weathered the crisis. It was a tremendous accomplishment, of course, but what has made the difference in the long run is how we stabilized after that so we didn't run into any more crises. Fly to Win was continuing to develop new partners, new destinations, and new services that our customers wanted. Now Fund the Future had to move from a respond-to-a-crisis plan to one that would *control* our finances—not only funding the future but planning it and responding to it.

Chief Financial Officer Larry Kellner shifted into high gear for us at this point with his team, including Mike Bonds and Gerry Laderman.

One of the first things he noticed when he came on board was that the daily, weekly, and monthly numbers he was getting from our forecasters were just this side of useless. That's part of what kept us so confused about our financial state for so long, and it kept us on the edge of our seats through the beginning of 1995.

One of the first things we did, even as we were climbing out of our chasm of debt and near-bankruptcy, was to start installing financial systems we could rely on. There's nothing worse as a pilot than to be flying and look down at your instruments and realize that you don't trust them—maybe your altimeter suddenly says you're 2,000 feet lower than you were five seconds ago, and you know you didn't drop. Maybe your artificial horizon shows you're in a turn and you aren't. Worse, maybe your airplane is turning sharply but your artificial horizon wants you to believe everything is just fine.

When you can't trust your systems, you never really know where you are. That's how it was with our financial systems. We generated daily numbers, but they meant nothing. We had forecasts, but we couldn't base any action on them. Now that we had a few dollars in the bank and could be relatively sure that we'd be in business for another quarter, we started putting money into new systems.

Our financial departments were much like our maintenance department had been—high costs and low productivity. A lot of people not getting a lot done.

So we spent some money and replaced our systems. As Larry said, you can make a cost estimate (say, for airport landing fees) at the beginning of the year based on industry averages and then just kind of keep track of it, *or* you can get actual landing-fee schedules for every airport we fly to, figure out how many flights a day will be landing at each one according to our schedule, how heavy we expect those planes to be, and what the resulting landing fees will be. Then you can update that estimate every month and every time landing fees or schedules change.

Which estimate do you think will be more accurate? Larry opted for the latter system, and before long, every single morning at 10 A.M., we had a report of the previous day's credit card receipts, which is our most important daily indicator of our earnings. That sounds like common sense until you realize that before I took over, we did *not* have an accurate daily cash report, so it was a big improvement.

As we implemented better financial systems, trained people to follow them, and hired the right people to manage them, we were soon generating a 40-item daily forecast every day at 4 P.M., including credit card receipts, maintenance costs, fuel costs, and revenue per available seat mile. We could track all our key measurements easily—every single day. As we learned more, the measurements became more and more accurate, which meant we could make better and better decisions with increasingly current numbers.

Another vast improvement. Information that's inaccurate isn't worth a thing, and it may be worse than useless—it may cause you to make mistakes based on misinformation. Accurate information is good, but accurate information four months late isn't much help.

Accurate information in time to help you make decisions, though? Now that's worth something, and in the longer term, of course, worth far more than the money we spent to implement it.

What's Going On?

The key to your financial health is simple: Know what's going on. That's step one, and the closer you can get to real time the better off you are. So we spent a lot of time and money putting the right people and systems in place to keep us abreast, as quickly as possible, of everything going on for us financially.

Larry Kellner helped us keep our eye on the ball—that is, know where your cash is. You can't afford to run out of cash. (We had learned that in spades.) All your accounting procedures should distill your numbers in a way that tells you, simply: How much money do you have? Where is it? How does that relate to how much you had yesterday or last week?

If a daily report varies from the forecast, you don't need to get worked up. But if a weekly report differs significantly, you probably should. A monthly forecast is off? You better get worked up.

Do you see where this is going? Once you trust your forecasts and your numbers, you're already able to start planning months, not days, in advance.

And once you have a handle on your cash and your accounting processes, you are at the planning stage. The first thing we had to do at Continental was to stop hemorrhaging cash and then get our earnings coming in. Once we were earning money and not burning money, we had to get control of where our money was going and coming from.

From then on, we could plan for the future. A great example is fleet planning. We were working on changing the makeup of our fleet, as I already mentioned. We knew that by having fewer types of aircraft we could run a better operation. But once we had financial systems we could trust in place, we could start learning things that would enable us to make much better decisions. How much are we earning per available seat mile on each type of plane? On each type of route? On routes from particular hubs? On planes at particular times of day? With particular types of connecting banks?

The more we learned, the better we planned. The better we planned, the better we did.

Another example is our European flights. When we were consolidating flights, cutting back, and learning where our markets were, we were discussing some consolidations in Europe. We had started to implement some of Larry's new financial systems at the time, and they revealed that we were making a remarkable amount of money on our European flights—so much, in fact, that we doubted the truth of the numbers.

We waited a month and checked the numbers again. When they again came up very strong, we did further analysis and learned that, almost unbeknownst to ourselves, we were doing great in Europe. So we didn't consolidate. Instead, we started charging more for our European tickets. And all of a sudden we had an additional $10 million for the next forecast period. Once you start getting good numbers, you stop working in hindsight and start making good decisions.

We all liked that.

Where's the Money Going?

Once we knew where our money was coming from, we had to make sure we knew where it was going. Larry Kellner likes to say that if you want to know what's going on in your business, follow one simple rule: Sign every check. For a long time after he got here, Larry did just that, signing every significant check we wrote. He's now delegated some of that responsibility, but even if he doesn't sign every check, there aren't any checks he doesn't know about. He knows—we know—exactly where our money is going.

Good point. Once we started getting better financial information, we could make better and better decisions about our flight plans because we knew which cities we were making money on by serving. We learned where we were sinking money into maintenance without sufficient return, for example, and where we were getting good revenues. In short, we were able to determine where to reinvest and where to pull out. Which was exactly the kind of information we needed.

The Thunderstorm

When explaining the importance of getting good information from good systems, I tell people about growing up in Texas. If you've ever been in Texas for any length of time, you've seen a Texas thunderstorm, which is a completely different animal than your garden-variety thunderstorm. Texas thunderstorms have hail; they have cyclone winds; they have dust storms. A Texas thunderstorm is a lot more than a rainy day.

Well, I watched those storms as I grew up, and I remember a very young wife at home with her baby, looking out the windows, watching one of those storms build up on the plain. As the lightning flashed and the thunder cracked, she patted the baby on the back, soothed it, and said, "Don't worry, everything is going to be all right. Mama's here."

Well, the truth is, it might *not* be all right. A huge storm was coming, and what the result was going to be, nobody could say.

I don't want to be like that baby. If the storm's coming, I want to know. I want to know as much about that storm as I can, as soon as I can, and in as much detail as I can get. Then I'll know whether to go down the cellar and hide, whether I can get away with just closing the shutters, or whether maybe all I need to do is take in the wash. But I want to know what the reality is. I want to be able to plan for trouble if it's coming.

The Downside

Unfortunately, there's always a downside. It was great to learn where we were losing money so we could cut service to cities that didn't appear to really want us anyway. Great for Continental, that is—not so great for our employees who worked there. Cutting our flights, cutting the cities we served, retiring airplanes to make us a better and more competitive airline meant, unavoidably, that jobs were going to be lost. If we weren't serving Greenville anymore, some Continental employees who worked for us in Greenville weren't going to like it.

But we did the same thing with our employees that we did with our suppliers and our other partners. We were honest and we asked for their help. We did everything we could to either move the employees to other Continental locations or help them find work with other airlines. We were able to find spots for most of the people who really wanted to stay with us.

The Ugly Reality

We were unable to save everyone's job, of course. We had to shut down our Los Angeles maintenance facility, for example. I announced the news the day I took over as CEO in November 1994. That facility was a leftover from the days long before I arrived, when Continental had been based in L.A. We were ferrying planes from all over the country to L.A. for maintenance, where the labor costs and taxes were higher and we had the additional costs of just getting the planes there. We didn't have that much service in L.A. by that point, because we were shifting our focus to our hubs in Houston, Cleveland, and Newark.

What's more, with fewer types of airplanes in our fleet, we were also getting rid of some of our older planes, which meant we'd be doing less major maintenance. We decided to outsource most major maintenance to either original equipment manufacturers or other third-party suppliers. We'd concentrate on line maintenance, which we could do cheaper in Houston or in maintenance facilities in our hubs or other cities.

We simply couldn't afford to keep our maintenance facility in L.A., especially in the midst of the financial crisis. We closed it, saving millions of dollars through the combination of cheaper line maintenance and outsourcing. Good news for Continental—bad news for the nearly 1,800 people who worked at that facility.

But again, we approached this step as a new company, not as the old Continental would have. One of the first people I recruited to Continental was George Mason to head our technical operations. George is the best maintenance and people manager in the business, and so instead of simply tossing people aside, as we had so many times before, we explained to them why we were taking the steps we were, and we set up a transition team. We showed them our books, and I mean that literally. We took balance sheets to employee meetings and had people explain them, showing employees what we were taking in and what it was costing us to remain in L.A. We were just losing too much money there. We moved those employees we could (and who were willing) to maintenance facilities elsewhere. And though we closed the facility in November, we kept people on until the end of the year, helping them to find other work and keeping them on a recall list.

Since then, virtually every employee who wanted to come back to work for us has had that opportunity—in fact, at our hubs now we're taking new hires because the recall lists are empty.

That doesn't mean that people liked being furloughed, or that it was a pleasant experience, or that it hurt us more than it hurt them, or that we would have done it if we had any other way out. But some furloughs were essential if Continental was to survive.

It was the same thing when, not far into the Go Forward Plan, as Continental Lite was completely scuttled, we closed our Greensboro, North Carolina, hub. We gave every employee working there an option to take a job elsewhere in the company, but we didn't pretend that they enjoyed that. We even went so far as to help pay relocation costs, because so many of the Greensboro employees had *already* moved from the recently closed Denver hub. Not everybody took the new assignments, and not everybody was happy with us.

Can you blame them? Here was a company that had been moving them around, asking them to forgo raises (sometimes take pay cuts), breaking promise after promise—and now was asking them to move *again*. It was hard to blame people for being frustrated.

And not only employees were dissatisfied. Greensboro-area civic leaders, members of the airport authority, and businesspeople had all worked hard to help us get our hub going there. We had all believed that the hub was going to be a boon to our airline and to their region, but it just didn't happen. The hub was bleeding us, so we had to close it. The community wasn't happy; our employees weren't happy; we weren't happy. But the reality was there, and by honestly addressing it and making the difficult choices, we at least took a bad situation and showed our employees and our partners that we were willing to face facts and do so as honorably as possible.

We earned our stripes by being up front with employees about these difficult issues. I personally went to tell the employees we were shutting down Los Angeles, and Greg did the same in the Greensboro hub. We didn't like it, but we didn't lie.

Wage Snapback

It was the same thing when a March 1995 wage snapback promised in the 1993 bankruptcy settlement had to be postponed until we reached profitability. During the bankruptcy, employees had been asked to take a wage cut for a brief time so the company could reorganize, and they were promised that their wages would snap back in March 1995. When we postponed the snapback, no one could blame our employees for saying, "Here we go again." But we opened our books, showed them why we had to ask them to wait, gave them a new target date for meeting our obligation, and never minced words or tried to soft-pedal the truth. Even the employees, as angry as they were, could see that bad financial news along with the truth was better than bad news along with a lie.

On July 1, we restored wage levels six months ahead of schedule because our financial situation had improved so rapidly. We weren't yet profitable, but we knew we were going to be. So instead of waiting until we reached the goal, we snapped back the wages right then. We knew we were going to make it, and we wanted everyone to get the benefits as soon as we could share them. So our employees learned something else: When we could responsibly put them first, we would.

There were other painful choices, too. At some destinations, as a way to apply the tourniquet to our cash crisis, we made what are called code-sharing agreements with other airlines. The idea is to combine forces in order to gain economies of scale. For example, if we were sending only a plane or two a day to, say, Phoenix or Las Vegas, we would allow an alliance partner—in that case, America West—to handle the groundwork on those flights, and we'd do the same for them in Orlando or Tampa, where we were a greater presence. The customer could still book the flight through us, and it would still be treated as a Continental flight, but the gate agents might be America West personnel. And, as I said, we'd do the same for them in cities we served. It's called *code sharing* because some of our flights would then share reservation codes with theirs, enabling both airlines to book passengers on the flights. In this way we could stop staffing gates that were only busy for a flight or two in the morning and the evening. Our colleagues could do the same thing, so both airlines came out ahead.

In total personnel it was probably a wash—we'd have to close some of our operations in some western cities, but we'd have to increase staffing in our eastern cities. Small comfort, of course, to the person living out West, but we gave those employees opportunities to keep their jobs by moving to other destinations. It wasn't pleasant. But we faced reality with as much grace as we could muster.

Creativity—and the Cost of Inaction

It was horrible to have to furlough employees, to postpone wage snapbacks, to close hubs (affecting not just our employees but entire regions). These decisions saved money—and probably saved the company—but there was a cost: in anger, in frustration, in deepened mistrust. Many people wondered whether the money we saved was worth that human cost.

One of the key questions in any decision is, not only what does it cost to do something, but what does it cost *not* to do something? You have to look at costs from every angle. We had to consider not only what it would do to our company if we closed those facilities and paid the price for it, but what it would cost us to shy away from that action to keep the employees a little happier.

Not closing those facilities would probably have put us under, and *all* the employees would have lost their jobs. We did the hard thing, and we did it in a cooperative way. We didn't regret it.

We had a somewhat similar situation in 19 cities we served, where it looked like we were going to save money by contracting out our ramp work (the work done by the baggage handlers, plane cleaners, and so forth). We were running only a few flights a day in those cities, yet in order to keep our gates staffed we had to pay people for full-time work even though they were spending much of their time idle. We had to weigh alternatives. If we kept our employees at the gate and ticket counters, dealing with customers, it looked like we could save money by hiring independent contractors take care of of the other, less visible tasks.

That's how it looked on paper, anyway. But hiring outside contractors and firing employees would have been the old Continental. We weren't doing that anymore.

Instead, we did the same thing we did in Los Angeles and Greensboro. We showed our employees what the problem was and why we were going to have to make a change: We were in a cash crisis; we were going to have to change things for the long term; and we were going to have to save a certain amount of money. Instead of letting them go, we asked for their help.

Our senior vice president of airport services, Mark Erwin, let the employees examine the books, looking over the costs of operation in their cities. He showed them competing bids from contractors and let them see if they could come up with a comparable alternative plan to keep our jobs in-house. In fact, he even put a team together at headquarters to help them sort out the staffing flows, work up their proposed bids, stuff like that.

Out of those 19 cities, 17 are now still fully staffed by Continental employees. Given the opportunity to contribute, employees came up with creative solutions. In New Orleans, for example, they did away with the distinction between gate and ramp personnel—some days you work upstairs, some days you work downstairs. But everybody kept their jobs.

The two stations that didn't manage to submit a competitive bid were cities where we were running only one flight in the morning and one in the evening. Even those employees could see we didn't really have a choice. We offered them all jobs at other locations, and those who were willing to move kept their jobs.

George Mason had a similar situation at a maintenance base in Houston. We were going to send some new aircraft maintenance work outside the company because we didn't have the capacity for it at our Hobby Airport facility. The people who worked there *wanted* the additional work, though, both for themselves and so we could rehire furloughed people. George said, "Fine, here's what it'll cost us to get it done outside. Why don't we sit down and see if you can bring it home at the same cost?"

Not only did these employees rethink their staffing and reorganize their procedures to handle the work, they actually solved a physical problem. One model of airplane they'd need to work on simply wouldn't fit into their building. The tail was too high to fit through the door.

Too high, at least, until they thought of jacking up the nose of the plane, which made the tail dip low enough to fit inside.

The line came to Hobby. And more people came back to work.

"These Guys Aren't Kidding"

The lesson our employees learned through all these actions was twofold. On the one hand, we weren't going to be shy about doing what needed to be done. We could slash jobs and routes, which would have costs in terms of how our employees felt, or we could refuse to make hard decisions and keep looking like the nice new management team, which would have dire consequences to our business. When we told them we were going to do what was necessary to save this company, we weren't kidding. We would weigh both the cost of doing things and the cost of not doing things, and we planned to make sensible decisions.

On the other hand, employees could see that our cost-cutting measures were not designed to squeeze out every last nickel we could find. We were interested in what we kept saying we were interested in: running the best company we could, making a profit by putting out a good product, and satisfying our customers and our employees. Cost was going to have to fit into that, but it wasn't the *only* thing we thought about.

The bottom line, for the first time in decades, wasn't the only line.

Keep on Climbing

That's how we addressed our financial problems. We took our Fly to Win strategy to heart and stopped doing things that weren't making money. We renegotiated our overwhelming debt. We renegotiated leases for planes and found a way to start making money on routes we wanted to fly.

We went to our creditors, told them the truth, showed them our plans, and asked for their help.

In some ways, of course, this is like a high-stakes poker game. Anybody can go to their creditors at any time and ask for better rates. People often do. It's usually not in the interest of the creditor to renegotiate—after all, the way they make money, the way they win, is to have the best possible rates on *their* side, not on your side. Our creditors could have decided we were just bluffing, or they might have been unwilling to take the risk. If they had had said no, Continental might not be flying now.

As I tell people, it *is* like high-stakes poker, and when we played our cards we didn't blink. We didn't blink because we weren't bluffing. We asked for what we had to have, and we got it.

We did the same thing with our employees. We told them what we needed from them, backed up our assertions with facts, let them look at the books, and worked with them to solve problems in a way that helped all of us. We had to make some tough moves, but we explained those, too.

From there, we worked hard on improving our internal financial systems. We hired Janet Wejman as chief information officer.

She helped us get better computer systems so we started getting better information, which enabled us to make better decisions and improve our cash flow. We found out where our money was, where it had been, and where it was going, and we started to control that. We hired better managers. And throughout the company, we got rid of people who weren't thinking creatively and people who didn't want to cooperate.

Once we got control of our money and our systems, we focused on keeping our eye on the ball and improving things. If we were doing well with a 10 percent interest rate on a loan, could we find a 9 percent loan? If we retired $200 million of debt, could we retire $350 million? If we saved $10 million with a fuel hedge, what else could we hedge that way? If we improved our cash flow by investing in computer systems that could give us monthly numbers two days after the end of the month, how could we get that down to one day?

Our company had been like that out-of-control airplane—spinning around and upside down. We got it to stop spinning and start flying right side up. Since then, our goal has been slightly different: to get control of all the things that got us spinning in the first place, and then to find a gentle rate of climb that would keep us gaining altitude without causing the same problems we just solved. Remember those wage snapbacks? Well, our employees would like more and better raises, because we've still got a ways to go before they're all paid the way they deserve, and the way we'd like them to be paid.

But we have to get there responsibly and slowly—sudden moves and too much too soon is what got us into trouble in the first place. So we carefully monitor all those numbers we've started generating. We share that information with our employees and our partners. And we take our steps where we can.

Better information, greater understanding, more control, better decisions.

We weren't just funding our future: We were choosing it.

Make Reliability a Reality,

or It's Time to Act Like

a Real Airline

L et me tell you the story of the ambulance in the valley.

There's a little town, and it's about halfway up a mountain in a bend in the road. That hairpin turn is a terrible hazard, and, about once a month, cars go flying off into the valley below. It's awful.

The town council gets together and they look into how much it's going to cost to regrade the road, put in signs, and install a guard rail—in other words, make the thing safe. Well, it's going to be really expensive. In fact, it's going to be so expensive that they decide they just can't afford it. But the cars are still flying off the road and people are getting hurt. They don't like that, and they want to do something, so they solve the problem of the dangerous road in what they believed was a less expensive way.

They put an ambulance in the valley.

It's a great story because it shows how hard people will work to avoid solving their real problem. At Continental before I came here, that kind of thinking was a way of life. The philosophy was that you couldn't solve a problem because it was too expensive to do what would solve the problem.

You know what? If you're asking how much it costs to solve a problem, you'd better ask the other question I've mentioned. You may say it's too expensive to fix the road. But you have to ask the other question: What does it cost *not* to fix it?

When we're talking about the core product of our airline, that question is central. At Continental, I guess I'm the guy who finally said, "You know what? It's *dumb* to put the ambulance in the valley. We gotta fix the road no matter what it costs, and that's all there is to it."

That's the difference between success and failure at Continental Airlines. We finally understand that it's dumb to put the ambulance in the valley. The whole point of a road is that you can drive somewhere on it and get there safely. If not, you can put an ambulance wherever you want to, you can put up billboards, and you can talk nice about the road, but it's still going to be a lousy, unreliable road—and sooner or later people are going to stop driving on it.

That's sort of where Continental was: It had become a lousy, unreliable airline and people had stopped using us and for good reason. An airline has no real value at all unless it's predictable and reliable, but for a decade Continental had been cutting costs so much that it not only wasn't improving the road, it had even stopped putting the ambulance in the valley.

So I started asking that question all the time. We know what it costs to do something—get the planes cleaned more often, paint them, hire an extra person to service the engines 10 minutes faster so we can schedule planes to fly when people want them to fly. Those things cost money, and there are always good reasons to avoid doing something that costs money. But what was it costing us *not* to do those things?

The answer was, it was costing us our business. We had cut costs so much that we simply had nothing to offer anymore. Our service was lousy, and nobody knew when a plane might land. We were unpredictable and unreliable, and when you're an airline, where does that leave you?

It leaves you with a lot of empty planes. You know the way customers fill stores to buy really crappy products? The way people line up to see a lousy movie? The way you hurry to a new restaurant with terrible food and bad service for an expensive dinner? Well, that's exactly the way people were lining up to buy Continental Airline tickets. They weren't. We had a lousy product, and nobody particularly wanted to buy it. You can't blame them.

I don't know of any successful company that doesn't have a good product. So while we were fixing the marketing, placement, and organization of our product with Fly to Win, and solving our financial crisis and planning for the future with Fund the Future, we had to do something even more important. We had to fix our product.

Continental was a terrible airline. For the better part of a decade, people had said it would cost too much to do things that would make Continental better. What are the fundamentals of running an airline? Reaching destinations on time. Being clean, safe, and reliable. To succeed, an airline has to be good at those things. Until it is, nothing else works. It's like the pizza story I told you—if you want to sell pizza, sooner or later you're going to have to make a good pizza, with tomato sauce, and crust. You can have fast delivery, pretty napkins, and real low prices, but if you don't do that basic pizza stuff, you can forget the whole thing.

We were an airline. We needed to be clean, safe, and reliable. We needed to operate our planes on time.

Just Be on Time

I already told you that every month the U.S. Department of Transportation measures large airlines according to on-time arrival percentage, lost-baggage claims, complaints received, and number of passengers involuntarily denied boarding.

All of those are important, but we figured out that the most important thing to passengers was getting where they were supposed to get on time. Any survey of airline passengers will tell you that. In fact, the 1997 J.D. Power and Associates Airline Customer Satisfaction Study showed that on-time performance was 22 percent of what determined customer satisfaction. No other single element was judged higher than 15 percent. I've already mentioned that you have to gauge the success of your product by whether it gives your customers what they want. When we chose being on-time as our most important goal at Continental, we were simply choosing what our customers wanted.

Thus, we chose on-time percentage as our macro metric—our basic indicator of whether we were doing well. Don't forget, Continental had been doing terribly for a decade. But we decided that what we were going to do was get our airplanes to land on time.

So we did one more thing.

What You Measure and Reward Is What You Get

We told our employees that if our planes landed on time, as our customers desired, we'd pay them extra. Specifically, we told them that every month our on-time percentage was good enough for us to be in the top five nationwide—again, according to those Department of Transportation numbers—every employee would get $65 extra. If the customers won, the employees would win.

Pretty simple, yes? But it was just another one of those things that used to be too expensive at Continental. We couldn't afford to pay employees to make it worth their while to get their jobs done. So we didn't—and they didn't.

Saving $5 Million by Spending $2.5 Million

I've emphasized that what you measure and reward is what you get. Put another way, what gets measured is what gets managed. It's simple: You measure the results you want, and you reward those results. To get Continental to perform better, we were going to have to both measure what we wanted people to do and then reward them for doing it.

So we said to our employees: Get us there on time and it's worth $65 to you—to *each* of you. Don't, and you don't get the dough—none of you. That's all or nobody—we win or lose as a team. Meet the goal and every single employee gets money. Although the pilots operated under their own union contract, this included every other employee—the gate agents, the flight attendants, the baggage handlers, the secretaries, the reservation agents. Every employee got $65 dollars. Simple as that.

Multiply $65 by 40,000 employees (fewer, actually, because we didn't include managers, who had their own bonus plans) and you've got around $2.5 million. Continental was going broke, and I decided to start giving employees an extra $2.5 million per month.

Where we got the figure of $65 is also simple. By being late, we ended up spending a lot of money. Late planes miss connections, which means passengers hang around airports, sometimes even overnight. You have to feed them. Sometimes you have to house them overnight. Sometimes you have to put them on other airlines to get them where you promised to get them.

We took a look at how much we were spending each month on costs associated with being late, and we determined that it was about $5 million dollars. That's $5 million that we were spending every month because we couldn't get our planes in on time. We figured we could take half that and give it right back to our employees if they were on time. Then if it worked, we'd actually be saving money—plus we'd have a product that people might actually want to buy.

This underscores what I said about the ambulance in the valley. It was going to cost us $2.5 million to pay an extra $65 a month to every employee, but an even more important issue was what it would cost us *not* to pay them that. The answer was $5 million or even more—possibly our business. In other words, we were going to save money by spending money—or, as we've learned, save money by motivating our employees to do whatever it takes to succeed.

Your Check Is in the Mail—and It Really Was!

You don't need me to tell you that it worked, but let me tell you: It worked.

We announced the new program in January 1995. I'm not sure that every employee truly understood it, and I'm not sure that everyone who understood it believed that anything good would come of it. Remember, these employees didn't trust us, and after the previous decade it was hard to blame them for that. That was one of the reasons we had chosen Department of Transportation numbers for our goals—in the past, anything to avoid paying promised pay was something employees would have expected from management. Until we re-earned their trust, at least nobody could accuse us of altering numbers supplied by the government.

However, it seemed as if employees gave us the benefit of the doubt right off the bat, because in January 1995, 71 percent of our planes landed on time. That wasn't perfect by any means—we ranked seventh among the top 10 airlines—but it was a lot better than January 1994, when we brought in only 61 percent of our flights on time and came in last. It was a start. We let the employees know we appreciated that and reminded them that if they did better, there was $65 in it for them.

In February 1995, 80 percent of our flights landed on time. That put us in fourth place—and, for the first time in years, better than the industry average of 79 percent.

Fourth. That's top five, and you know what that meant: Checks worth more than $2.5 million went out to our employees.

Please take note of that. We didn't just drop $65 extra dollars into their paychecks and have the whole impact of their bonus disappear. Nor did we let them start calculating how much of it they lost to taxes. We gave each employee $65 in a special check—we took the withholding out of their regular paychecks, so they got $65 actual dollars.

It was exciting to walk the halls during early March, when employees were buzzing about the $65 in what seemed to them to be found money. You would hear stories—one woman wasn't going to tell her husband she got the check, so she could use the $65 of extra-budget money for something special for herself; another employee used the $65 to celebrate by letting his children choose whatever sugary cereal they wanted when they went grocery shopping. For people on tight budgets—and Continental employees were definitely among them, though they've certainly made strides since then—$65 was something.

Do you think they noticed? Well, in March we ranked first. More than 83 percent of our planes landed on time, and nobody did better than that. We were in first place—for the first time in our entire history. They got $65 more.

Yep. They noticed. We were first in April again. We didn't do so great in the next couple of months, the result of a work slowdown by some of the pilots, who were in the midst of an understandably frustrating union contract negotiation. But when our contract with the pilots was settled, we were right back up: second in August and September, third in October, fourth in November.

Raising the Bar

We got so much better so quickly that we raised the bar. With all the praise we were giving everybody for the great job they were doing, we told them that things were going to get a little harder. For 1996, instead of getting paid for being in the top half, we decided we were going to have to finish third or higher to get the bonus. But because we were raising the bar, we also wanted to raise the reward, so for finishing in first place, employees would get $100.

The employees, who had learned a thing or two about themselves by then, shrugged their shoulders and came in first in December 1995—before they were even scheduled to get paid extra for doing so.

Well, I one-upped them: I *paid* them $100 for their December performance. You see, they had shown all of us in management that all they needed was a good reason to believe they would be rewarded for success and they'd succeed. Hell, all they really needed was for us to get out of their way. So I wanted to show them that we appreciated their accomplishment—and even though the $100-for-first policy didn't start until 1996, we paid them for December 1995.

Remember the discussion in Chapter 2 about how we did things to show that Continental was different? Everything from sitting in different places in the meeting rooms to repainting all the airplanes showed employees, suppliers, and customers alike that this company was different.

I think that payment in December 1995 convinced any remaining doubters. We had promised to give them $65, but instead we gave them $100. The Go Forward Plan had been in place for a year. The company's financial situation was vastly improved; people were flying our airline; the on-time percentage was better than ever. We hoped employees could see that the management was behaving better, too—and in December, anybody who couldn't see it before finally saw it.

Since then, we've had to keep readjusting the bar in different ways. Directives have to be responsive, not set in stone. For example, our policy of measuring on-time percentage and rewarding it got a lot of press, and we started getting passengers back. Naturally enough, other airlines started doing the same thing and working as hard as we were to be on time. In 1997, we started noticing that we could have, say, our best August ever for on-time percentage, but we'd still come in fourth if a couple of other airlines had great months.

So we adjusted. Now we either have to rank in the top three nationwide or we have to be on time with better than 80 percent of our flights. Even if we're only fifth-best in a month, we figure that if we're on time 80 percent of the time, that's very good work and worth the reward. So that's perfectly clear to our employees now: Get better than 80 percent of our planes in on time and get the bonus. If we can't do that, we can still get the bonus if we're in the top three nationwide. It's clear, and it rewards everyone together for what we want them to do.

Getting the planes in on time became a central part of Continental's culture. Just as important, we were getting things done together—as a team. It's important that we learned to focus on getting things done right, that we set specific goals, and that we rewarded people for achieving them as a team.

Here's shorthand for Make Reliability a Reality: First, we focused on the basics of our business. Second, we rewarded collective behavior. We were winning, and we were winning as a team. That changed our company completely.

Oh, You Want the Bags, Too?

At first with the new on-time policy, we saw something that in a way wasn't too surprising: The planes were landing on time, but the numbers of lost bags were going up. Planes were leaving on time and getting where they needed to be—but not always with their bags. Slow bags, late bags, problem bags wouldn't always make the plane.

It makes sense. If you're getting paid to get the planes in on time and baggage handling is perceived as incidental, what's your priority going to be? You think another baggage cart might be coming with a couple more bags, but if you wait you might miss the 15-minute leeway for being judged on-time. What would you do?

So we had to get the word out that if the number of baggage complaints was increasing, that wasn't going to make it. We didn't want on-time flights without bags, or without people, or with dirty aisles. On-time meant the whole system was working on-time, not just part of it. So we explained this to our employees, and baggage started making it onto the planes. Baggage has ever since been one of the areas in which we excel—we recently went through a period during which we were in the top three airlines in baggage handling for 30 out of 31 months. That's people getting their jobs done.

This requires further explanation. When baggage became a small problem in our effort to get the planes on time, we didn't say "Okay, we need to offer people money to get the bags on the planes." That's their *job*. What we needed to do was explain that we wanted those planes to be on time, and we wanted people to get their on-time bonuses. But just as it wasn't going to do any good to get planes out on time if the passengers weren't on them yet, it wasn't going to do any good to get them out on time without those passengers' bags, either.

The whole point of on-time ranking as a metric was that it measured our entire operation. A plane that got out on time was a plane that had its supply of meals, all its passengers, and all their bags. It was a clean plane and a safe plane. It was a plane that was giving our customers exactly what they wanted.

Bit by bit we were learning to focus our employees on their real jobs. We were paying them to do better, and they were doing better. They quickly learned that their job wasn't to save money anymore. Their job was to run a good airline—an airline that got planes in on time, with their bags; that fed its passengers and treated them well; that showed them nice-looking planes all painted the same color, with first-class seats, frequent flyer miles, and polite people working at the gates and on the reservations lines. That's how our employees would win—that's how they got paid. So that's what they became: people who did their jobs so that the airline could do its job.

A Word on Safety

Let me say a word about safety. We had to remind our employees that they had to get all their jobs done in order for us to succeed the way we wanted to—it was a fundamental change in our company. But it is worth pointing out that one thing we never had to remind them of is that we weren't willing to compromise safety for any other goal. There isn't one person—not one—in our company who would sacrifice safety for financial or any other goals.

The main reason for this is, of course, that safety is just plain important. But if you push the moral importance of safety aside for a moment and presume that we're all greedy supercapitalists here who would gladly send up rattletrap airliners so long as we made a profit, take a look at any other company that has suffered the loss of an airplane lately. Crashing airplanes can put you out of business.

If you lose an airplane and it turns out that your operation's safety standards looked a little uncertain, you're in big trouble. You won't be making a profit for a long while. Just like with food and medicine, first it has to be safe.

People appreciate landing on time and getting their bags, but above all, they want the plane to *land*. They want you to land them alive. Everything else is negotiable. Once you lose their confidence in that, they're gone. If you make pizza and you cut costs so much that you're making lousy pizza, you can start putting more cheese on it and people might come back. If you're making pizza and you stop refrigerating your ingredients so that your customers start spending time in the emergency room, all the cheese in the world isn't going to get your business going again.

So for a moment, let's just leave the moral imperative of safety out—we never do, of course, but just look past it for a moment. An unsafe airline is the worst business in the world.

So safety at Continental—and I believe this about our worst days as much as about our best, about Continental under my predecessors as well as Continental since I've been there, and about every top 10 U.S. air carrier—is sacrosanct. We don't take risks with safety.

Here's an Idea: How about If We Let *You* Do Your Job?

That said, what did we do to get our planes on time? Yes, it's great that we showed our employees that if they got those planes in on time we'd pay them extra money. That gives them incentive. But surely before we instituted the incentives, our employees weren't getting up in the morning and saying, "What the heck, I'm going to work but who cares whether I do any work today." We couldn't presume that just tossing a little money at them was going to suddenly fix what was wrong. Money could get their attention, but we didn't think it was just lack of money that had been causing our operation to stink.

In Chapter 2 I told you that we burned the employee manual. That's one of the most important things we did, and it had a profound effect on the reliability and predictability of our airline.

Under the old style of management, as symbolized by that authoritarian manual, employees were limited on every side. A passenger with an unusual situation was a dangerous character to be avoided, not a challenge to be resolved. No matter what employees did, the manual probably told them it was wrong—and if the manual didn't, one of their perpetually annoyed supervisors in our generally cranky airline surely would.

Here's an example. We used to have what were called Add-a-Penny-Add-a-Pal fares—you'd buy one ticket at full fare and someone would fly free along with you. Say you're flying with your husband on a companion fare to your daughter's wedding in Chicago. However, there's a problem with the plane, and your flight is canceled. We're going to put you on another flight to Chicago, on another airline. The old manual was crystal clear about procedure in this situation: We put people paying full fares on other airlines; people flying free or paying other special fares had to wait for the next Continental flight. There's no room for interpretation: Mrs. Smith, your flight leaves in 20 minutes, sorry for the trouble, and have a nice flight with our competitor. Mr. Smith? Not so fast—you'll be going out five hours from now.

That's World War III right there in the airport, and if you're Continental's gate agent, you're not any happier than the Smiths. You know it's a stupid policy, but you know that at the old Continental Airlines we followed rules and that was that. So you had a choice: You could take the heat from the Smiths and hate it, or you could break the rule—and maybe lose your job.

Not any more. With the symbolic burning of the manual, we changed that. We set up a committee to reorganize and rewrite that manual. And we don't call it a manual any more, we call it guidelines. The new guidelines are supposed to help employees solve problems—give them a sense of where the boundaries are when they run into trouble. But in the general pursuit of their jobs, we want them to use their heads and use their resources. We don't want robots, we want team members.

Now the guidelines say, for example, that if someone is flying on a special fare or a free fare, we'll try to put them on the next Continental flight, because that makes sense. But if you find yourself in the middle of something complicated, something unusual, something that just doesn't fit, then you use your head and make the best decision that you can. Do what's best for the customer and the airline. Not one or the other—use your head and do what's best for both the customer *and* the airline.

We want employees to use their judgment. And to be honest, this scared some of our managers to death. "They're going to be giving away the store!" was the basic fear. And there was some grounding to that fear. When you've got irate customers yelling at you in an airport, it may be tempting for an employee to just give them what they want—whatever they want—to make them stop yelling, especially when Continental management has made clear that *we* want to stop yelling, too. Some managers feared that whatever the problems were, employees would solve them by spending money—giving away fares, buying new parts when old ones could be fixed. Given free rein, what would our employees do?

I didn't worry. Sure, I figured, 5 percent or so will run wild, take advantage, screw this up. But the other 95 percent are people who probably will be so glad for the opportunity to do their jobs that they'll easily manage the balancing act between the good of the airline and the good of the customer. Then we can let our entire management team worry about managing only 5 percent of our employees, because the other 95 percent will basically be managing themselves.

It's worth making one more point about the employees giving away the store. Once we started making profits, we started writing profit-sharing checks. Each year, around Valentine's Day, 15 percent of our pre-tax profits are distributed to our employees. Therefore, it's their own money they'd be giving away.

Let me tell you, they think twice. And our success shows that I was right. The combination of the freedom to do their jobs and the incentive to get results was the recipe for a miracle.

Working Together

Here's an example. Say you're a flight attendant, looking to close the airplane doors and get your airplane ready for takeoff, but you're five meals short. You go to the catering person servicing your plane and you ask for five more. He's got a problem: His cart is empty, and he's got to go back to the kitchen and get more.

In the old days, that meant a late plane. But it wouldn't be the flight attendant's fault. Catering would have to answer for the delay the following day. Besides, she didn't want to handle the irate customers who didn't receive meals if everyone decided to eat.

So that flight attendant was going to hold the plane, and if anybody asked why it was late, she was prepared: "His fault," she said, pointing at the catering guy. He could shift the blame to his kitchen staff, I suppose. But the point is that people wouldn't stick their necks out to solve problems. That's what the situation demanded. That was how to be successful at Continental Airlines. That's how Continental worked.

Now it's different. If that flight attendant is five meals short, the catering guy says he's got to go back to the kitchen, and the plane will be late, she's going to get creative. First, of course, she's going to tell him not to put her in that position again. Then she's going to close the door of the plane and get ready for takeoff. She knows that those passengers think getting where they're going on time is more important than their meals—and she knows that she'll be rewarded if they get there on time. She'll figure she can find five investment bankers on the plane who'll trade their meals for drinks and she'll solve the problem that way.

The difference is that she now has the ability to solve that minor problem—we *want* her to solve that problem. We figure that's her job, and we want her to do it to the best of *her* ability. More important, she's got that $65 or even $100 on-time bonus helping her to stay focused on getting that plane off on time.

As I said, that catering guy is going to get a dirty look—and the flight attendant is going to save his butt by getting the plane off on time anyhow. The catering guy, in turn, is going to work hard to do better next time, because he doesn't want to be the reason that nobody in the company gets their on-time bonus next month.

Take that little example and multiply it by more than 2,000 flights a day, by millions of telephone calls to our reservation centers, by thousands of bags that might have missed a plane if somebody didn't hustle, by thousands of gate agents making thousands of decisions to keep passengers happy and planes moving. You can see the impact our new policy has.

A similar situation exists with our pilots. Instead of an ironclad rule to take off at the scheduled time, our pilots now have the authority—the *responsibility*—to take off when it makes sense. That means that a pilot—who's got the flight plan that shows the day's winds, the time between cities, the situation in the destination city—can make decisions. If the plane is waiting on a couple of bags or a couple of pass riders but the pilot has got a tailwind and no traffic problems at the destination airport, then maybe he or she can wait 10 minutes and still land on time. On-time arrival, by the way, is measured by the Department of Transportation as arriving at the gate within 15 minutes of schedule. We figure that our pilots should use that leeway to the best advantage of our passengers and our airline. Again, we want them to make smart *decisions*, not blindly follow rules.

Suddenly our employees are running a good airline.

The Checklist

I can't stress enough that getting people to understand their jobs and how they are measured made their lives easier. This was the complete opposite of how it used to be, with an employee manual that boxed them into ridiculous procedures for every element of their work. Now we give them actual goals instead of rules—and rewards if they make the goals rather than punishment if they miss them.

It's a kind of checklist. Go into the cockpit of an airplane—or the galley, or anywhere that airline people do their jobs—and you'll find checklists: takeoff checklists, landing checklists, supply checklists. Doctors have diagnostic checklists that they run down, at least mentally. Maintenance technicians have checklists to make sure they've checked everything about an engine.

When your job is broken down into a series of steps that you know need to get done each time you do it, it becomes easier to do that job. The key here, of course, is that the jobs are now defined in steps that actually get the jobs done—and in ways that the people doing the jobs have signed on for.

I told you in Chapter 3 that one of the keys at Continental was to get different employees and different groups working together rather than sabotaging each other. That meant that by the time we made a flying schedule, or a new cleaning procedure, or a fee structure, or a maintenance estimate, the people who were expected to do the work had signed off on what it was we were asking them to do, whether it was fly between Houston and Miami in less than three hours or perform a certain maintenance task in 45 minutes.

People were being asked to do things they had agreed could be done—so suddenly it wasn't as hard to do them. They could review the checklist of their responsibilities and not see anything that didn't make sense. They could run down the list, saying, "I can do that . . . yeah, I agreed to that . . . yeah, that makes sense . . ." and then realize they had an entire job that made sense. They knew what they were supposed to do, they agreed that it was possible, and then, to top it off, we would pay them extra if they reached a goal—*and it was a goal they had already agreed was possible to reach.* Suddenly Continental was getting to be a nice place to work.

The checklists themselves are a series of important steps to achieve their goals, whether the goal is to get the plane off the ground, to approach an airport from a certain direction, or to make sure the entire plane gets cleaned, including the galley. The checklists keep the employees focused on the tasks at hand.

The Go Forward Plan itself is a checklist. When people in the company lose their direction and start coming up with schemes to, for example, save money or improve paper flow around the office or change the music on the planes, the Go Forward Plan reminds them what their goals are. The plan encourages the employee to ask how this scheme, whatever it might be, will help to ensure flights that people want to take (Fly to Win), keep the company financially responsible (Fund the Future), improve Continental's service (Make Reliability a Reality), or improve the way employees work together as a team (Working Together)? If a proposal doesn't do one of those things, it's off-base. The checklist helps identify that.

Under Make Reliability a Reality, we worked on making that checklist really easy to understand: Get the planes to their destinations in a clean, safe, and reliable manner, with their baggage. That's it—that's the job.

Now that management is out of their way, the employees do it every day.

More Help from Above

Meanwhile the managers sit around and take the credit, right?

Wrong. A manager's job, I think, is simple. A manager wants to hire the best people for the job; make sure they have the proper training, resources, and support; and then *get out of the way*. When employees have problems, the manager should take the problems off their hands if possible, so the employees can keep doing their jobs well. Basically, managers do their best work by letting employees do theirs.

You have to choose right, of course. You have to choose good employees, and you have to make sure that they get the necessary training and support. You have to do other managerial things such as plan and schedule and organize, but all that is really just a way to clear the runway for the people who are doing the work—and to keep that runway clear.

Once we saw how well our employees were doing, keeping the runway clear was pretty simple.

Call Me

We had to keep improving, of course. We kept asking our employees what would help them do their jobs better, and they kept telling us things. They felt cut off from management when they had problems. A plane could have a broken oven in the coach galley, for example, and those who had to cope with it had the feeling that all the forms and requisitions in the world wouldn't get it fixed—it would cause trouble for six flights instead of two before it was attended to.

This was an excellent point. If broken things weren't getting fixed in a timely fashion, flight attendants couldn't be expected to do their jobs. To make sure that they could get directly to help when they ran into trouble, we set up an 800 number for them to call when they had any kind of technical operations problem, such as a broken oven, a stuck jetway door, or a balky computer. We set up an operational response team, staffed seven days a week, to help solve these kinds of problems. C. D. McLean, our top operations executive, formed a special team to help solve problems. He placed a talented DC-10 captain, Debbie McCoy, in the lead of an effort to really solve operational glitches daily.

We even set up an 800 voice-mail number directly to my office. We were still dealing with employees who, for good reason, didn't trust management. I was new, and I was the guy who was saying that everything was going to be different. So if they could trust nobody else, they could call me. On a good day, I'd get a couple of calls. On a day when a policy changed or something unusual happened, I'd get a couple of dozen.

And here's the secret: *We responded.* If an oven had been broken for six flights, we got it fixed—and then figured out why it wasn't getting fixed more promptly. Sometimes we found communications glitches. Sometimes we found that employees had so completely lost confidence that they weren't even filling out the repair requisitions any more. Whatever problems we found, we solved.

Word got around. After one or two crew members called the 800 number and got something fixed, other crew members started to believe that maybe what was broken *could* be fixed. Then instead of ignoring problems or grousing about how nothing ever gets done around here, they'd dial that 800 number, get results— and do better work.

My favorite story about earning the employees' trust by responding to their needs came from one of the pilots. He had written to me in the early days—late 1994, I think—with a complaint. I don't remember what the specific complaint was, but I do remember that it was justified. So I picked up the phone and called the pilot. It was seven or eight o'clock in the evening, and he was sitting in his hot tub with his girlfriend when he answered the phone. When I identified myself to him, he was so shocked that he spilled his wine into the tub. I thanked him for his letter and told him we were working on the problem. I asked him to keep the faith. He said he would.

Afterward, he told everyone he worked with, "You know what? If you write Gordon, he'll actually respond!" The same thing happened over and over: I'd call an employee, identify myself, and, at first, people wouldn't believe it was me. After a while, though, word got around that if somebody called up and said he was Gordon Bethune, he probably was.

That management message helped people believe that if they needed help, they could get it—because they could.

"Sorry You Hated Your Flight—See You Next Time!"

Of course, what works for our employees, as always, works for our passengers.

We surmised that those complaints about Continental that were going to the U.S. Department of Transportation and were killing us in the statistics and ruining our reputation must have originally come to us. Most of them had. We were real good at *getting* complaints back then. We just weren't too good at *doing* anything about them.

When we dug into our customer service response to complaints, we discovered that if you had a bad experience on a Continental flight and took the time to write us about it, you might not hear from us at all. If you did hear from us, you'd get a form letter— about five months later. The letter would say something along the lines of: "Sorry you hated your flight. Hope you fly with us again! Sincerely, Continental Airlines." I don't need to tell you what kind of repeat business that was getting us. It was those people we were ignoring who were then getting so disgusted that they would call or write the Department of Transportation.

Larry Goodwin, our vice president in charge of reservations and customer care, changed that. Besides improving our service and doing everything we could to stop giving people *reason* to complain, Larry decided to head the complaints off at the pass. We did everything we could to encourage people to contact us, so that we could solve any problems they had, instead of sending them to the government.

We made it easy for them. We put postage-paid cards in our in-flight magazines, asking for their response and opinions. We set up and heavily promoted an 800 number (800-WECARE-2) to enable people to get to us immediately. We made it a priority that if you wrote Continental Airlines, you would get a reply from us within five days. No other airline did that.

The number of complaints started dropping. In 1994, we averaged 68 complaints to the Department of Transportation per month. By April 1995, that number had dropped to 26. By April 1996, we were down to less than one complaint for every 200,000 passengers, which ranked us third nationwide. We've never looked back.

Once again, we encouraged the people who handled those complaints to use their judgment in solving problems. If someone had a legitimate complaint, we did what we could not just to hear them out, but to satisfy them. Our customer service people had at their disposal first-class upgrades, coupons for discounts and free food, and even free flights when necessary to assuage disgruntled customers. If a service representative thought that a customer had been treated poorly and the rep wanted to send a card or some flowers, or take another extra step, that was okay with us. If someone was truly giving away too much, we'd pull in the reins, but that made up the smallest portion of what we were doing. By and large, our employees, given the chance, loved to do good work.

Going Forward

Once our new program proved successful, keeping employees' attention was simple. We stuck with what worked: We kept tinkering with what wasn't working perfectly yet and solicited input on other areas that needed attention.

For example, we found that we were getting passengers and their bags on the planes and the planes were getting out on time, but, in our focus on the passengers, we were sometimes missing the boat on each other. Employees flying on passes, as well as their family members and their baggage—in other words, nonrevenue passengers and bags—were sometimes failing to make flights that had empty seats on them. This was easy to understand. When you're focusing on getting things done right for the first time in a long while, something like employee travel can seem secondary or get lost in the shuffle.

That wasn't good enough. In the same way that it was not acceptable for our planes to be on time but without their passengers or bags, we didn't want the planes to be going without the pass riders they could carry. That's one more example of a price we didn't want to pay for being on time.

Pass riders don't generate any cash for Continental, but those flight privileges are part of the compensation we offer our employees—for some of them, those privileges are every bit as important as the money. Ignoring those employee pass riders was just a sneaky way of not paying them what we had promised them. So we made that a priority, and we started measuring it. We checked flight manifests and pass rider requests; we compared cities on the basis of their compliance with on-time departures and empty seats when there were pass riders waiting.

Surprise! Once we started measuring it, people figured out ways to get everybody on the planes. This was just another indication that our commitment to doing things right went one layer deeper. As usual, when the employees understood how it had to work, they found ways to *make* it work.

We took the same approach to lost baggage on these flights. On most airlines, lost baggage for pass riders—employees or their family members flying on passes—is just that: lost luggage. These passengers aren't reimbursed in the way that paying customers are, because the tickets don't generate revenue. Lost luggage is looked at as the risk you take for flying free. Continental followed this policy, too, until a flight attendant called my 800 number to complain about that.

We changed it immediately. Our employees are our most important resource. If we want them to fly free on our airlines as part of their compensation, then we ought to take care of their bags as well as we take care of any others. After all, we weren't losing many bags anymore. We reimbursed the flight attendant who had complained and we made this a provision of our policy.

Employees learn about changes like that all the time, because we send out memos and notices and post information on bulletin boards I'll tell you about in Chapter 10. More important, they hear about them from their coworkers—from the pilot who got the call in the hot tub; from the flight attendant who got the oven fixed; from the employee who was reimbursed for a lost bag.

Things are *working*, they keep hearing. And that feeds on itself.

Would You Please Pick Up the Phone?

Everywhere we looked we found ways to improve. Larry Goodwin did some pretty simple testing of how long it took our reservation agents to answer the phones, and he didn't like what he found. You could call Continental Airlines and be on the phone for more than a minute before someone would answer.

For people whose job is basically to answer the telephone and get people's money, that was not going to work. So we did two things. The first was to tell these employees that wasn't going to be enough. They were going to have to start getting the phones answered a lot faster. The second thing we did was to give them the opportunity to do that. By talking to our reservation agents and their supervisors, we discovered that the reservation system they were using was balky, old, and unreliable. One of the reasons they were taking a long time to answer calls was that it was taking so long to help the people whose calls they *were* answering.

We took measures to improve the situation. For one, we increased capacity, so we could handle larger call volumes. For another, we automated everything we could. A large amount of airline phone traffic consists of simple questions—What time does a flight leave? Is it on time? Is Denver snowed in? That kind of stuff was easy to automate—all you needed to know was your flight number and you could get all the information without having to speak to a reservations agent. That helped.

We also staffed the reservations centers correctly. With better staffing, better systems to support their work, and the offloading of calls they didn't need to handle, Continental's reservations agents quickly became the fastest in the business. If you test this yourself, you'll find that it's true: Call five airlines and I guarantee you that, overall, we're going to be the fastest to take your call. We want you to spend your money with us.

Reliability Is Everywhere

As with all our other initiatives, our reliability initiatives built on themselves and combined with the others we were working on to reinforce the improvement of this airline. In Chapter 3, I talked about getting the scheduling and operations people to work together to design a schedule that would work and that would build in time for required maintenance. Well, that started working, too.

I've always said that you can either schedule routine maintenance or let the airplanes schedule it for you by breaking down because you don't maintain them. Once we had a schedule in place, by which the mechanics had time to perform the maintenance the planes needed, the planes started breaking down a *lot* less. That improves on-time percentage. It sends employees home with $65 a month extra, which makes happy customers and employees—and makes employees who work harder and better next month.

It's just not that hard to figure out, honestly.

Copycats

Nevertheless, some people in our business couldn't do it! They say that imitation is the sincerest form of flattery, so when other airlines started coming up with their own variations of on-time pay, I thought, good enough.

Only here's the thing: *They got it wrong.* Earlier in this chapter I told you that the figure of $65 for our on-time bonus was equivalent to half of the money we were losing every month by being late. Funnel half of that $5 million or so to your employees, and you improve your product and at the same time take better care of your employees, while giving them the incentive to continue to improve. You win; the customer wins; the employees win. Pretty simple, right?

Well, not to one airline that copied our program directly—only they got it wrong. For one thing, they chose $65 because it was the same amount we used—it had no real relevance to their own profit and loss statement. For another, they didn't take the scheduling, maintenance, and support steps that we did, so their employees couldn't meet their goals. This company did exactly the wrong thing: They set up a reward but made it one the employees couldn't attain. So who wins there? The customers lose because the flights don't get any better—in fact, they may get worse when the employees get good and frustrated. The employees lose because they can't meet their goals. With annoyed employees and disappointed customers, do you think management wins or loses? Good guess.

But even if they didn't completely understand it, our competitors realized they had to respond to our program. Whether by somehow copying it or at least by acknowledging it, they had to respond. Suddenly they had a new competitor, and we planned to be a problem for them.

You see? It's a competitive business. We've made reliability a reality so completely that we're being copied by our competitors, which is natural. And fun's fun. And I'll stay real cheerful as long as we stay right up near the top in all the ways we're measured.

And the Details Never Stop

At Continental, we keep doing new things to improve our service. We asked our passengers what kind of food they wanted on their flights, and we made corresponding changes—they wanted Coca-Cola instead of Pepsi, so now they get Coke. They wanted variety in the beers we offered, so now they get that. They wanted priority baggage handling for first-class passengers, and they got that. We learned that food was a priority, so now Greg and I taste new food offerings ourselves, before we put it on the planes.

We keep asking, they keep telling us, and we keep changing in response. Reliability is truly a reality now.

Phones Are Good—Phones with Dial Tones Are Better

Not that it's always easy. We learned that our passengers wanted in-flight phones, and even before I took over from my predecessor, Continental had worked hard to get new, high-tech phones in our planes. These phones were supposed to be able to make calls, play video games, do everything but put your luggage in the overhead compartment and bring you a scotch.

But they didn't. So we put some effort into finding a new partner, GTE, who could supply us with reliable phones that not only look kind of neat, they actually work. By the end of 1997, most of our jets had them.

Remember the Fundamentals: The Product Is the Point

Do you see how all this worked?

In the Make Reliability a Reality phase of the Go Forward Plan, we demonstrated the most important part of our new focus. Everything we did was based on making our *product* better, as defined by our customers. We wanted to be on time, and then we had to remind ourselves that we needed to be on time *with* the bags and *with* all the nonrevenue passengers and *with* the food and *with* a clean airplane, and with all the other things passengers expect of their product.

First, we said, we'll pay our employees better to do better. Pretty simple. At the same time, we gave them the tools to *be* better— better systems, better planning, and the time to do their jobs. Naturally, that worked pretty well.

Everything else flowed from that. We started putting out a better product, so, naturally enough, people wanted to buy it. Then we had a little more money to further stabilize our financial situation and do a better job of providing the tools our employees needed to do their jobs. That led to further improvements, better pay, and so on.

Our progress built on all the things we were doing in all the other phases of the Go Forward Plan. Remember I said that newer planes mean less heavy maintenance? That in turn meant that we could get more flights out of our planes, which also meant better schedules. Remember I talked about putting scheduling and technical operations together? That paid dividends not only in itself but in better planning as problems and opportunities came up.

Suppose someone suggested that we could save money by repacking the wheel bearings on the landing gear every six months instead of every three months. That's fine as far as it goes, but what will that do to the wheel failure rate? Because we have better and better systems, we could actually track that and see that, if we saved a little by performing maintenance a little less frequently, we'd end up paying more in occasional wheel failures. That is, we'd be saving money, but we'd be decreasing the reliability of our product. Suddenly that's an easy decision to make. We aren't in business to save money—we are in business to put out a good product. Keep repacking those bearings like we always have.

Or say we found that a plane coming out of Newark was regularly late, simply as a result of the incredibly complex airspace around Newark. To a certain extent, that problem is unfixable—all we can do is get our planes away from the gate on time. If they end up sitting on the runway for 45 minutes, that's just reality.

But what if we looked at isolating that problem, so that instead of a plane leaving Newark for Washington and then Houston and then Miami, which would mean that three more flights would be delayed, we kept flights into and out of Newark as straight out-and-backs from our hubs? That way, if Newark was delayed, it would delay the passengers on that flight, but no others. Better scheduling and operations reliability enabled us to figure out things like that.

Remember Fund the Future, the segment of the Go Forward plan in which we decided to fly fewer kinds of planes so we'd have fewer kinds of maintenance? That made our maintenance more reliable, which in turn made our airline better and brought us more passengers.

Continental had regained its focus. From the old days when cutting cost was what we did, we had remembered that, fundamentally, *flying airplanes* was what we did. It always comes down to that: Focus on your job; focus on what people want from you. We figured out that customers wanted us to be clean, safe, reliable, and on time, with their bags. So we gave them that, and they came back to us.

Continental has some 2,100 flights every day. I ask my employ-ees sometimes, Which one is most important? Which one above all else has to be on time, has to give the customers what they want? There's only one right answer: *The flight you're on.* That's the only one you can control, the only one you can directly affect. Therefore, focus on making *that flight* a great Continental flight, and everything else will take care of itself.

The best example I can find for how thoroughly that culture has made its way throughout our organization is a flight I took recently from Washington to Houston. As I've told you, when I get on a flight I stick my head in the cockpit to say hello, intro-duce myself to the crew, and chat for a minute. But I often get on at the last minute, which this time meant I was getting on just as the gate agent was hustling to get the plane out on time.

My back was to him, and I heard someone say, "Excuse me, sir, you'll have to sit down. The plane has to leave."

One of the flight attendants was horrified. "Do you know who that is?" she hissed. "That's Mr. Bethune!"

The agent said, "That's very nice, but we gotta go. Tell him to sit down."

I sat down. You see? He didn't care if it was Gordon Bethune or George Bush. His job was to get the airplane out on time. His pay was connected to that. That was his focus. So, whoever I was, he wanted to get that plane out on time.

That is how Continental Airlines stays on time.

Working Together, or Which Part of This Watch Don't You Think We Need?

In early 1995, as part of Continental's efforts to make sure our
employees knew that finally their voices were being heard, we
took our show on the road. We expanded the open houses we
were holding in the Houston headquarters. We started holding
employee meetings twice a year all over our system—mostly in our
hubs. The point was that we wanted it to be easy for any employees to get to top management and ask any questions that were on
their minds. Things were going better for us—a lot better. But as
things changed, we wanted employees to stay comfortable. We
wanted to make sure they had the chance to ask questions directly
of me, of Greg, and of other big shots.

At one of those meetings, in Newark, I asked the most important question I have ever asked my employees, and I still ask it
every day. I was telling them a little about the $65 bonuses they
had started to receive. They were thrilled, of course, but people
being people, they had some questions.

One employee stood up and asked a tough question.

He could see why the pilots would get on-time bonuses. He could see why the gate agents and flight crew would get the bonus. He could see where the baggage handlers would come into the picture, and maybe even where schedulers and mechanics fit in. But why, he wanted to know, did people like reservations agents— the people who answered those phones I was telling you about in the preceding chapter—get bonuses? They weren't loading the planes; they weren't flying the planes; they weren't getting passengers on and off. They were just selling the tickets. Their actions seemed to have nothing to do with whether we were on time. So why were they getting a share of the dough?

Before I tell you how I answered this question, you should know that I collect watches. I admire watches—they're miracles of cooperation—dozens, even hundreds, of parts all fitting together to do a single job, and they create value for you by letting you know exactly what time it is. Every part of the watch does a job—and any part that fails can impair or destroy the function of the entire watch. It's no good to you without the hour hand or the clock face, certainly, but it's just as useless without the tiniest screw that holds the escapement together or the mainspring on. It's an all-for-one kind of proposition.

So I looked out at all these expectant faces, all these employees who wanted to see how I'd explain why everybody in our company got bonuses. How was I going to justify giving away money to people who never, as part of their jobs, actually saw the inside—or even the outside—of an airplane.

I held up my watch.

"Which part of this watch," I asked the employee, "don't you think we need?"

The employee couldn't answer and sat down. Not embarrassed, mind you—his question made sense. But I think we all learned something about teamwork and the value that each member brings.

What We Learned

What that employee learned at that moment, and what every Continental employee has learned over the several years since I took over from the old regime, is that, just like that watch, Continental Airlines is an all-for-one kind of proposition. All that talk about not having internal winners and losers, about making sure that everybody wins and loses together, was true.

It wasn't any good to us if the pilots were happy and the gate agents weren't, or if the baggage handlers were getting paid and the reservations agents weren't, or if the mechanics were getting awards and the people in accounting hated to come to work—or if the big shots were taking home big canvas bags with dollar signs on the side and the flight attendants were taking pay cuts. That kind of stuff breeds internal dissension, unhappiness, and, eventually, poor performance. *Everybody* had to be winning, or Continental wasn't going to fly successfully.

And, do you know, I think that after that meeting, as word of the exchange between the employee and me started to filter out into the company, was the point where people started to believe in the new Continental. After giving on-time bonuses, burning the employee procedures manual, painting the planes, renegotiating the leases, replacing the first-class seats and the OnePass, and making profits—after all that, still, I think our employees were pretty cautious. They'd been burned before by trusting new management schemes, and they were willing to give us a chance but they were still unsure.

I think that when we started to tell them—and show them— that they were *all* part of what we were doing, they truly started to believe it—to believe that we could be a different kind of company, that this could be a place they'd enjoy coming to work.

The People Are the Company

And that's what Working Together is, at bottom. It's about making Continental a place where people are happy to come to work.

I've said many times that I've never heard of a successful company that didn't have a good product and where people didn't enjoy coming to work. You can see, from what I've explained so far, what we did for our product—all the improvements in its marketing and presentation in the Fly to Win segment of the Go Forward Plan, all the improvements in what we did and how we did it in the Make Reliability a Reality segment. You can see what we did to solve our financial crises in the Fund the Future segment. All that goes toward keeping us in business and making a good product. And it's pretty obvious that employees who come to work at a successful company are going to be happier than employees who work at a company that's going down the tubes.

In Working Together, we said that we didn't want happy employees just because we wanted our company to do better. We wanted that, too, but in Working Together we made employee satisfaction and comfort one of the *ends* of our business.

Whatever problems you run into in running a business, they are all people problems. Cash problems, reliability problems, marketing problems—whatever your problems, they all have at their base the people who are doing things that don't make sense. It may be because they're being told to do so by leaders who have the wrong idea; it may be because they think that if they point out a problem they'll get into trouble. It may be because they're so frustrated they've given up.

Never forget: Businesses are run by people; businesses are made up of people. So at the root of whatever problems you have in your business, you'll find people.

I think that's what finally distinguished this plan from many other plans put into effect by managers all over the world. We didn't just change the symptoms of what was wrong with Continental. We changed Continental. We changed its corporate culture from top to bottom. In fact, we changed more than any other corporation this decade. In *Fortune* magazine's 1998 report on the most admired companies in corporate America, *Fortune* called us a "star" and said Continental "raised its overall rankings more than any other company in the 1990s."

The Revision of a Corporate Culture

Changing a corporate culture is a complicated thing. I've told you about the culture of mistrust and cost cutting that I found when I got to Continental. And I've told you about a lot of things we

changed in the way we did our work and paid our bills and presented our product.

But those are all things people *expect* you to change when you
come into a company. Those are all the places people are used to
go to look for problems, and there are all kinds of common solutions, most of which we used. It wasn't really a stroke of genius to
look at our debt and say we had to get better interest rates or to
look at our service and say it had to improve.

But I think a lot of managers and executives trying to solve
problems miss the forest for the trees by forgetting to look at their
people—not at how much more they can *get* from their people or
at how they can more effectively *manage* their people. I think they
need to look a little more closely at what it's *like* for their people to
come to work there every day.

Before the improvement, people came to work knowing that
our flights were so unpredictable that they didn't really know
when they'd be going home; knowing that they were going to
spend all day dealing with frustrated and angry customers, whom
they could not satisfy; knowing that they would be working with
dispirited and unmotivated coworkers. They didn't like it, and I
couldn't blame them. And that's why I knew that, whatever else
we did, we had to find a way to make the employees of Continental Airlines like coming to work.

A simple enough idea, it seems—but how do you do it?

It sounds almost silly, but we simply started talking to them. We
told them, from the first introduction of the Go Forward Plan,
that everybody working together and everybody getting along was
a big part of what we were working toward, and that would be
measured and evaluated just like everything else. We wanted to
find the people who couldn't adapt to the new way of working and
either reeducate them, retrain them, or move them out.

That is, we wanted our culture to be different, so the first thing
we did was to start *acting* different. Not only that, we *told* everybody it was different. Remember all the stuff I talked about in
Chapter 2, about letting people know that things were different?
We showed them not just in their pay or by the color of the airplanes that things were different. We *treated* them differently.

Most Important Thing: Let Employees Do Their Jobs

Remember that we ritually burned that employee procedure and policy manual and then had employees come up with a new set of guidelines?

That was probably the most important thing we did as far as managers making employees happier. If we had learned nothing else from our decade in inflexible management, it's that cram-downs don't work. That's just human nature. People like to buy into what you're doing rather than have you force it on them. With the old manual and the old way of doing things, people barely had the freedom to decide what color underwear they wore—everything else was crammed down their throats.

Therefore, without the manual—and with the new guidelines, designed by people *doing* the jobs themselves—people were suddenly permitted to think for themselves. In fact, they were *encouraged* to. And I have to tell you, all the talk in the world won't get that across—you have to live it.

Here's an example.

I was getting ready to get on a plane in Washington, D.C., one evening, having spent some time with legislators during the day. I usually wait for the last minute to get on the plane, as I've said, and I stopped for a moment to chat with the gate agent before boarding.

"Did you hear about what happened?" she asked. I said no, I hadn't. So she told me about the plane that had just landed.

Lady with Lapdog

High above the eastern seaboard, a Continental flight attendant looked into the seat of one of the passengers and went to remove a woman's fur coat. She chided herself for having forgotten to take the coat before takeoff, but she jerked her hand back when, as she reached for it, the coat moved. The woman had taken her tiny lapdog out of its flight carrier—where it was required by FAA regulations to remain for the duration of the flight—and put it in her lap.

The flight attendant kept her composure. She politely explained to the woman that the dog had to be returned to its cage, that there were federal regulations about that sort of thing. The woman resisted, so the attendant went on, pointing out the danger a loose dog could pose in an emergency or even under normal circumstances in a cramped airliner thousands of feet above the ground.

Nothing doing. At first appearing merely reluctant, the woman became intransigent and angry, bordering on ugly. The dog was small and, at least, quiet. In the interest of keeping the peace and not disturbing the flight for the other passengers, the flight attendant decided to flout the regulation and let the woman keep her dog in her lap. It seemed as if arguing with the woman was only going to ensure exactly the kind of disturbance she feared, so she took a chance and hoped everything would go all right.

Pretty good call. She did her job and did it well, making a smart decision. Only here's the thing: With some customers, you just can't win.

The flight continued as hoped. The dog kept quiet and never seemed to bother anybody. When the flight neared Washington, though, the flight attendant approached the woman again. She politely requested that the woman put her dog away so the other passengers wouldn't be upset by it as they left the plane. The woman wasn't having any of it, and she began to grow loud, finally becoming upset enough to cause a scene. When they landed she even, bizarrely, refused to get off the airplane.

The flight attendants helped everyone else off the plane, and with nothing else to do, called the site supervisor. The site supervisor had no more luck with the lady and finally called the police. However, the woman had agreed to leave the plane before the police got there, and she demanded to see someone in charge.

The supervisor asked me if she should have called me. She knew I was in the airport Presidents Club. The lady might write a letter of complaint to the Department of Transportation; she might do any number of things.

I said no way. What was I going to do that the supervisor wasn't doing? I would have called 911 and told them to get this nut off the airplane. She had already done that, and a lot more besides. No, I didn't want to tell her how to do her job or tell her what was wrong or right with her job after she had done it. She made a decision on her own about whether to report the woman to the FAA as a disturbance, and she decided it wasn't worth the bother since it hadn't disrupted the flight. We both rolled our eyes and, along with the passengers to Houston, I got on the plane.

I think those flight attendants, gate agents, and supervisors got a lot of benefit from our new employee guidelines, and I think they get a lot from having more responsibility. But I don't think you can quantify the relief they felt at that moment: They had solved a problem, the big boss was around, and he didn't want any part of Monday-morning quarterbacking. I told them "good job" and went about my business just like they had gone about theirs.

So now, instead of being nervous about doing their jobs, employees feel that sense of freedom, of relief, of power. Their jobs are theirs, they know, and we want them to *do* them. Unless there's a good reason for it, we won't bother them about decisions they make. It turned out that I was right when I said in Chapter 5 that only 5 percent or so of our employees would take advantage of our policy giving them more responsibility. Actually, I overestimated—I think closer to 99 percent of our employees have proven extremely trustworthy, and the more responsibility we give them, the more effective they become.

No Monday-Morning Quarterbacking

I didn't just make up the idea of trusting your employees. I learned it for myself—and powerfully—when I worked for Piedmont Airlines in the 1980s.

I was the operations executive, and we had a flag stop one day. That means that a plane had been scheduled to go nonstop from, in this case, Houston to Charlotte; however, the last Piedmont flight from Nashville to Charlotte that night had been cancelled and because the Houston flight had to fly right over Nashville on its way, the systems control center decided to stop the Houston flight and pick up the Nashville passengers. The term *flag stop* comes from the old railroad days, when the station manager would put out a flag if he had any passengers waiting for the train.

My boss, the company chairman, was grousing the next day because he had a call at 6:00 A.M. from some customer who was irate because his nonstop from Houston had been stopped. The chairman wanted to know what happened and why. So I went to the systems control center to ask questions.

The guy there was pretty straightforward. He could see the downside: We had irate customers in Nashville, and if we stopped the Houston plane for them they were at best going to think that was the *least* we could have done, although they were probably going to be annoyed no matter what. And we had passengers in Houston who were perfectly happy with their flight, but stopping in Nashville was probably going to upset at least some of them. On the other hand, we had promised to take those Nashville passengers to Charlotte, and if we could do that it seemed worth doing.

So it was a tough call. The systems control operator weighed his options and made the call. After he explained it, he turned and looked me in the eye. "Mr. Bethune," he asked, "do you want us to call you at home at night when these things come up?"

I thought for a minute and then smiled at him. "Nope," I said. "You did a good thing. Way to go."

I went back to my boss and said we had empowered these people to make these decisions. Given the facts, stopping in Nashville seemed like the right thing to do. It's a shame someone was irritated by it, but it was a close call.

And that's what we pay the systems control operator for—to make those calls. It doesn't get us anywhere to sit there the day after and complain that he turned left when he should have turned right or that he served chocolate when he should have served vanilla.

I tell the people I work with now: I don't want to fly the airplane. I don't want to serve the meals. I don't want to help the passengers off the plane and I don't want to take the tickets. We have good people that we hired and trained to do those jobs.

Let them do them. Monday-morning quarterbacking not only defeats the purpose of training employees to do their jobs, it also makes them unhappy and teaches them not to trust themselves. They feel constrained and restricted. With no options, they either blindly follow rules or give up and work depressed. You don't want either of those scenarios.

But pick the right people and trust them to do their jobs, and you've unleashed a tremendous and talented creative force in your company. Our employees demonstrate that.

But Pay Attention

Working Together and trusting our employees didn't mean ignoring the business and letting it run itself, and it didn't mean that no matter what anybody did it was okay. An example is the way we handled two different pilot errors.

One error got a lot of attention. A pilot—in fact, one of our best—preparing to land in Corpus Christi was following his flight plan, checking the instruments, looking out for the landing field. He looked out the window, saw the runway, saw he was approaching it from the correct heading, and landed—only he landed at a Naval Air Station four miles short of his destination. It happened to have a runway at exactly the right heading to his approach runway. He was checking his instruments, he looked up, and there was the runway, so he landed.

Naturally, nobody was happy. The passengers, confused and not a little terrified, had to be bused to the airport. The captain and crew were mortified. The company was embarrassed because it was a pretty big screwup, and it made all the papers. Jay Leno even had a skit about it, in which a passenger on a Continental flight spun a roulette wheel to see where he'd land.

It was a big mistake, and the captain and the copilot had to spend some time on probation, and go back for some training. We didn't just pat them on the back and say, "Oh, well, stuff happens." It was the result of human error, but nobody was hurt and no regulations were flouted. It was a mistake made by responsible and hardworking people, and we corrected it.

In another case, though, a crew landed a plane with the landing gear up. They, too, had explanations—they neglected to perform the tasks on the landing checklist and the landing gear was not locked in the down position. But the warning horns sounded—and I mean warnings. Remember what I told you about flipping the plane upside down in the simulator? These planes actually yell at you that your landing gear isn't down and you're too close to the ground. Buzzers go off. Lights flash. There are ways you can double-check whether the gear is down if you're at all concerned. These guys ignored all those and landed the plane—on its belly.

Fortunately, nobody was hurt, but those two pilots were fired as soon as we established that they had neglected their duties. We know that errors happen. In the first case, the pilots made an error but followed their procedures and were completely safe. In the second case, the pilots willfully disregarded volumes of safety procedures that should be so ingrained they do them in their sleep. Those guys don't work for us anymore—nor should they. If they did, would you want to fly with us?

Therefore, let me stress: Working Together doesn't mean have a party, be nice to everybody, and let the business run itself. But one essential part of it is letting the people you hired do their jobs without your second-guessing them all day long.

How about We Try This on Each Other, Too?

So that says a little bit about how management began to treat employees differently under Working Together. We made a much bigger point of getting out of their way—and that goes from the top down. It applies just as much to what Greg Brenneman and Chief Financial Officer Larry Kellner got from me as to what baggage handlers got from their supervisors. We pushed it down from the top, and made sure everyone knew: We wanted employees to do their own jobs, and we wanted second-guessing to stop.

I've already told you volumes about how we tried to improve our relationships with customers, suppliers, and creditors by treating them with a little respect, taking them into our confidence, sharing information with them, and explaining what we were doing. As a result, we were doing better with our customers and our suppliers. And because of changes like the manual reorganization, relations between supervisors and their employees were improved.

That left only one more change to make—the most important one.

I told you right up front, in Chapter 2, that I could tell what was wrong with this company the minute I walked in: *It was a crummy place to work.* Not just because of the bad pay and the mistrust of the managers and the lousy service and the angry customers. But because, in that environment, the employees no longer trusted even each other—and they treated each other like they didn't.

Remember what I said about businesses being about people? Nobody likes going to work to be miserable. Nobody likes being miserable or being mistreated by anybody. This isn't Harvard Business School stuff—this is human being stuff.

Therefore, one of the most important points in our management philosophy was that it was time to start treating each other with dignity and respect.

Team Sports

Let me remind you once more that this was all happening at once. Working Together didn't occur in a vacuum. We could get our employees to be a little more patient with each other because they were a little more cheerful. They were more cheerful because they were getting on-time bonuses. They were getting on-time bonuses because they were doing a better job. They were doing a better job because they had more sensible schedules and better equipment. They had more sensible schedules because our planning finally made sense, and they had better equipment because now that Continental's debt structure and finances were getting back in line we could start spending money on the equipment we needed, rather than on debt service.

So you can see that it's all a huge spiral, and it's going to go either up or down. For the record, I prefer up.

Calling the Right Plays

I've said over and over that running an airline is the biggest team sport in the world. A key to Working Together is choosing things the team actually *can* do. The buy-in between the scheduling and the operations department, discussed in Chapter 3, was a great example of Working Together. Groups found a way to stop fighting long enough to try to solve the problems they could solve together and quickly learned that they got so much done working together that solutions for many of the remaining problems came much more easily.

Nothing can be more dispiriting to a team—to any group—than being given a task that it simply knows it can't accomplish. Tell operations people that they've got 10 minutes to perform maintenance that they know takes 30 minutes, and you've broken the spirit of an entire department effortlessly. On the other hand, get them involved in scheduling the maintenance so that they *can* perform it in the minimum time, and suddenly they'll buy into the whole *idea* of getting maintenance done on time.

A friend tells a story about Brian Sipe, onetime NFL quarterback for the then Cleveland Browns. Sipe, he tells, followed a simple rule: You gotta call the plays for the guys you got. It wouldn't have done Sipe any good to call pass plays that would have worked great if he had had the wide receivers that the Steelers had, or runs that couldn't miss if he had had the Cowboys' offensive line. He had to call plays the *Cleveland Browns* could run. He wouldn't call a pass play that required him to complete a pass longer than he could throw. Instead, he'd listen to his teammates and call plays that took advantage of the skills they had.

It's just the same in his team as in ours. Ask maintenance crews to do the impossible and they'll go through the motions, at best. Ask players to run plays they know they can't run and you get the same thing. But set goals they can really achieve and they'll begin to believe in themselves.

Once they believe in themselves, maybe they *can* do the impossible once in a while.

Dignity and Respect

The final ingredient missing in our teamwork was treating *each other* with the dignity and respect we had learned to give to our supervisors, the people who reported to us, and our customers. We had a lot of scar tissue built up in the morale of our company—scar tissue from all those years of mismanagement and wretchedness. Even the best people working here were unhappy and depressed, and even the most naturally nice people had learned by experience to be suspicious, mistrustful, and defensive. It only made sense. The baggage handlers looked at the gate agents as people to be mistrusted, not as people who helped them.

Think back to that football team. How are they going to play if the linemen say to the wide receivers, "You guys just run around and catch the ball—the *real* work goes on down the line, and we're much more important than you are." How will they play if the quarterback figures he can throw the ball *and* catch it *and* run with it? You can't do that. A team is made up of a number of people doing different jobs, all of which are important. The biggest, meanest defensive tackle has some respect for those little wide receivers. He knows that person is crucial to the success of the whole team. There's a mutual understanding: You've got your role and I've got mine, and we don't jam each other because we're not the same.

An airline works the same way—we have 40,000 people doing literally thousands of different jobs, but as I said in that famous meeting, *every* part of the watch is not only necessary but *as important* as every other part. Everybody thinks he or she is the hour hand—everybody thinks he or she is the most important part of the watch. That's just human nature. But for the watch to run, all the parts have to be working. And when you're dealing with human parts, the best way to keep all the parts running is to treat them all well.

So that was the final part of Working Together that we implemented: the goal of treating every coworker like a customer or like a family member—like a basically nice person who deserved to be treated nicely. Everybody, we said, deserves dignity and respect.

Many Watches in One Case

That seems obvious enough, but remember who we were dealing with. Not only had our employees put up with years of terrible management and confused business policies, they had another problem. In reality, they weren't really just one watch.

Continental had been cobbled together during the deregulation era out of the parts of several different airlines. That's kind of like trying to make one watch out of pieces from a bunch of different ones. Some of the gears don't fit; some of the pieces clash and rub. Several different cultures were bubbling around in one company, and the dominant culture was one of mistrust and wariness. So we had plenty to do to get everybody working together and treating each other the way we thought people ought to be treated.

If You Need a Reason for Kindness: A Big Piece of Pie

Everybody be nice. It's a great idea. But is it really worth the effort? I know that sounds like a silly question, but someone out there reading this is thinking, "Let the damn employees be nice on their own time—we're trying to run a *business*, dammit!" This person is focusing on cost of goods sold or cost per available seat mile or some such thing—and missing the point. But if you need a reason *beyond* the fact that dignity and respect improve everybody's life, here it is.

I tell a story about something I learned when I was in the Navy, serving in the Philippines, living in bachelor officers' quarters. It was a pretty cushy deal—stewards, who were enlisted men, served you your meals and managed the quarters. These stewards were usually Filipinos, who, in case you don't know it, are about the most gracious people in the world—and the most open.

One evening I was dining with three other guys at a table in the officer's mess. Every time one of the stewards would bring out something or pick up a dish or refill my water glass, I would look up and say, "Salamat po," which is a very polite way of saying "thank you" in Tagalog. Of course, like anyone, Filipinos appreciate the effort any visitor makes to understand their language. So I saw a lot of happy nods and beaming smiles.

One officer asked me why I did that. I said, "Let's see who gets the biggest slice of pie for dessert." One of those stewards went back and cut up the pie, and another one brought it out and served it to all of us. And who do you think got the biggest slice of pie?

Now, what did that cost? And what was the reward?

So if just making your employees happier and having your business run in a more pleasant fashion isn't enough reason for you to believe in being kind and pleasant, do it for that reason: You get more pie.

Swell, Be Nice—But How?

Simple: You act nice. And you insist that everybody act nicer. Whenever possible, you react to their understandable hesitance with more niceness. It all sounds almost silly, but the fact is that the only way to change a corporate culture is to just change it. How do you eat an elephant? One bite at a time. So we all just started working at that, from the top down.

I treated my direct reports the way I would want to be treated. They treated theirs the same way, and on down the line. We used discussions with their own direct reports as part of evaluations—everybody knew that part of their compensation after each evaluation would be based on whether the people they worked with said they were pleasant to deal with and whether they were working as a team.

By the middle of 1995, we were able to make this a priority. Continental's financial situation had improved so rapidly, its service was so much better so quickly, and the tickets for our flights were being sold so much better that almost everything was looking up.

In fact, at that point we checked out our budget and realized we had to make our final hard decision. We could see that we were going to make a profit for the year. We could see (we were measuring) that our product was getting better. We could see that our changing market strategies were helping us find our customers and helping them find us, and that once they showed up we were giving them what they wanted and doing that well.

But we still had too many people in our airline. Not on the line—not pilots, not baggage handlers, not reservations agents, not accounting people. We had too many managers, and especially too many middle managers, which you commonly find when you have a company that has been running on automatic pilot for a while and is made up of a bunch of different companies tossed together anyhow. We were going to have to tighten things up a little and get rid of some people.

We did exactly the opposite of what people expected. No buyouts, no early retirement—the people who take buyouts and early retirement when they're offered tend to be the people who can best find other jobs. We didn't want our best employees to leave, we wanted our least effective employees to leave.

So we asked them to. During the year, as we implemented some of our new programs and changes, not only did we put those personnel matters into the mix for evaluation, but we asked all of the higher-level managers to rank every supervisory employee they had. Every employee was ranked on the quality of their work and, especially, on whether they were team players. They were ranked on a scale of 1 through 4, with 1 being as good as it got and 4 being someone who was not treating people they way we wanted them to be treated at all.

All through 1995 we talked to people about their performance, giving them a chance to either get on board with the company's new direction or not, as they saw fit. We kept those rankings fluid until later in the year, when it became pretty clear who was a 1, who was a 4, and who was in between.

Then in October, when we looked at the numbers and saw there was one more personnel cut to make, we simply asked all the 4s to leave. I don't say it was easy, because you never want to fire employees. But we didn't have to wring our hands over who should be let go—we already knew that. We let people go either because they weren't doing well enough at their jobs or because they weren't team players. If you weren't both, you might not be with us.

And you know what? That final cut didn't cause the smallest amount of unhappiness or fear or dissatisfaction in the ranks. Instead, there was a big sigh of relief. Employees said, "Jeez, they got rid of Harry—that jerk should have been shot 20 years ago and somebody finally did something." Employees suddenly saw they had not only fewer bosses but *better* bosses. The atmosphere kept improving, and it began feeding on itself.

We explained simple things to people, and they listened. For example, we talked about those automated reservation telephone lines we had put in. Larry Goodwin also installed special lines for employees who wanted to travel on passes to call on to make their reservations, to find out whether they'd be likely to make a certain flight, and so on. The reservations agents didn't need to be involved at all, freeing them up for other things.

However, people don't always learn real fast. Mechanics or accountants would always be calling overworked reservations agents and filling up their time with something they could have done themselves. So we told the agents to be nice to such people.

Instead of saying, "Listen, you dumb jerk, there's a special number you're supposed to call so you don't bother me," just treat them the way you would want to be treated. Tell them, "Let me check that for you, and by the way here's the 800 number you can call next time." That mechanic is going to be the guy who sees that your next flight out is on time—and that mechanic is a person just like you who deserves to be treated nicely.

For example, say there's a family member of an employee hanging around by the gate waiting to see whether she'll make a flight. Don't tell her, "I'll let you know—if you hear your name called, you're on the plane." Tell her what the likelihood is that she'll make the flight. Treat her like she's important. Remember, this is somebody's mother you're dealing with. Not just our customers are valuable—we're *all* valuable.

We put our focus on solving our financial problems and got control of them; we focused on our marketing problems and changed those. We addressed our performance problems and started outperforming the entire industry. And when we turned our attention to improving the way it felt to come to work at Continental Airlines, that worked, too. Before long, things really did change.

The Day the Problems Started Walking Out

In fact, the biggest change came at one of those monthly meetings, this time in Denver.

I was talking about how things were changing and how much better things were going, and, as usual, people had questions. However, the number and tenor of the questions had already changed. We were getting more substantive questions—"How should I do that?" "When will that program kick in?" What if this should happen?"—than expressions of disbelief or disgust.

But there was still plenty of disbelief. At that meeting in Denver in late 1995, an employee stood up and said, "It sounds fine, but I still don't believe it. We've had too many new programs here and I don't believe it."

I reasoned with him a little, explaining why things were working. I tried telling him about pieces of watches. I tried going on a little more about Working Together. No dice. So I told him the same thing I told the pilot in Newark—that the jetway was still attached, and if he didn't like the direction in which we were going, maybe he needed to get off the plane. Amazingly, he spun on his heel and walked out the door—perhaps expecting his coworkers to follow him.

Nope. His coworkers did something else: They applauded. They're not stupid. They could see that things were getting better for us—and fast. So when someone who wanted to be part of the problem instead of part of the solution walked out, they applauded.

Working Together was establishing itself as the way Continental worked.

The Pilots Slow Down

The best example of that dignity and respect taking hold concerns our pilots. When we started to change things at Continental, the employees had plenty of reasons to be unhappy, not the least of which was pay. They were grossly underpaid—we weren't just a low-fare airline, we were a low-*wage* airline. The company had been run on the backs of the employees for too long, and the first thing we did was delay a scheduled wage snapback. Although by the time you read this, we'll have worked our way right back up near industry standard, in 1995 industry-standard wages were a long way away.

In the midst of all this, the pilots' union was negotiating its first contract. It takes a long time to get a union organized and an even longer time to hammer out a first contract. We were scrambling to keep the company solvent and our planes in the air; at the same time we were trying to change a lot of things about how we worked *and* start paying on-time bonuses to make our employees realize there's something good waiting for them for all their hard work.

In the middle of all that, in early 1995, a small minority of the pilots decided that the contract process wasn't going quickly enough, so they organized a work slowdown. We were working hard on improving the percentage of Continental flights that arrived on time, so that's where they struck. The union sent out a long list of checks and double checks for the pilots to complete before takeoff—the British call this "working to rule," and it's just a way to slow things down.

Of course, that's just what it did. Because of the slowdown, Continental stopped being among the leaders in on-time percentage. And we stopped paying $65 bonus checks. You don't need to be told that whatever attention the pilots were getting from management was overshadowed by the attention they got from their coworkers, who were suddenly being denied the on-time bonuses that were the first good things they had received from Continental in a decade.

The contract was eventually signed, and the planes started moving again. Before long, whatever friction had developed between the pilots and their coworkers dissipated. The point that I want to make here is that *during* that protracted and difficult negotiation, we in management purposefully chose *not* to capitalize on the vulnerable position those pilots had put themselves in with their coworkers. We made our statements regarding the negotiations and kept the information flowing, but we never tried to use the friction between those pilots and the other employees to our advantage.

More, their coworkers, angry at the pilots and frustrated, still refrained from mistreating them. I'm not saying they always, for example, gave a pilot traveling on a pass the best available seat on a plane, but they kept their heads and avoided troublemaking.

It's hard to explain this without sounding self-congratulatory or like I'm saying I told you so, which I don't want to do. A labor contract negotiation is a grueling thing, as anyone who's ever been through one on either side will tell you. The tactic those few pilots chose didn't do them too much good in the final analysis, and it didn't help them that their coworkers were unhappy with them for costing them $65 per month for two months. Still, we managed to keep our focus on the good of the company—on the good of *all* the employees.

Dissension, as part of Working Together and as the central point of the overall change in Continental's corporate culture, was exactly what we were looking to avoid. We didn't want internal winners and losers. We wanted to all win or all lose together.

Regardless of what happened, eventually we were going to come to an agreement with the pilots—even the longest and most fractious negotiation eventually ends. And what then? If we had been pointing fingers at the pilots and driving wedges between them and their coworkers, how would they feel once they were back inside the fold? How would their coworkers be able to forget the mean things we *had* been saying and start believing the nice things we suddenly *started* saying?

The same thing applies to the strife between the pilots and their coworkers—both sides seemed to realize that sooner or later they'd all be back on the same page. They managed to avoid caus-ing any lasting damage during a difficult period. When the pilots went back to the negotiating table in 1997, once again, after a long and fractious negotiation ended, everybody was comfortable and on the same side.

Before the Go Forward Plan, the tiniest miscommunication between employees, or between managers and employees, was enough to turn employees off for a week: "Here we go again." Now even a protracted labor negotiation is just a bump in the road. We've been treating each other better for several years now, and that's the norm. Thus, a mistake is just a mistake—and when such mistakes happen, employees are more likely to think of manage-ment or of one another, "They probably didn't mean that," instead of "Uh-oh, I knew it—here it comes." We're giving each other the benefit of the doubt.

The Pilot's Next Wife

Still, I don't want to say things went easily. It takes a long time to win over employees who have been mistreated for years. In 1996, we actually made "Dignity and Respect" our slogan for the year and enlisted comedian Rodney Dangerfield to make a video for some of our meetings, because we were still trying to convince some people.

And then there are some people you may never reach.

One day during the pilot slowdown, I took a plane to Acapulco to give a speech to the tourism council about what we were accomplishing at Continental. I got on the plane, and, as I usually do, I stuck my head in the cockpit to say hello to the crew. I saw that the pilot had the union safety checklist the pilots were using to slow down takeoffs. I said that I was sorry to see it and that I hoped we could get all those issues behind us.

The pilot said, "Gordon, maybe it isn't you, it's the nine guys ahead of you. Every one of the previous CEOs lied to us. The only way you get anything around here is to do what we're doing. You're going to have to take this because of what we've been through."

I stood there for a moment. Then I said, "How many times have you been married?"

He started laughing. He said, "I'm about to get married for the fourth time if you can believe it."

I said, "Oh, I can believe it. But I want you to tell that fourth wife, when you start acting like a jerk, that it's got nothing to do with the way she's acting—it's those first three wives you're paying back. And I want you to tell me how that relationship is going to work."

I guess he didn't think that was too funny. I think that pilot took longer than any I've ever known for his preflight checklists. Like the rest of the passengers, I just sat in the plane and waited.

So you're not going to win over everybody—there are always going to be employees who, given the choice, would rather operate *without* dignity and respect. This pilot is the exception. The vast majority of our pilots didn't—and don't—behave that way. As Continental continued to change, we had fewer of those people around. And things kept getting better.

Reminding People That Things Are Going Better

Things started to go better to the degree that we sort of had to tell people it was time to stop complaining. We explained to them that most of the stuff they wanted to complain about had stopped happening. We didn't mind listening to their complaints for the first year or so after we took over, but after that we had to draw the line.

It was natural for people to complain—we knew that. We let them do a certain amount, knowing that it would help. After all, that was a big part of what all those employee meetings were for.

After a time, however, it got to the point where we had heard it all before—and more than that, the things people were complaining about hadn't been happening for a while. It was—and is—still important for employees to be able to air their grievances, but we started to realize that the incessant griping was just another part of the corporate culture that we were trying to change.

So we changed that, too. Whenever we had one of those employee meetings, near the end I would say "Okay, we've got 15 minutes left. Let's go around the room and everybody tell me one thing that's better today than it was a year ago." One person would start—and the next person would say, "That's right, and here's something else." This would continue around the room until I'd say, "Thanks a lot you guys, everything is really looking up, and you're doing a great job." Then I'd get out of there.

Now remember—this works only if you really do have 30 or so things your employees will be able to come up with off the top of their heads that actually are better. So if you expect to jolly your employees into realizing how good they have it this way, they'd better really have it good, or else they're going to run out of things to say.

Our employees didn't run out of good things to say.

The Biggest Picture: Winning and Losing Together

The last thing I want to say about Working Together is that it is, at bottom, about sharing. Let's go back to that football team analogy. The offense can't win if the defense doesn't win, right? The kicker can't go home a winner unless the rest of the team goes home a winner, right?

Right. That's why a team sticks together and works on what it needs to as a *team*—because that's how it's going to win or lose. The team members come to treat one another with respect, first because they need to for the good of the team and after that because they learn things about one another that remove their misconceptions.

So that's what happened to us. First our employees, distrustful of management and each other, started treating each other well because it was in their interest to do so. Happy employees did better work and were more likely to help everybody get their $65 on-time bonuses. In addition, they knew they were going to be evaluated on their treatment of one another, so they just tried harder.

Soon, as we all worked together, we learned that it was a *lot* more fun to work that way. That made us work even better. Then we made more money, and, as I've said, that spiral kept going up, which leads ultimately to that final and best reward of Working Together.

You can talk to employees about watches, and you can tell them they're members of a team. You can urge them to be nice to each other, and you can be nice to them to show them how. But this is reality, and sooner or later they're going to want to see results.

For management, the results came quickly. We saw the numbers of complaints we got from employees *about* coworkers start to diminish right from the start. As soon as we gave them the opportunity to reach us, we received notes, phone calls, and e-mails from employees telling us they felt better about each other. Absenteeism decreased. So did turnover and on-the-job injuries. That showed *us* that the employees felt better, which was key, but I think they, themselves, still wanted to see something tangible.

Fortunately, we could show them something tangible. On February 15, 1996, I got a chance to do something that no chief executive at Continental had done for a decade. We finally had a little wealth, so we shared it.

In meetings all over our network, with balloons and press photographers and crowds of utterly disbelieving employees, Greg and I handed out the ultimate fruit of Working Together, and the clearest demonstration that we mean it.

We gave out profit-sharing checks. Fifteen percent of our pretax profits go directly back to our employees through profit sharing. In a series of meetings nationwide, the executive team brought the employees together, thanked them for their excellent work, and gave each of them a check worth actual money—money *they* had earned by working hard to make Continental a success. If you remember the fears some people had about giving employees more opportunity to control their own jobs, this ensured that they'd forever after gladly protect that money through responsible problem solving. It was their money.

If there was anybody still wondering whether this Working Together stuff was for real, I like to think they started believing when they got those first profit-sharing checks.

Success Has No Autopilot

Through the Go Forward Plan, we addressed all of Continental's major problems—marketing, finances, product, and employee morale—and wouldn't you know it, it worked.

And so . . . then what?

Well, I have to tell you that it's a lot harder to *keep* things going great than to get them going great in the first place. When you're turning a company around, at the start you have all that wonderful energy and excitement—each month something new happens that shows people that, by God, it's *working*. It's exciting and people are high-fiving each other and the world is your oyster. You can all go through tough things—a round of unavoidable layoffs, a postponed wage hike—together without too much ill will because you know that the alternative is immediate and terrible failure.

But once you're moving well, you get a few good quarters behind you, and your ship is stabilized, things change. Continuing to work at the same level of intensity is harder, because that wolf isn't quite so close to the door anymore and the consequences of slowing down don't seem so dire. People who have put in long hours willingly during the crisis can start to relax a little, enjoy the success, and maybe figure that they're good enough, unless they get more motivation to keep getting better.

Naturally, part of your planning must be to give your employees that increased motivation—to up the ante in their bonus pay while your company is improving, to up their base pay as soon as you can so that they see that the company's rewards are theirs. We've kept doing all that, and in fact now, from a company that had some of the lowest-paid employees in the industry, Continental has become an airline where virtually everyone is paid at or near the industry standard. And we'll keep going from there.

However, there's something else going on, something that doesn't really have to do with money at all. It has to do with human nature. I can't say often enough that business is about people, so it's the human nature stuff that you really need to keep your eye on.

The Future Is Not the Past

When I worked at Braniff in the 1970s, we could see that the airline industry was going to change. Braniff was the main air carrier for Dallas. When you went to the Dallas–Fort Worth airport in those days, all you saw were the multicolored Braniff planes. As far as you could see, it was bright Braniff colors.

I remember standing on the Dallas airfield with a Braniff mechanic. I was trying to talk to that mechanic about being competitive, the new threats, deregulation—all that stuff. I told him I had my worries. He looked at me and said, "What are you talking about? I've worked here 20 years. My father worked here. See all those colored airplanes out there? See these hangars, all those passengers? This is our stuff. We don't have to worry about that."

I said, "You know what? That's what they said at the Packard automobile plant." And you know that Packard didn't exactly last for the long haul.

You know what happened to Braniff: Deregulation came, the industry changed, and Braniff ran out of money. The company had a bad business plan, high costs, poor management, and, when all was said and done, a poor product. All that stuff the mechanic was referring to is all gone now.

And all those mistakes came out of one big mistake: taking success for granted. Relying on the autopilot for success. I'm here to tell you that there's no such thing.

It's human nature to want things to get easier. It's human nature to think that if good things happened to you it must be *you*, not your hard work or your long hours, not your coworkers and your team and everything else that went into making you successful. I could easily fall into the trap of believing that things are going so much better at Continental just because my name is Bethune or just because I'm such a great guy. And then things would stop going great at Continental in the blink of an eye.

You Still Have to Keep Winning

Because the answer is, you can't win forever unless you excel forever. I like that. It gets harder and harder to keep it up, and that's the next challenge you have to focus your business on.

Think of a great football team, like the Dallas Cowboys. You can win the Super Bowl once and you're great, but the next year everyone's gunning for you. It's much harder to win that second time. Everybody else gets better. Everybody else sees all the things you did to get so good, and they start to do those things. Plus everybody else wants to beat you because, by beating you, they've beaten the best.

They're going to keep getting better to try and beat you. So if you want to keep winning, you'd better not just stay great—you'd better keep getting even better.

Keep Raising the Bar

The best way to accomplish this, of course, is to just do that: Keep practicing, keep getting better, keep your eye on the ball. At Continental, that means never losing track of the things we changed that made us good in the first place. I told you in Chapter 5 that once we started ranking in the top five in on-time percentage I raised the bar for the on-time bonus to the top three, increasing the reward for finishing first, too.

That's good, but sometimes the bar just raises itself. That's happened to us at Continental. In mid-1997 we experienced a bumpy period during which we fell out of the top five for a while. We had a couple of tough months, a couple of storms hit our hubs, but more than that, we simply lost our focus.

When you're at the top of your game, it sometimes doesn't take much to knock you down a peg. It can be compared to a musical performance or figure skating in the Olympics. You take that solo or that jump for granted because you've done it right so many times. Then suddenly you start missing it. Maybe the people at the operations hot line stopped following up in one day and would take a couple of days to do so. Maybe the people in scheduling didn't refine to the second permutation because they figured they got it right on the first. It's little stuff—but it's enough to take you from first to fifth in a tight, competitive market.

The best thing about a good company is that the employees don't *like* not winning. Now when we're not in the top three in on-time percentage for a couple of months, the employees say, "What's this? This isn't where we belong!" and they hustle like crazy to get back to the top. They like those on-time bonuses, but, more important, they're used to being winners and they want to be winners. They know they can be, and so they do what they have to in order to win.

When you start from a hole, just breaking even looks pretty good to you. In 1995, we thought Continental was going to make a profit of $45 million, and we were ecstatic. We're winning! We're not going out of business! We can pay our employees! Now, a profit of $45 million for a *quarter* would make us bust out in a cold sweat—we'd wonder what happened to us and start turning over every rock to find out where our success went. If we made a lot less money because we were spending more on improving our food or putting better magazines on our planes, we'd better think again. Risking our basic success for what might be a small improvement isn't worth it. We want to keep getting better, but we still have to run an airline.

Our job, after all, is to do several things at once. First, we have to run more than 2,000 flights a day and ensure that every one is perfectly safe, clean, and reliable. If we lose track of that, we're sunk. That's still the life's breath of our operation—if we stop being reliable and safe and worth the price we charge, all the improvement in other areas won't get us anywhere. We've got to start by doing all the things we've already committed ourselves to do well.

Second, we have to do that and make money at it. That's the blood of the operations. We can't stop being financially healthy—not for a year, not for a quarter, not for a day.

So that's an awful lot to get done every single day before we even think about how to get better.

The third thing, though, is where the art comes in. It's doing those things in a way that makes our employees and customers happy, and that makes us win. That's where the cycle starts—with people who are happy to come to work. And they're happy to come to work if everything is going well. Since everything is going well if we do what we must to make sure we keep winning, we have to keep raising that bar and challenging ourselves to do even better.

Keep Measuring

The best way to keep the bar going up is to keep measuring. In mid-1997, for example, Continental had a period during which our on-time performance slipped badly—one month it even dropped to ninth place out of the 10 largest airlines.

We had to take a look at what had happened, and we found the problem pretty easily. We had taken our eye off the ball. We had assigned the head people in operations to other jobs where their help was needed, and nobody had backfilled their jobs with quite the same level of scrutiny. Attention was withdrawn, and things weren't running as well as they should have. Like I said, it was little stuff—but enough little stuff.

Because what gets measured is what gets managed, we learned very quickly that our performance was slipping. It never got a chance to get out of hand because we knew within a *month* that we had made a mistake. I made a few speeches at a couple of meetings, and word got around: "Uh-oh, Gordon's on the warpath, we'd better get back on the stick." We refocused and in only another month or so we were back up to number five, and then number 3, at which point our employees resumed getting their on-time bonuses, as they have come to expect.

The recovery just took a little more attention—we had to get our eye back on the ball. We didn't panic; we didn't point fingers; we just took the information that we got and acted on it.

The key here is *never* to stop measuring. Remember: You have all those instruments to tell you where you're going. Keep an eye on them and believe what they tell you.

You see, this is all human stuff.

It's All Relative

Another thing we had to be aware of at Continental was that other airlines were catching up to us. For example, in absolute terms, during our down months in 1997, we were coming in on time as much as we had been a year earlier. In fact, on an absolute basis, we were doing fine or even better than before.

However, it's not an absolute world—it's a relative world. In January 1996, a little less than 70 percent of our planes arrived on time, putting us third in the nation. It wasn't our best month, and there were storms that slowed everybody down, but it was good enough for our employees to receive their on-time bonus.

In March 1997, almost 78 percent of our planes were on time. Pretty good—but only good enough for us to rank seventh, and nobody was getting bonuses for that. So we had raised the bar, not only for ourselves but for everybody. Every other airline, reading about our success, had naturally enough worked hard to chase us and compete with us. Some of them worked so hard that they surpassed us.

Therefore, we weren't necessarily doing any worse, but everybody else was doing better. Just like I was saying about the Cowboys: You can win once, but then everybody sees how good you are. They work extra hard to catch up to you and beat you, and then everything gets harder.

Staying on Time

The hardest thing about maintaining success is that it's not like failure. There was a lot of trouble at Continental during the decade before I came here, and people are very slow to forget that.

They remember failure, and it plants seeds of doubt that you have to spend years eradicating. However, people forget success in about a second. If you take your eye off the ball and slow down a little, let things fall back even a small amount, people forget real fast that you were successful.

I liken it to the psychology of perfect attendance. Say you have an employee, Bob, who has perfect attendance for 15 years. He's better than an atomic clock—he's there on time every time. Then one day he's late, and everybody says, "Holy smokes, this is terrible—Bob must have been in an accident." When he finally arrives, he says that the alarm didn't go off, or he had a fender bender, or whatever. Everybody's amazed: Bob was late. They think they've just seen Halley's comet.

The next week, Bob's late again, and everybody says, "Jeez, what's up with Bob all of a sudden? This is really weird. I hope he's okay." Then he's late the week after that, and everybody says, "Ah, jeez, that Bob, he's always late." See how fast you can lose it?

That's what we're up against now, and we're up against it every day. Yeah, we've won two J.D. Power awards in a row; we've been chosen Airline of the Year; we've been on time and profitable and a good place for our employees to work. But put a business-class traveler on a few bad flights in a row and she's going to tell her assistant to book her somewhere else. I can't emphasize it enough: A company can't just stay good. It has to keep getting *better*.

For example, as I've already mentioned, we've been trying hard to increase the percentage of business travelers that fly Continental. Business travelers make later reservations and require more special services, so they're the best-paying customers. We don't ignore our other customers, but we can see that the more business customers we get, the better we do. Over the past several years, we've seen our fortunes improve as our percentage of business travelers has increased. Do I need to tell you that we shouldn't stop trying to get more business travelers?

It is surprising that some people do not recognize this. There are managers out there who spend three years increasing their share of business travel and watching their airline's fortunes improve. Then they sit down one day and think, "Well, we've got our business travelers, so that's that. Now let's focus on something completely different." Or worse, they think, "We've improved our company, now let's spend some time on the boat, or at the casino, and let the company run itself." You know people like this; you've worked for people like this. So have I.

Complacency Kills: Don't Take *Anything* for Granted

This is simple, but true.

For example, when flying an airplane, you can't take anything for granted. *Nothing.* You're hurtling through the air at hundreds of miles an hour thousands of feet above the ground, and the smallest thing you fail to pay attention to could cause the worst possible failure. You can't figure, "Oh, we've been doing great on fuel this whole year, so I don't need to worry about fuel." That's when you run out of gas. You need to make sure that *this plane* was filled before you took off. That's why you do the preflight check-list before every single flight. You check everything before you start, every time. Ignore anything in an airplane and it can ruin your day.

It's the same thing in your business. Ignore anything and you won't be successful. Think of a relationship. If you take your girl-friend for granted and assume that she'll always be around, what happens? One way or another, she's going to show you that you shouldn't have been so complacent. Business works the same way. If you ignore your employees, your cash flow, your service, or your product, it'll disappear on you. It happens that quickly—and that simply.

The thing to remember is that everybody is looking for the equivalent of autopilot—everybody. It's human nature to want to say that things are going great now, I can go back and joke around with the flight attendants and have a good time. But you'd better stay up front and fly the airplane. If you want to stay successful, *there is no autopilot for success.* You can't take your eye off the ball.

The good news is that it's a pretty simple thing to keep doing as long as you don't forget about it. It simply means living by those principles you instilled during the big turnaround from mediocrity to success. I told you about the pilots' negotiations, when some pilots used slowdown tactics to allegedly strengthen their bargaining position. Their coworkers were pretty frustrated with them, since they were losing their on-time bonuses. It would have been easy to press that advantage, to isolate the pilots from the other employees to improve the bargaining position of management. But that's exactly what we didn't do, because that was exactly what we *didn't* want. Everything that we discussed in Chapter 6 about working together and finding a way for everybody to win would have been easy to forget in the heat of the negotiation. But we didn't forget—we kept our eye on the ball, dealt with the pilots on their own terms, and came up with a solution that didn't demean anybody. We didn't want the company to lose and the pilots to win, nor did we want the pilots to lose and the company to win. We all had to win together.

Thus, when the negotiation was over, those pilots just slipped back into the fold. There were much smaller messes to clean up than there would have been if we had pulled out all the stops and pressed our point, because the goal was to get a contract everybody could live with. Sooner or later, we were going to have a contract, and the worse things got before the contract, the longer it would have taken us to recover from the negotiations. So we kept our eye on the ball—total company success—and didn't get lost in the minutiae of winning or losing the particular negotiation. We considered the big picture and everybody won in the end.

It's the same everywhere you look. We saw that the convenience of getting to a lot of desirable destinations from Continental's hubs was bringing us more and more customers as we cut service to the places people *didn't* want to go. So to keep improving, we kept adding more destinations from our hubs. We didn't add more hubs, which would have spread us thinner again and sent us down the road we had just pulled ourselves off of. Instead, we added new destinations *from* the hubs and increased service to the places people *did* want to go. We added Portland, Oregon, for example, as a destination from Houston. Not Portland to Seattle, which wasn't our territory—people up there don't know Continental. But people in Houston know us, and they'll take our planes to Portland. That's a service to them.

When we added more destinations, we kept finding out what people wanted. To increase service from our Newark hub, we added more international destinations—Rome and Milan— entering partnerships with companies like Alitalia, Air France, and most recently Virgin Atlantic, to provide our customers with the destinations they wanted.

We continued to work on all aspects of our operation. We kept looking at ways to make the food better *and* more reasonable. If we found that improving our product required improving the food, we did that. Sometimes we found that we were offering so many different kinds of food that we weren't adding value (remember the row-five test?), so we improved our cash picture by reducing the number of choices passengers had to wade through in selecting their meals.

None of this constant effort should stop, and the different aspects don't stop being related to one another just because the overall effect is working, either. For example, we kept trying to raise employees' pay to get them up to the industry standard, but it had to be done slowly and responsibly. True, Continental was making more money, but if we had given it all to the employees in one fell swoop to make them extremely happy, there would have been no money on hand to replace or maintain the planes, or to pay down debts, or any of the other things we needed to do to keep improving as an airline.

Thus, we had to keep making trade-offs—balancing all the elements of the operation. Most especially, we had to keep talking to our employees, honestly and constantly.

Keep Talking

Communication is often one of the first things to go when a company gets fixed. The people who get the credit for fixing something that's been broken often start to believe all the nice things people say about them. They stop listening to the people who helped them in the first place ("Hey, *I'm* the one who's so smart; who needs their opinions?"), and those people stop telling them what's going on ("Don't you worry about anything, I've got it all under control").

Both of those failures will kill your momentum in a second. What made Continental go forward as well as it did was keeping everybody involved—winning and losing together as a team, listening to those messages we got on the 800 numbers, responding to the problems the employees and customers showed us were the most important. If we had become self-satisfied and vain about our success, we'd have gone from first to worst faster than we went the other way.

There are lots of ways to keep from getting your head swelled up and believing your own press clips. Make sure you only hire people who will be willing to kick the door open if you lose direction and close it; make sure you constantly measure your success in every way you can. You may be able to ignore somebody's opinion if you don't like it, but if the person has data to back it up, your intellect should be able to overwhelm your vanity. Always listen to your employees and your customers, and remember that nobody can do this alone: Your whole team is what got you to the top, and if you discard them because you're at the top, you'll go to the bottom in a hurry.

All of this simply means *don't stop*. Keep doing what you did to get there, and you'll probably be all right.

Banana Management

One of the ways Continental stays on track now involves meetings. We've continued the rules about meetings starting and ending on time—once that becomes part of corporate culture, it sticks. But we now have a way within meetings to keep them on track: If somebody loses focus and wanders off into the kind of flights of fancy that success can lead to, somebody else in the meeting just says "Banana."

That comes from something that happened to me when I worked at Piedmont. Piedmont ran a great airline, but it was taken over by USAir. Suddenly, a whole new group of executives sat in on our meetings, and they didn't see things in a way that made sense to us. The old Piedmont crew tended to see things the same way, and this clearly had worked for us. Suddenly, here were these new guys telling us to change stuff that was working.

The analogy we used was that we'd all be sitting in a meeting and counting by twos—2, 4, 6, 8, etc.—and we didn't have to discuss too much because we knew we were headed to 100 by twos. So I'd say "two," the next guy would say "four," and then the new guy from USAir would say "Banana." It was our way of saying that they were not making sense, that their solutions didn't fit the problem we were trying to solve. We called it "banana management."

So I've brought that saying to Continental. It's a code word we use to stop a meeting in its tracks, to let everybody know we're off the track. We might be patting ourselves on the back or we might have strayed from the topic into what-ifs or wouldn't-it-be-nice, and someone will make a suggestion or present an idea that's just off the wall and doesn't make sense. Someone else says "banana," which is code for "Wait a minute—that doesn't make sense at all." At that point, we stop talking and find our way back to the topic at hand.

The key, of course, is to keep people around who are willing to say "banana" when you're off track—and to be willing to hear them when they say it.

Object Lesson

What happened at Piedmont is the best example I've ever seen of what happens when you stop listening.

I worked for Piedmont Airlines in the early 1980s, when it was what Continental is now: the darling of the media, named Airline of the Year for 1984. I was senior vice president of operations there, and we did a lot of the same things to be successful there that we've done here. We focused on the basics, making our product first class and working together as a team. We updated the scheduling process and some of the technology (when I started there, Piedmont was still using rotary dial phones!).

However, when Piedmont got all that media attention, the people at the top took their eye off the ball. Some of these executives really liked being successful, and when things would go wrong—things inevitably go wrong in the real world—they stopped listening.

When you're really successful, you can hire a bunch of people who will tell you everything looks good, if that's what you want.

And who could blame you for wanting that? Every time I go into a meeting now, I want every one of my employees to tell me everything is great, that we're making record profits, all our planes are on time, nothing ever breaks down, there are no storms, no employees are sick, nobody makes mistakes, there are no scheduling disputes, and the Houston Astros won the World Series. Of course, they don't. Things do go wrong—our on-time percentage slips, there's a problem with a particular plane or a particular route, an employee mistreats a passenger. But I listen, and then we figure out what to do—and we constantly try to improve.

At Piedmont, the guys who kept bringing up the problems started getting left out of the loop. The guys at the top started listening to the guys who said everything's perfect. That makes for a lot more pleasant meetings. But it's not so great for your airline. In fact, at Piedmont, things started to unravel somewhat. They unraveled to the degree that, when people at the top weren't paying attention, Piedmont was taken over by USAir. Although Piedmont had all kinds of protection against takeover, a few people took their eye off the ball and we woke up one day to discover that our airline was owned by someone else—a company that was inferior in the marketplace in quality rankings, a company that we beat handily in the markets where we competed. All of a sudden, we were theirs.

I was devastated, as were a lot of other employees, because I'm like anybody else—I was working at Piedmont for more than just wages. I thought I was making an investment in the company. I loved that company, and I loved the people in it. Even though I had a five-year contract with Piedmont and all kinds of stock options that the takeover was going to make worth a lot of money, I wasn't happy. I felt betrayed.

And I showed it—like any other employee, when I felt betrayed I behaved badly. I spoke out of turn in a few meetings, including some pretty public forums. At a large pilots' meeting, where I was asked how the company could have been sold out from underneath us, I responded pretty angrily, pointing the blame where I thought it lay. A Piedmont airplane had run off the runway at Charlotte a few months earlier, and I brought that up. Nobody had been seriously hurt, but it was something that had shaken us.

"You remember that plane we lost at Charlotte?" I said. "When the FAA and the NTSB wanted to know why that plane was in the mud instead of the sky, they didn't go talk to the first officer or the flight attendant. They asked the captain. So if you want to know where our airline went, I can't answer that—I think you'd better go ask the captain"—meaning the guy at the top, who I believed had let this thing happen. I later heard that many of those pilots did ask.

I wasn't the only one who was upset, of course—the whole employee base was angry. A couple of days after the sale was announced, I walked into a hangar and found that the mechanics had hung a corporate executive in effigy. The foreman saw me walk into the hangar bay and he was horrified, saying, "Oh geez, we've got this guy hung in effigy and here comes Mr. Bethune." He rushed up to me and apologized—the guys were angry and upset, he said. They'd get that effigy down immediately.

"Well," I said, "yeah, see that you do. Sometime in the next couple of weeks, you get that down. You guys look like you're pretty busy getting the airplanes fixed. That's what I'd focus on for now." I believe the mechanics appreciated me for that—we were all in the same boat. We all felt betrayed and let down by people who didn't have their eye on the ball.

Of course, after a few days of speaking out of turn I was asked to keep my mouth shut. That was fair, so I did. But when all was said and done, my time at Piedmont ended unhappily, with harsh words between me and people from whom I had learned a great, great deal.

But I've never forgotten the final lesson I learned: Just because you're successful doesn't mean you can stop doing the things that got you there. You *must* keep paying attention. You *must* remember that your business is more than just getting or making money. And you *must* remember that, as chief executive, when something big happens, the fingers are going to point at you. So *you* are the one who'd better set the tone by sticking to the basics.

Staying Successful in Two Simple Words

I can say this over and over again in different ways: Keeping your company successful is actually pretty simple. Here's the key. After all the platitudes and all the plans and structures that you put in place to produce and maintain the success of your business, there's only one thing you need to do to keep that success up—one extremely simple thing.

I'll explain it to you with a story a friend of mine tells. He's a longtime hiker, and he remembers his first backpacking trip. He was packing and worrying about the upcoming trip—he wanted to make sure he got everything right. He researched and bought the proper tent; he bought the appropriate sleeping bag; he bought and broke in the right boots.

But he knew that all the planning in the world wasn't going to make sure that he made it to the end of his weeklong hiking trip, and he asked question after question of the guy who was organizing the trip. What if he realized he had brought the wrong kind of food? What if his sleeping bag got wet? What if the tent ripped? What if he broke a bootlace and he forgot to bring an extra and he hiked along with a loose boot and he got a blister but he kept hiking and the blister broke and his foot got sore but he still kept going and the foot got infected and he got blood poisoning and they hiked to a road and flagged down a car and he was rushed to the hospital and the doctors did everything they could and had to cut off his leg but it was too late and he went into a coma and he lingered for a while and then he died?

The leader grew weary of providing reasonable answers—we'll share the extra food, we'll dry your sleeping bag, we'll repair the tent—and finally just sighed. He told my friend that he had two words of advice that, if my friend followed them, would guarantee that he would successfully reach the end of the trail.

My friend held his breath, waiting for the two magic words of wisdom that would solve all his problems.

The leader said, "Don't stop."

And, of course, that's all it is. If you want to remain successful, *don't stop* doing what made you successful. It's difficult, it's unavoidable, and it's the simplest thing in the world. To become successful at Continental, we improved our financial situation, worked harder to give our customers the service that they wanted, improved the product, and took measures to make our employees happy and satisfied.

To remain successful, we couldn't just *keep* our financial situation good—we had to keep making it *better*. We couldn't just keep our planes coming in on time at 1996 levels—we had to make them come in on time at 1998 levels. It gets harder every year.

So that's it. To become successful you address every area of your business; you put plans and measures and programs in place to make it work. You start treating your customers right; you start treating your employees right; you start marketing your product right; you start making your product the best product out there. And it works. You become successful.

To keep it successful?

Don't stop.

part TWO

A Flight Plan for Success

8

How the Sickest Patients Need the Best Doctors, and concerning Tapeworms

fter I took over as chief executive of Continental Airlines, as
you can well imagine, we had quite a turnover in the executive ranks.

I've already told you about the forced ranking we did for all
management employees during my first year as CEO, which made
the difficult job of thinning the ranks somewhat easier. At the top,
the job wasn't much different.

Of the 61 Continental vice presidents working here when I
took over, about half quit or were asked to leave. We never really
had a purge—but we kept turning over rocks, and if we found people who weren't doing their jobs or weren't team players, they
didn't stay. And those who did seem to be doing all right didn't
always want to stick with us when they saw how we did things.

But we were changing our spots big-time here, and in order to be different you have to want to be different. People who were pulling in good salaries doing poor jobs for a floundering company didn't always want to suddenly have to work harder to do a good job in order to make a good company. No problem; we asked those people to leave, and people around them knew exactly why.

Managers were let go here for two reasons: Either they weren't getting the job done, according to the measurements we put in place to determine that, or they weren't team players. Those were the new rules at Continental: Get your job done and work together. If you couldn't or wouldn't do either one of those things, you didn't work here anymore.

To replace the people we let go, we went looking for the best people in the business. And we paid top dollar for them, just as Continental paid me a lot of money to stay here in 1994 when United made that attractive offer to me.

People sometimes ask about that. How could you justify paying all that money for executives when your employees had been taking pay cuts for years? How could you start paying people *more* when the company was running out of money as it was?

I always answer, "Simple." Here's an example: By getting control of company finances, by doing what only he can do, chief financial officer Larry Kellner saved us $6 million in the first few months he was here. Looks to me like if we pay him a dollar less than $6 million, we're already ahead of the game. Of course, we don't pay nearly that much, but the point is, you get what you pay for. If you want great performance, you're going to have to pay for it.

When I first took over and people talked about the salaries of my predecessors, I used to say, "You're right! Seems like if you want someone to lose $200 million a year, you could do that yourself in your spare time. But if you want someone to *make* money for you, you'd better spend the money to hire someone who can." And when those first-rate executives you hire are compensated with bonus and stock programs intimately tied to the performance of the company, then you're probably going to feel pretty good about the work they do. Same thing with our employees, who turned out to be pretty good doctors once we made it clear we'd pay them like good doctors if they acted like good doctors.

Put it another way: When you need brain surgery, do you look around for the best—and maybe most expensive—brain surgeon in the business, or do you hire a proctologist who's willing to learn? Nothing against proctologists—if I had that kind of problem, I wouldn't want a neurologist trying to solve it. But in all cases, I like to say that the sickest patients need the best doctors. And let me remind you, Continental Airlines was a very sick patient.

So we went out and got very good doctors. We got them where we found them. Larry Kellner came from a big bank. Jeff Smisek, our general counsel, was a partner at a big law firm. We hired talent and team players, not airline expertise. We offered them a lot of money, we offered them performance bonuses tied to having them do what we needed them to do, and we let them do their stuff. And the patient got better in a hurry.

Now I'll make one more point, which I've made before. If you're going to choose these folks and pay them great and pin your hopes to them, you'd better choose right.

Fortunately, choosing right isn't that hard. I've been in the aviation industry my whole life, so I've worked with a lot of fine people, and I went looking for some of them. C. D. McLean, our executive vice president of operations, is an example. He was my first hire—I called him for help even before I took over as chief executive. I could see that operationally this company was in trouble. C. D. had worked with me at Piedmont, and I knew he could get things in line. He was in charge of the pilot training at Piedmont, and we needed someone to help restore our relations with the FAA and the Department of Transportation. I called C.D., told him he'd have a good salary, resources, and autonomy, and he came. He likes to say now that when he took over we had what we called a control center, but we didn't control much. He's responsible for updating a lot of our technology, and his people work on the operations hot lines. It was great to get C.D. on board.

Soon after I took over, I called George Mason, the technical operations guy at Piedmont. He came, too. The three of us had worked well together at Piedmont, and with C.D. already here he was glad to come. He likes to say that when he came here, "There were people around here who hadn't hit a lick at a snake in a long time." George is the type of guy who doesn't like those people working for him. He's come up with improvements in everything about the way we maintain our airplanes. When I called him to offer him the job, I told him there were a lot of risks here, and he practically hung up on me in his haste to come to Houston. I've always been gratified by how quickly he was willing to come work with me again.

Greg Brenneman, of course, I simply co-opted. He was already here as a consultant for Bain and Company, and he had a hard time seeing why he'd leave a great job to take over a position at a failing airline. I'd say, "Greg, it's an opportunity to be the chief operating officer of a $6 billion company." And he'd say, "Yeah—the world's worst $6 billion company."

But he worked hard for us anyway. He was in reality the chief operating officer and my partner, even if he technically still worked for Bain and Company. I just wanted him full time. Greg enjoyed doing things—he's good at it and he liked the job. He's too full of energy to just give advice to people, and by March 1995 he accepted the chief operating officer's title and joined us.

Another guy I grabbed from the old days at Piedmont was Jun Tsuruta, who had been vice president of purchasing there. I looked into Continental's purchasing, and everything there had an uneasy feel to it. I knew I could trust Jun, and he came.

But I couldn't rehire everyone from my Piedmont days. In other cases, I asked around. You ask a dozen people you trust who's the best in the business at, say, scheduling. If six of them say the same name, you have to figure that you're onto somebody worth hiring. Then we did what it took to hire those people. Some of them came because they wanted to work with me; some of them came because they liked the challenge of turning around a company in trouble. Some of them came because we showed them they could make a lot of money here if they did their jobs and wanted to be team players. Most of all, they loved knowing that I would give them the autonomy to run their part of our business.

We kind of had to sweet-talk Larry Kellner, but given the opportunity to have free rein over the finances of a company our size, he was willing to take a chance. His chemistry was good with Greg and me, and that's a positive sign for Working Together.

Remember that we only wanted people who were the best at their jobs and who were team players. We were building a team here.

We needed a general counsel, and it was the same thing—a lot of people suggested a prominent local attorney, Jeff Smisek, a Vincent & Elkins partner, so we contacted him. Jeff likes to point out that his secretary had standing orders never to book him on a Continental flight because our airline was so lousy. But he had lunch with me one day, and I asked him if he was the type of attorney who saw a contract as an inviolate document or the kind of guy who could use it as a negotiating instrument. I asked him if he was a T-bill kind of investor or whether he took gambles.

It turned out he took gambles. And he's turned our legal department from a place people regarded as a stumbling block into a department people work with and turn to for help.

I wanted risk takers; I wanted achievers. I wanted people who could see past the airline we were to the airline we could become. And I was willing to pay.

During our protracted negotiations with Delta and Northwest in late 1997 and early 1998, the people at Delta told me we had the best management team in America. I agreed, and I mentioned that we didn't inherit most of them. They came because they'd be free to do their jobs and if they did well, they could make a lot of money here. But the important thing is, they came. We got who we needed.

Keep Those Doctors

After hiring them, of course, we had to keep them. Headhunters call the folks at the top levels of Continental every day. Some managers here figure on at least two calls a week from people trying to lure them away. But they don't go. They don't go because nobody can match what they've got here.

For one thing, we've put into place a pretty powerful salary and bonus system that makes it possible for them to make a lot of money here as long as the planes keep landing on time and the company keeps performing. All this team stuff we talk about, we actually put into practice. Just as the employees are in line for on-time bonuses (which they directly control as a group by their performance) and 15 percent of company pretax profits through profit sharing (which is tied to overall company performance), our executives get bonuses partially based on overall company performance and partially based on individual goals we set for them, all based on the Go Forward Plan. They know that if they do the jobs we hired them to do, nobody else could reward them the way we will.

And besides the money they stand to make, they get to work in an environment where success is the norm; where they are left alone to do their jobs to the best of their abilities; where, when they need help, all they need to do is ask for it; where, if they make a mistake, we're going to correct it and learn from it. So they know they're not going to get hammered from above if they take risks or get creative. That's what they're hired to do, and they're encouraged to do it.

There's one more reason that's worth pointing out for why it costs a lot of money to get the people you need to save your company. In Chapter 2 I told you that the first question in solving a problem is this: Whose problem is it? When you're a sick company hiring people to save you before you finish your self-destruction, who's got the problem?

You do. And top-flight executives are going to need a little more than the thrill of problem solving to get them to leave secure jobs at successful companies to come and save your butt. The bad news is, what makes it worth their while to take a chance on you usually involves a lot of money. The good news is, once you get them, they're usually worth it. In our case, they were really worth it.

Can I Say This Again? Working Together

More than the money they can make, these executives are in an environment in which they don't have to worry about getting undercut by coworkers. Part of this, of course, is general corporate culture now. Once you stop micromanaging from the top and start managing for results rather than compliance, people get much more interested in doing their jobs and much less interested in doing other people's jobs. Managers worry about each other's work when they're frustrated and can't do their own. They take that frustration out on each other.

There's no question that even in the best companies little turf wars spring up now and then and you have to stamp them down, but, overall, the entire culture of the company—whom we hired, whom we rewarded, whom we promoted—showed that the way to success was to do your own job as well as you could, to help other people if they needed your help, but not to undercut people and not to waste a lot of time wrestling over power. To make sure that message got through, I made some very specific statements about it.

The first week after I took over in late 1994, I assembled the 20 or so people who report directly to me. We sat around a board-room table, and I gave a little lecture. I said, "I want you to look around the room. You're all big shots here. You're the vice president of maintenance, you're the vice president of sales, the vice president of this, and the vice president of that. You have your jobs because that's what you're good at."

I let that sink in for a second, then I got to the point.

"And if one of you decides to spend your time knocking off one of the others, I'm going to pay you exactly what you're already getting to do your job. And while you're knocking someone else off, your part of the company won't work well, because you'll be too busy subverting someone else's. And so none of us will get a bonus, because the company won't succeed.

"So I want you to see that you won't get a nickel for taking someone else's job away, and you probably will cost yourself—and everyone else—a lot of money. Because none of you are going to get anything extra unless we all win as a team. So why don't you stick to being a good vice president of whatever you're vice president of, hope the others do the same, and we'll all get along great when we count our bonuses at the end of the year?"

Everyone nodded politely, but the message got through. The era of jockeying for position and backstabbing that made the old Continental such an awful place to work was over, starting *now*.

This worked as well with the people in the management positions as it did with the people answering the phones and loading the planes. We've never looked back.

"That's a Lovely Tie You're Wearing Today, Boss"

One of the first questions I'm asked by reporters investigating our success is how we manage to avoid a culture where ass kissing works. Most people seem to work in environments where the people who get ahead are not necessarily the stars. Often the people climbing the ladder are yes-people, ass kissers, corporate clones willing to engage in skullduggery.

True enough. Wherever you look, people work for companies where no good deed goes unpunished, and the soulless lead the clueless as they try to frustrate the capable. That's deadening to workers, especially talented workers. That means that sooner or later it's destructive to product, service, and profits.

It's something you won't run into much of at Continental. How, I'm asked, do we do it?

Well, first, I've got to tell you that it starts from the top. I like to think that I'd rather hear the truth than a bunch of B.S. that sounds good and will make me feel better, and that I demonstrate this on a daily basis—think of what would have happened to us if Greg Brenneman had been afraid to tell me we were going to run out of money in January 1995 because he thought I would yell at him. I'd rather have the bad news in time to do something about it. For example, once when we were picking up a new plane from Boeing, I had planned to have our board of directors meet in Seattle, and we'd fly them to Houston on our new plane. It was going to be an event.

However, things didn't go just right at Boeing, and the plane wasn't ready. Boeing knew my board was coming, and they weren't too happy, but they called and told me. We were supposed to take delivery of another plane a month earlier, so I said, "I guess we'll just have to leave the other one there and fly home on that one." I wasn't happy; I wished everything had gone right. But they gave me time to react, and the board and I had a nice flight—albeit on another plane. So I don't want flattery, I want information.

But I'm human like anybody else, and that oily flattery eventually works on anyone. It happened to Napoleon and it's happened to plenty of business leaders who have been successful, started to believe their own press clips, and fallen in love with their own images.

Think of it this way. Remember the analogy of the sickest patient needing the best doctor? For your brain surgery, are you going to hire the surgeon who's your nephew, or your buddy, or the guy who says you have the nicest tie? Nope. You're going to forget who's your pal and who talks the nicest to you, and you're going to hire the surgeon who's most likely to have you wake up after the surgery.

To protect myself—and Continental Airlines—from that, I make sure that at every level we keep the focus on results. We keep measuring—we keep our eyes on the results that made us successful, according to the measurements we determined.

Believe Your Instruments

In my own case, I keep in mind that bullshit in a business is just like bullshit on an airplane. And let me tell you a little something I learned as a pilot: *You can't bullshit an airplane.* You either know how to fly it or you don't. The fuel level on board is whatever it is, even if you adjust the gauge to make it read "full." You might feel better looking at a fuel gauge reading "full," but the engines don't run on the gauge. They run on the *fuel.*

The thing is, if you find a first officer willing to curry favor by ignoring the truth about something going wrong, you've forgotten a pretty important fact: *You're on the airplane, too.*

If you put on insufficient fuel to make it to your planned destination, it's preferable to change the plan before the airplane changes it for you.

Since I've been captain, we've only been hiring people who like to tell the truth. We hire people who, if they were encouraged to B.S. the captain, would rather strap on a parachute and jump out of the airplane. We hire people who will take their chances, who trust their own judgment, and who won't shut up.

It's okay to be overruled—I sometimes overrule people who tell me things, and sometimes the people I work with overrule me. But we do that after we've checked all our information.

I want people working here who don't mind standing up and saying we're low on fuel and are willing to stick up for their beliefs. And they've also got to be ready to understand that when the decision is made—we're going on to L.A., or we're stopping in Phoenix—the decision is made and it's time to get to work.

What I *don't* want is people who won't tell me we're low on fuel because they think they'll get a bigger raise if they keep it to themselves or blame it on someone else. Because you know what? *Nobody* gets a raise if we don't reach our destination safely.

The Tapeworm

If you're willing to look at it from all angles, you can see that, apart from what it does to a business as a whole, ass kissing is self-destructive to the people who practice it, too. The problem with ass kissing, the problem with being somebody's pet, is you're like a tapeworm. You have to go where the person goes, eat what the person eats—and you die when the person dies. If you're some-body's pet and that person gets fired or retires, you're dead, too. Instead of having your success defined by the success of the company, by being part of a team, your success comes down to the well-being of one person. You can't like those odds.

Plus, once you're somebody's pet, you have to spend all your time looking out for *that person's* health as well as your own. You better look both ways when *that person* crosses the street as well as when *you* do.

Thus it's not a very effective way to marshal your own forces, to use your own time and energy. Instead of working for the good of the whole company and your own good, you're looking out for one person. Like I said, you can't like the odds.

The Booger

Ass kissing isn't good for the company as a whole, and it's not good for the person doing it. But it's seductive to the person who's receiving it, yes?

In the short term, it is. But take a look at the long term. In the short term, I might feel real good about someone who stands around telling me how great I am. But in the long run, if the person doesn't tell me the unpleasant facts—we're low on fuel, we're going too slow and we're going to stall, whatever—we're all going to fail.

In fact, in that meeting where I told everybody that the days of rivalry and undercutting were past, I told them something else straightforwardly: You're going to have to tell me the unpleasant facts when you know them.

If I'm supposed to make a presentation and I have a booger hanging on the end of my nose, one of you has the unpleasant responsibility to tell me about the booger. It's going to be an awkward moment for both of us, but it's going to be a lot worse for *all* of us if you don't.

If I walk into that meeting with that booger, I'm not going to get the respect of whomever I'm meeting with—the board, the stockholders, the people trying to lease us airplanes. The meeting won't go well, and that won't go well for Continental Airlines, which means it won't go well for you.

So tell me about the booger, won't you?

I represent Continental Airlines, and it's in everyone's interest for me to do so as well as possible. You can't be an effective leader if someone has put a "kick me" sign on your back and none of your subordinates will tell you. So being willing to listen to criticism from my subordinates allows me not to do anything stupid around here.

I surround myself with the smartest people I can hire. And then I listen to them.

You know what? It works.

Of course, all the ass kissing in the world isn't going to get you too far at Continental anymore, because we do something different now.

Measure, Measure, Measure

We measure.

Have I said it often enough? Identify what you want to accomplish, explain it clearly to the people who need to accomplish it, and then find ways to measure whether it's being accomplished. In that situation, how could anyone survive by flattery?

"Geez, boss, that's sure a nice tie and you're the greatest guy there ever was plus I think Hodgkin is a big jerk, don't you?" Well maybe so, bub, but according to these numbers, you are *still* not bringing in your planes on time. Tell me I'm great all day long; I love that. But you're not getting the job done. According to the numbers, Hodgkin is. Hodgkin gets to keep his job; you don't. But you can still keep telling me I'm great; I don't mind it.

There's no way to bullshit if you're measuring the right stuff. In fact, that is how I know I'm doing a good job. We measure. Our profits keep going up, as measured on our financial statements. We keep getting more customers, as measured on our daily bookings.

We keep getting *better* customers, as measured by our percentage of business passengers and our average revenue per available seat mile. Our employees keep getting happier, as measured by their reduced sick time and on-the-job injuries, their diminishing complaints to management, and their declining turnover rate. Our service keeps getting better, as measured by on-time rate, lost-luggage rate, complaints to the Department of Transportation, and so forth.

If the emperor had no clothes, somebody would have kicked me out by now—I know it. Continental is now the kind of place where the employees would stand up and shout that the emperor had no clothes if that's what they thought.

But in whose interest would it be to kick me out? Stockholders are richer, employees are happier and better paid, managers are happier and better paid, corporate lessors and other partners are doing better business and getting paid more promptly.

Simplicity Itself

There are a million reasons to do whatever you can to get the best people to work for you and to make sure you don't reward toadyism, instead rewarding what people accomplish.

But to get to the ultimate point, you have to return to the people you work with. Where do people work happier and better—for people who reward excellent work and accomplishment or for people who reward sneakiness and ass kissing? Where would you rather work—and which kind of manager would you rather be?

Oh, Yeah—Don't Be a Jerk

There's one more way to reduce the incentive toward ass kissing and other destructive kinds of behavior, and that's to never, ever emasculate someone publicly for making a mistake. That's how it used to work at Continental—people working in this executive suite still shudder about the things that were said and the way people were treated. It cast a pall over the entire company that took an entire Go Forward Plan to dispel. Therefore, even if a mistake is bad enough that someone has to lose a job over it, do that in a humane way and in private. Worrying about public humiliation just doesn't promote good work.

People will make mistakes—in an environment where chance taking and independent thought is encouraged, they may at times make *more* rather than fewer mistakes. A sure way to prevent them from getting defensive and secretive and toadying is not to excoriate them for those mistakes.

That's what causes ass kissing in the first place—if people are afraid of what will happen to them if they make some kind of well-intentioned mistake, they'll start finding ways to pretend those mistakes don't happen or to curry favor to prevent the consequences of those mistakes from being as unpleasant as they might be. So if I were upbraiding people publicly for mistakes—calling them on the carpet, emasculating them, humiliating them—or if their immediate supervisors were, they'd learn real quick that all our talk about teamwork and employees being our most important asset was just talk. And everything would fall apart in six months.

Part of that is general common sense. In Chapter 6 I talked about Working Together and how we never used differences among employees to separate them. We knew not to do that because sooner or later whatever problems you're having will be solved, and there will be a lot less scar tissue if you've avoided mean-spiritedness or divisiveness on your own part. People will have a much easier time getting back into the fold if you don't beat them up too badly when they've wandered out of it.

That's one reason not to excoriate people who make mistakes: It makes enemies out of them, and even when they come back into your good graces, they don't forget how you treated them when you were unhappy with them.

The other reason is that that kind of treatment encourages people to hide their mistakes and do whatever they think might prevent you from treating them that way again. You get yes-people that way, not strong and helpful employees. If you make a mistake and I stand there in front of your coworkers and call you an idiot and say I don't know why I'm paying you to do such a half-assed job, how are you going to feel the next time you have a chance to make a decision? Chances are, you're going to hide behind the counter and pass the problem along to somebody else. Pretty quickly people inside the company and outside it are going to learn that we're not solving problems here, we're ignoring them.

Remember that I said the job of a supervisor isn't to look over people's shoulders, it's to hire good people and let them do their jobs? It's the same principle here. If you're there to help employees solve problems that come up and recover from mistakes they make by virtue of your wider view and your greater experience, you can expect employees to come to you with problems and own up to mistakes in the hope they'll learn from them—and learn from you in the process.

Mistreat them, and you can expect your employees to hide problems from you and try to curry favor with you rather than simply do their jobs. It just makes sense, from their point of view. Now what makes the most sense from yours?

Nobody Loses When the Whole Team Wins

I say it all the time: An airline is the biggest team sport there is. It's 40,000 people working together, day after day, toward the same goal: getting 2,100 planes loaded with people to their destinations in a clean, safe, and reliable way.

If you want to make the most sweeping statement you can about the change at Continental since I came on board, it's that now everybody's on the same team and everyone knows it. Everyone knows what the goal is and what his or her part is and how it relates to the goal. Everyone knows what the reward is for making the goal and what happens if we fail.

We're all working from the same plays, the same playbook— plays everyone's had a chance to buy into, plays the people who will be running them had a chance to help design, plays everyone believes in, plays everyone believes can win.

You want your company to run well? Here's an ironclad rule: Get everyone on the same team. Get everyone working for the same goal; get them to win or lose together.

Bad Teams Don't Play Together

The other way doesn't work.

When a team has a bunch of plays it doesn't think will work, the team doesn't win. When team members are beating up on each other, the team doesn't win. It's when the team beats up on *other teams* that it wins. Beating up on itself just causes trouble and makes noise.

Look at a good team. The quarterback isn't looking down his nose at the guards because they can't throw the ball. The quarterback knows that without those guards, he gets flattened on every play. His running backs can't run and he can't throw the ball to his wide receivers if the guards aren't doing their jobs. So he has a real clear sense that those guys are doing a pretty important job—a job he couldn't do himself.

Same with the guards. They're not griping that the wide receivers might be making more money than they are; they recognize that the receivers are the guys who carry the ball, so they might take home more pay. But the guards know that if they're not blocking for the quarterback, he's not going to throw too many touchdown passes to those wide receivers, and the team won't score too many points. So they know what their contribution is, and they know their contribution is valuable. On good teams, the quarterbacks and the wide receivers know the same thing. They have respect for each other's jobs, so they don't try to do them for each other.

Good Teams Win Together

All team members know that getting the ball across the goal line depends on all of them doing their own jobs. That's why a team— or a company—is more like a watch than anything else you can think of. Every piece has to do its job for the whole thing to work. If even the smallest piece of the watch fails, the whole watch can fail. Either the watch works and you can depend on it, or it doesn't. It's pretty simple.

Look at the Super Bowl. When a team wins the Super Bowl, who gets what? Everybody on the team gets $48,000. That's *everybody* on the team. The star quarterback doesn't get more, the reserve linebacker who only plays on special teams doesn't get less. Everybody gets the same thing, because the team won. That quarterback could throw three interceptions and cause the team to lose, or that reserve linebacker could recover a fumble and cause the team to win. In fact, that kind of helps to ease the heartburn of that star quarterback taking home such a big salary. If it's his passing and play calling that got you to the championship game, you tend to feel pretty good about that salary. At the end, everybody is equally important in winning, and everybody's working for the same reward.

Same with our airline. For a flight to be on time, everybody has to do his or her job—catering people, cleaning people, pilots, flight attendants, mechanics, gate agents, baggage handlers. And behind them, the ticketing people have to have done their jobs right long before the plane ever got off the ground. Having three passengers ticketed for seat 17E can hold up a flight every bit as much as a slow baggage cart, a missing meal, or a late flight attendant—or for that matter, a big storm. Any one thing can throw the whole team off.

Running Plays the Team Believes in: Buy-in

Remember in Chapter 6 I talked about calling plays that your players can run? That's teamwork, and a pretty important part of that is getting the players themselves to buy into those plays. That means getting their input before you call the plays.

Say you've got a wide receiver who isn't too fast but has the knack of getting open. Well, for crying out loud, don't call a bunch of fly patterns that call for him to flat out run past defensive backs. He can't do it—he knows he can't do it, and sooner or later he'll quit trying. On the other hand, call plays that require him to make a lot of cuts and shake free, and he'll be begging for the ball.

That's exactly how our maintenance and scheduling and marketing people work together to design our schedule. When we had that schedule, we sent it around. Everybody took a look at it, and—whoa!—for once, they saw something they liked. Operations guys looked at it and saw that there's 25 minutes on the ground here to get this plane clean. Can we do that? We'd better be able to—we said we could in the meeting a month ago. Pilots look at the schedule and it says that the plane has two hours to get from Houston to Nashville. Can we do that? We'd better—that's how long we said it would take in the meeting.

It was all stuff everyone had agreed to. Why *wouldn't* it work?

On the other hand, design a schedule that calls for planes to get 45-minute maintenance procedures done in 35 minutes or fly a two-hour route in an hour and a half, and sooner or later employees get disgusted and hang their heads. That's how it used to be done at Continental: Marketing said we needed 10 daily departures from Fort Lauderdale, and the flights needed to go to these particular cities. Scheduling drew up a schedule, threw it over the wall at the operations people, and ran, in effect, saying, "Our end is straight, if those guys in operations can't get it together, that's their problem."

When I took over I cut that stuff out.

Now the team works well because everybody knows the definition of winning. Everybody knows what his or her role is. Maybe they get mad about this or that, but we've got ways of dealing with that. Upset about your schedule? We've got supervisors who will listen to you and maybe show you how you can work your way up to getting better choices. Annoyed at those guys in maintenance? Call the 800 number and let us know. We'll address it. Have a benefits problem? Call the 800 number for that. We'll help you. Mad at somebody for treating you badly during your shift? Let us know, we'll work it out.

However, once you're at work and trying to get those planes in the air, let that go. That $65 monthly on-time bonus—and the profit-sharing money it eventually leads to—are on the line every day just as sure as that $48,000 is on the line for the guys in the Super Bowl. Our employees know it. It's all for one, so they put problems aside in order to win.

They're a good team now. And on a good team, players don't lose sight of that ultimate goal: getting the ball across the goal line and having more points on the scoreboard than the other team at the end of the game.

Everything Is Relative—Even Winning

Because winning in the airline industry is just like winning at any team sport. You want to be as close to perfect as you can, but in the end, you're only judged against the other guys. You'd like to score a touchdown on every play on offense, return every kick for a score, and sack the opposing quarterback every time he takes a snap.

But it ain't going to happen. So you do your best and you find a more reasonable goal: You want to score points, keep the other guys from scoring too many, and end up with more points than they got. That'll work. You can have a bad game, where everybody seems to be having a rough time getting their jobs done and nobody's too happy about anything, but if you have one more point than the other guys when the gun goes off, you still win. That's the point.

Same with us. We'd love to run an airline where every flight departed on time, full and in perfect condition. Where we never lost a bag or missed a connection or did anything wrong. Where bearings never wore out, where fuses never blew, where communications always worked and every time a flight attendant opened the door to a plane there was a catering person with a cart full of the right food for the right passengers. We'd be perfect, and why would anybody fly any airline other than Continental?

As long as people are people, that ain't gonna happen. People make mistakes. They read baggage claim tickets wrong or misunderstand directions—or forget to cater the ice on the flight . . . or land at the wrong airport. So we have to make do with a more reasonable goal: being better than the other guys. We'd like *every* flight to be on time. But if we can keep it so that more of our flights are on time than anybody else's, that's still going to win for us. We'd like to *never* lose a bag. But if we can lose fewer bags than anybody else and make sure that if we lose your bag we take care of you, that's still going to win for us.

We'd like it if our employees linked arms and sang "Kumbayah" before every shift and remembered us and each other in their prayers every night. But if we can get them to enjoy coming to work for us and to believe that we treat them better than they'd be treated at any other airline, that things are going pretty well for them here and they have a fair deal and the opportunity to do their best work and get paid fairly for it, that's still winning for us—because that makes them happy, and that makes them work well. When they work well, our planes land on time and we attract more passengers.

And that's winning for us. As long as we never lose sight of that, we'll probably keep winning.

Winning Is the Ultimate Goal, but Not the Only Goal

I say *winning* over and over, and I say so because, at bottom, I think it's the thing everybody wants.

Business, or management—or, better, leadership—is all about people, don't forget. People have pretty simple needs and requirements, and we know pretty much what they are. Abraham Maslow published his hierarchy of human needs decades ago, and it's just as true today as it was then. It starts with basics like oxygen, water, food, and shelter and works its way up through self-actualization, where you're in swim with the universe and everything is kind of perfect.

We all want to get to self-actualization, and winning is a sort of shorthand for that. It's getting what you want. It's one of the most fundamental human motivations—everybody's got it. Everybody wants to do well, to do better than they did yesterday and better than the other guy they can compare themselves to.

The key, of course, is the same in running an airline—or a pizza parlor—as it is with a football team. If you've got your fundamentals straight and you've made it all the way up the ladder to that final step, you'd better not forget to keep those basics in line. Don't concentrate so hard on that last step to self-actualization that you forget to make sure you're still breathing.

If a football team has been blocking and tackling and doing everything else just right and they've been getting to the Super Bowl every year but just can't win, they'll keep trying to figure out that last thing. Maybe it's a better punter; maybe it's a trick play; maybe it's even just a change of uniforms to somehow alter people's attitudes. It's something—you can always improve—and they'll keep looking for it.

But while the coaches and managers and players are searching hard for that tiny missing element, the players better keep blocking and tackling well, because if you finally figure out what that tiny missing piece is and you've lost track of everything else, you still ain't gonna win.

Keep Maslow's hierarchy of needs in mind when you're work-ing on your business. For us at Continental, that means we don't want to get so interested in the kind of food we serve that we lose track of getting our planes in on time. We're not going to go too far if we've got one little element right but we're missing the basics. After all, look at our OnePass frequent flyer program, which year after year was voted the best in the business—and all the while we were losing bags, screwing up flights, and losing cus-tomers.

It's great to have the best frequent flyer program. But we had to have the basics—clean, safe, and reliable flights to places people wanted to go (the food, clothing and shelter of an airline)—before that was going to get us anywhere.

Here's an example. One of the things we were working on in 1997 was appropriate boarding music for our flights. It's something we play on the planes to soothe the passengers as they're going through the stress and bustle of boarding the plane. Pleasant, familiar music helps people concentrate on something other than the hassle of finding an overhead baggage compartment, or the fussing baby sitting a row behind them, or the worry about making a connection.

I happened to step onto a transatlantic flight, and I heard something that sounded like somebody was killing a cow. I couldn't believe that was supposed to be soothing our customers. So I called up the big shots in marketing and asked for an expla-nation.

"You gotta understand," they said. "You heard the soundtrack to a video—it's whales swimming, and that's their call." I said, "You know what? The passengers aren't watching their little video screens when they're boarding. They're standing around or fussing with their armrests or trying to get the flight attendant's attention. I want you to rethink this and let's have a meeting and see what you come up with."

So they did, and we had a meeting. They said, "Okay, we've got this much better for you, Gordon, let's take a look at this new video." And I turned my chair around and looked at the wall and said "Okay, shoot." They said, "No, Gordon, you don't under-stand, it's a video, you have to watch it."

And I said, "No, *you* don't understand—during boarding, people do not watch videos. We need music that soothes them without making them watch TV."

They forgot the basics of what they were doing—the basic blocking and tackling, the food, clothing, and shelter of their task. The point is to soothe customers. If it works in video, that's even better. But that's up at the self-actualization end of the scale, and if we lose track of the primary goal—making the passengers a little more comfortable as they board, regardless of whether they can see the video—then we're doing the wrong thing. If I were spending all my time on boarding videos while our on-time percentages were going to hell, I'd be spending my time on the wrong thing.

You see? It's the same way you build a great team. You need to get the basics done first. It's great to have a terrific fake punt play, but if you can't make two yards on third and one, that fake punt is only going to get you so far.

Getting People to Win

Okay, Gordon, if that's so obvious, if everybody wants to win, what do they need you for?

Good question. An awful lot of management at an awful lot of places not only doesn't help the team win, it prevents them from winning. Continental was a great example of that before I got here. The company took resources away from people; it prevented them from cooperating; it rewarded them for all the wrong stuff. Continental took a staff of people capable of winning and taught them that not only were they never going to win, but their only recourse was to keep a low profile. Even surviving was in question as far as they were concerned.

The definition of winning changed from week to week. Credible, consistent communication was almost nonexistent.

That was just about the opposite of helping your team to win. It was the equivalent of the coaches getting paid while making the team practice plays they'd never run against teams they'd never play. Not exactly "Win one for the Gipper."

And that's where you come in—the leader, the coach. You're the guy who designs the plays, who helps everybody get on the same page.

If the Coach Wins, the Team Wins

Wherever I've worked during my life, I've made this clear: If I win and you're on my team, you'll win, too. Every time something good has happened at Continental, it's been that way. Our planes started being on time more, and what happened? Employees got $65 a month. When the company became profitable, everyone received extra pay through profit sharing. When I received a bonus, so did my top managers.

I started getting interviewed by newspapers and magazines about what was going right, and every time I talked to someone I said the same thing: This entire team at Continental, working together, made this change happen. Not just me, not just Gordon Bethune. I'm the head coach, sure. I'm getting the right players and hiring the right assistant coaches, and I'm listening to them. So we're designing plays we can win with, and we're calling the right plays at the right time because we're all together. It's not me—it's us.

Do you get that? If Gordon wins, you win. Now, which team do you want to be on?

I figure you'll want to be on my team, and that's half the battle right there. Now all we've got to do is decide what we need to do to win, what the reward is going to be if we win—all the stuff I've been talking about—and then just do it.

So wherever I worked, people worked really hard. I'm a good leader for a simple reason: I know that everybody likes winning better than losing. Everybody wants their chance to contribute.

You Gotta Be a Leader

If you want the team to win, it's better to have a good coach. Isn't that right? You can put all kinds of talent on the field, but without the coach to get the players organized, without designed plays and plans and some kind of structure, the team might do okay, but it's not going to win the championship. That's the bottom line. Part of what a team needs is a good coach, and if you're the leader of the company, you have to be the leader of the team.

There are different kinds of leaders, and you have to be the kind of leader you're comfortable with. But if you're not a leader—if you're just an administrator—you're going to be in trouble. A business is a collection of people, and people need leadership.

Think of football coaches. Some are ranters and ravers. Some are arm-around-the-shoulder types. Some are cool strategists. Some are pleaders, and some are threateners. But they all deal with their players. They don't treat them like interchangeable parts; they treat them like individuals who have emotions and needs and their own points of view. The successful ones, you can bet, are honest with themselves, honest with their teams, and willing to change a strategy that isn't working.

If you're an arm-around-the-shoulder type, you might not have too much succcess with a player who needs a kick in the butt. But if that guy's the best player at his position and you need his contribution, he needs a kick in the butt, regardless of whether you're good at giving it to him. So you'd better either get one of your assistants who's good at that sort of thing to kick him in the butt or learn to do it yourself. One way or the other, that guy needs a kick in the butt. And if he doesn't get it, you're not going to win.

The thing is, you have to figure out not just what would make *you* want to win in his situation. You have to figure out what motivates *him*. This is about people, not about job specifics. You can't go out and do his job for him—you can't go out and catch the passes yourself or block for the running backs yourself. Then who's gonna call the plays? That's your job, and you can't forget it.

You have to motivate people, and that means finding the incentives that work for them.

Why Isn't the Horse Fast?

That's one of the true challenges of taking over a business that's in trouble, as I did at Continental. You walk into a situation that you know beforehand isn't good, and you have to start fixing things. You have to figure out when to use a hammer, when to use a screwdriver, and when to just use duct tape. And sometimes, if you're not paying close attention, the situations are hard to tell apart and you can cause more damage than you prevent.

Think of it as a horse race. A jockey is riding a horse in a race, and the horse isn't winning. The jockey is dissatisfied, so he gives the horse a little whack with the whip, and the horse goes faster. The jockey figures that, without the whip, the horse was running at about 80 percent. After being whipped, the horse is giving a good 90 to 95 percent.

The horse is going faster, but it's still not winning, so the jockey whips it harder. The horse really throws it into gear now, and it moves up to second place, probably running about as fast as it can go. The jockey, still not satisfied, whips the horse even more, and the horse gives everything it's got—it goes up to 110 percent, and it really can't do that for more than a short burst.

The jockey still sees another horse in front of him, so he keeps it up with the whip—and before long the horse is pacing along at about 80 percent again. The horse has learned something: It doesn't make any difference how fast it runs, the jockey's going to keep whipping it. It may as well just run at 80 percent and be comfortable.

The board of directors says, "We ain't winning with this jockey; we need a new jockey." The new jockey comes in and finds a horse that's running along at about 80 percent. So what does the new jockey do—start whipping the horse?

The Psychology of Horses and the Psychology of Humans

The answer is, you have to know *why* the horse is running at only 80 percent. You have to figure out where the horse is in the evolution of things. Is it running at 80 percent because nobody ever thought to whack it a little? Or is it running at 80 percent because no matter what it does, somebody whacks it? In that case, you might be better off to just stop the whacking and see if the horse speeds up. It all depends on the horse.

That's the psychology of horses—and the psychology of humans.

I came to Continental and things were just barely moving along. I could have easily decided that this team needed me to yell at them, threaten them, fire a few people, and make a lot of noise. That would have got their attention.

However, the people here were just struggling along because they had learned that no matter what they did, they were going to get yelled at. They were going to have their pay cut; they were going to have layoffs; they were going to be undercut by their teammates and yelled at by their customers and by their bosses. It was all whipping for these guys.

I always think of the image of a gate agent driving to work at the Newark airport in a snowstorm. It's already a bad day, and he has to go to work knowing that planes are going to be late, people are going to be disappointed, and he'll have a lot of angry passengers on his hands. We weren't running a good airline in the first place, so this gate agent had to drive to work just dreading the day ahead of him. It didn't matter now nice he might be, people were going to be frustrated, because even if the plane was late because of the weather, he was dealing with passengers who were used to Continental being late. These people were angry going in.

How's that guy going to feel? I liken it to being in a nuclear war, and all this guy has got to defend himself is a rifle. There was just nothing that gate agent could possibly do to fix or improve anything. Sooner or later he's going to figure out that his best bet is to just dig a shell hole, cover up, and start trying to save his own butt.

I took the trouble to figure that out. These people needed to learn that they *could* make a difference before we could expect them to *want* to. I knew right off that whipping this horse, being the kind of coach who ranted and raved at these team members, wasn't going to get us anywhere. I could have fired people and jammed a whole bunch of new stuff down their throats. But that wasn't going to get us to win, and I sure wanted to win.

This was a horse that needed us to *stop* whipping it. So this was the first thing we did. We determined goals that everybody could buy into. Then we added a reward for reaching these goals—that famous $65 on-time bonus—and it turned out that we had a pretty fast horse after all.

I'm not saying that whacking is never the answer. Sometimes it is. But not always. Just as yelling isn't always the answer and rewards aren't always the answer.

You have to understand the psychology of horses to get them to run fast. And you have to understand the psychology of people if you want them to work well together.

It's about People and Nothing but People

So is that my advice? You have to pay attention to the people who work for you? That doesn't sound like anything too ground-breaking.

Yep. That's it exactly. It's not groundbreaking, but how come so many businesses forget it? Just about everything I've said in this chapter is pretty basic, I think—but you have to remember to do it. As the leader of your team, you have to be willing to make sure it happens.

You have to be willing to sit in a different position in the meeting room; you have to be willing to open the doors to your office. You have to be willing to return those phone calls your employees make to you. You have to be willing to take all those good ideas you and your cronies come up with in meetings and actually put them into practice.

In short, you have to lead. You have to *do something about it.* That's how you get people's attention. Employees, like football players or soldiers or any other group, need someone to show them the way. That's just human nature. But if you show them the way, if you treat them fairly and do all the stuff we've been talking about in this book—communicate with them honestly, help them do their jobs, set goals they can actually believe in and achieve, and then reward them for their efforts—sooner or later they'll follow you anywhere, because you will have taught them to believe in themselves, and that's what they want. That's coming close to the self-actualization that Maslow talked about.

Here are a few words from the *Tao te Ching**:

When the Master governs, the people
are hardly aware that he exists.
Next best is a leader who is loved.
Next, one who is feared.
The worst is one who is despised.

**Source:* From *Tao te Ching by Lao Tzu, A New English Version,* with foreword and notes by Steven Mitchell. Translation copyright © 1988 by Steven Mitchell. Reprinted by permission of HarperCollins Publishers, Inc.

If you don't trust the people,
you make them untrustworthy.

The Master doesn't talk, he acts.
When his work is done,
the people say, "Amazing:
we did it, all by ourselves!"

Lao-tzu wrote that some 2,500 years ago, and it's every bit as true today. Why? Because basic human nature has not changed.

People still read Shakespeare today, 400 years after he was writing. Why? Because people have not changed. Shakespeare got his characters right on the money, and when people see those plays today, they think, "By God, that's true. My boss is just like that guy. My mother is just like that woman. I'm just like that person." Our fundamental motivations and needs, wishes and desires, are very much the same as they've always been. The truth just doesn't change.

People want to do their work. They want to get paid well for it. They want to be appreciated. They want to work together. They want to win. And if they have a stake in what they're trying to win—whether it's profit sharing, an on-time bonus, or $48,000 for winning the Super Bowl—they're going to give it everything they've got.

People like to cooperate, to be part of a team. They want to win, and they want someone to take charge and lead them there. They don't mind short-term pain to achieve long-term goals. In Chapter 6 I told you how we force ranked our managers on a scale of one through four, where four represented the poorest performance. When we let all the number fours go, there wasn't too much heartburn among those who remained. The number fours were the people they wanted to see go.

This is like a coach who lets go players who aren't carrying their weight. Players are pretty smart. They know who's getting the job done. The coach is the guy who has to make the hard decisions about what to do with those who aren't. A coach who is willing to do that, in a reasonable and honest way, can expect more, rather than less, respect from his team.

One Other Winner

There's one final similarity between a team and our airline. When a team wins, the team members get what they wanted, and the coaches and everybody else get what they wanted, too. But who else wins?

The fans, that's who. The people who put their energy into supporting that team. They are just as happy as the team members. Which celebration is bigger: the one in the locker room or the one out there in the stands? Everybody looks pretty happy to me.

That, finally, is the thing to remember. If an airline is a team, then its fans are its customers and owners—and nobody wants the team to win as much as they do. When Continental is doing well, it's satisfying its passengers. Clean, safe, and reliable flights produced by a safe, happy, and cooperative staff mean that everybody wins—inside the company and outside.

This is the kind of teamwork that lasts.

Keeping the Lines of Communication Open

When Continental announced that the controlling block of our stock had been purchased in our new alliance with Northwest Airlines in early 1998, I learned how successfully we had changed the way we communicated at Continental.

See, I felt as if I had spent the first two years as chief executive of Continental telling my employees we weren't merging with America West Airlines. Chapter 4 discussed the code-sharing arrangement that Continental entered into with America West. Faced with some western routes that were losing money but that we felt we still needed to serve, we consolidated some destinations with America West, which was in the same situation with some eastern destinations. America West took over staffing of some of our western gates in places like Phoenix, combining our operations with theirs to enable them to run one profitable gate with, say, eight flights a day instead of each of us running unprofitable gates with four a day. But the city was regarded as one that Continental served, and the flights both companies shared had a Continental flight code so that our passengers could fly there, even on an America West plane, and never feel as though they had left Continental. The converse arrangement was made for America West in places like Orlando and other east coast cities.

This meant that we had to increase staff in some cities and drop staff in others. We had to ask some employees to relocate, and people didn't always want to. It wasn't pleasant, but it helped stabilize the company, although it caused some heartburn to our employees overall.

Naturally enough, when that happened, the employees thought that we were going to completely merge with America West—that we were going to end up laying people off, canceling jobs, and downsizing our airline. At all those employee meetings we were starting to have, the questions continually came up: Are we merging with America West? Am I going to lose my job? The answers to both questions was no, but it didn't matter how many times I said this, the questions were sure to be asked again at the next meeting. Word didn't yet travel very well at Continental, and when it did travel, people didn't believe it. So I had to say things over and over.

Now let me tell you what happened late in 1997, when we began to publicly discuss a somewhat similar but much broader arrangement with Northwest, which got a lot of attention in the business press. It looked like this arrangement would actually go a long way toward preventing any kind of merger or takeover. The result was going to be exactly like the America West agreement, only we weren't going to do any kind of consolidating, so nobody's job would change at all. We were going to add some of Northwest's destinations and they would add ours. But we weren't going to change a single job, or add or remove a single airplane. No consolidation. No layoffs. No takeover.

Still, the same questions came from employees: Are we merging with Northwest? Am I going to lose my job? The answers were again no. But this time, Greg and I said so once, and everybody got the idea. That was that: pretty simple.

The excitement wasn't over, though. It turned out that the Northwest pilots, who had the right to approve any joint marketing deal, demanded more time to review it, so it was delayed. The bidding war between Northwest and Delta that I told you about in Chapter 1 ensued, the result of which was that the controlling stock was acquired by Northwest but allowed us to continue running as an independent airline. It was in some ways the best of all possible solutions for us.

Throughout, our employees kept working. Instead of running to the newspapers and hanging around watercoolers trying to figure out what was up, they went about their jobs and kept our airline running.

Think about what this looked like to these employees, as well as how they responded. Initially, it looked like the deal with Northwest was going to happen; we explained it, and they kept working. Then the deal with Northwest was put on hold; we explained it, and they kept working. We went through a period when things looked pretty dark to those of us involved in the negotiations with Delta, and we had no information we could share. It's possible that the employees sensed something was up, but they kept on working. Then the final deal was struck with Northwest, which worked out pretty well for us. We explained it, and the employees kept on working.

So what had changed?

Two things had changed in three years.

All the News, All the Time

First, when we had breaking news, we wanted to keep our employees in the loop. Employees had countless new places to turn for information about anything company-related they were hearing about. Instead of going to the watercooler or the Houston *Chronicle*, the Cleveland *Plain Dealer*, or the Newark *Star-Ledger*, they could go to their daily update from corporate headquarters, which explained it. They could go to my weekly voice-mail message, which explained it. They could go to the monthly employee newsletter or the employee quarterly, which explained it. They had other internal resources to turn to for information.

When the final deal with Northwest came through, we did the same thing. We put the employee bulletin out at the same time we did the news release. We kept employees posted; we told them everything we knew; we answered all their questions. If, after this, they were still worried, they could turn to their supervisors or read a question-and-answer sheet, which would explain it.

Second, when we said it, something remarkable happened: The employees believed it. After three years of experience with me at the top and my management team in place, they knew. We don't lie to them. Sure, the business pages of every paper in the country were speculating about what tricks Continental and Northwest or Delta might have up their sleeves for the future. But after three years of constantly telling the truth, we were in a pretty good position. Our employees know we're a better source of information about what's going on in Continental Airlines than even the *Wall Street Journal* or the *New York Times*. That's how we want it to be.

We had changed from a culture where we instinctively kept information from our employees into one where we naturally shared it with them. Unless there was a good reason not to share information—it would have broken a law, ruined a negotiation, caused misunderstandings or misinterpretations—we told our employees everything we knew about Continental.

We had changed from a culture where much of what management said was misleading or just plain false to a place where we simply told employees the truth—all the time.

Never Lie to Your Employees

These two points—informing employees and being honest with them—are basically the same. In court you must promise to tell the truth, the whole truth, and nothing but the truth. If you want to be honest with your employees, you have to do that. Not telling them stuff that will deeply affect them is just lying to them in a sneakier, less overt way.

We stopped lying to our employees; we stopped withholding information from them.

In fact, there are three golden rules about lying: Never lie to your doctor. Never lie to your attorney. *And never lie to your employees.*

Employees are the people who can save your bacon, and they're the ones who have to know the whole story, however painful it is to tell them. You may need to lie to your girlfriend or boyfriend; you may even need to lie to your spouse (you may not really like that new wallpaper). You probably need to lie to your kids sometimes, and you almost certainly need to lie to your parents. If you're negotiating something, you manage information to your benefit. In just about everything you do, there's an element of untruth or of keeping part of the truth hidden. That's just reality. That's life.

But don't lie to the people who are gonna save you, because if they don't know the whole story, they might not be able to save you.

That's pretty simple, and it takes a long time for people to believe this change to a policy of honesty has occurred. But once it has, employees modify the way they view what they hear from their company. Once they start believing that the information they're getting is complete and true—as they do now at Continental—then communication with your employees becomes much easier. You simply tell them everything you know. They listen and believe you. And then they know.

That's good.

Communication Works Both Ways

Of, course the other side of the communication coin is listening, and we do that now, too. We have 800-number hot lines for our employees to call for information about ground safety and operational performance. We have hot lines for them to call for information about benefits, about payroll, about their 401(k) program. We have numbers they can call for nearly anything that comes up—anything they want to know more about or anything they want us to know.

And when we get employee calls, *we respond—fast*. They know that their questions and concerns aren't going into some black hole, rotting in some in box somewhere. Employees are treated just like our customers now. They know that if they call with a problem, somebody's going to help them get that problem solved soon.

Sometimes questions can become repetitive, but we avoid squawking about that. You can't bark at somebody for asking a question—whether through an 800 number or in an employee meeting—and then expect the next person to ask a question. You have to keep making it clear: There's no penalty for asking questions. All the penalties come from *not* asking questions.

Get the Right People Communicating

I don't respond personally to every message and letter I get. To be honest, I'm not a nice enough guy—I get too frustrated, whether by complaints from customers that I might think are too picky or demands from employees that I might think want too much too fast. That's not my best suit, so I let people who are good at that do it. We make sure every piece of mail we get and every phone call get a response, but we make sure it's an appropriate response.

Here's an example. I once got a message from a flight attendant. She was mad because the rear ovens had burned out on one of her flights. She had to work the whole flight from the front galley, making a lot of apologies. She came back the next day, she said, and the plane was three hours late, but nobody had notified her at the hotel, so she spent three hours hanging around the airport.

She went on for a while in the same vein: Where do we get those incompetent people, there's nobody who knows how to run an airline in this company, I'd better get back to her because she was calling me on her own time, and so on. I got kind of annoyed. She was having a triple-zero day (people have those), and she vented. I was chosen to hear it.

My first reaction was that I wanted to call her and say, "Hey, I'm glad to learn that there are at least two of us who are perfect now." But that wasn't going to help anything. So I handed it off to Debbie McCoy, our vice president of flight training and inflight, asking her to check with the maintenance department to see why the ovens hadn't been fixed. I also asked her to remind crew scheduling that they need to let crew members know if their flights are late so they can use their time at hotels or at home instead of hanging around crew rooms in airports.

Finally, I asked her to check the employee's record. Often the people who make the most angry complaints are the ones who are having the most problems in their own jobs. In this case, we needed her supervisor to say to her, "Gordon thought enough of this that he contacted us personally. The ovens are fixed and you'll be notified at your hotel next time your plane is delayed. Thanks for bringing that to our attention. However, the delay in fixing the ovens was because you never notified maintenance that they needed to be fixed. Things will probably go more smoothly next time if you come to us before going to Gordon. We can help you a lot faster, if you'll help yourself."

Thus, there are kinder, gentler ways to pull this employee back in and to help her find a way to start seeing the problems as small problems—problems we can solve together, rather than demons she has to fight.

When I'm in meetings and people start picking at things like that, I say, "Look, you know anybody that doesn't have a zit on them somewhere? We're buying Clearasil in 55-gallon drums here, and we're working like hell to clear up every blemish on this company. But try to remember, three years ago we were worried about this company surviving. Isn't it kind of nice to be worrying about minutiae like this?"

They usually get the picture.

The Point of All This Communication

What's the point of all this?

The point of all our good communication—the point of everything we do at Continental—is to offer a good product that people want to buy. The point is to have an airline that's clean, safe, and reliable, as well as reasonably priced. We have to set priorities that will get us to that point, figure out what each employee has to do, *and then make sure everyone knows and understands what that is.* After that, it's easy.

In order to improve your product, you have to figure out what the key to your product is. You have to focus on that and let that define your goals. You have to do the kind of cooperative planning that gets everyone to voluntarily buy into those goals, rather than having them shoved down their throats. You have to measure those goals. And you have to reward people for achieving those goals.

Obviously, for all this to happen, you need to communicate all those things to your employees, in ways that make it easy for them to get the information and in terms they understand. If you haven't made sure your employees know and understand what they're supposed to do, you can't be mad at them if they don't do what you want. How are they supposed to know they need to get the planes in on time if you just figured that out around a board table one day, then mentioned it in some boring staff meeting, and never did another thing about it?

If You Don't Know, It's *Your* Fault ·

I've already told you how we worked together to choose the right goals, how we got everyone to buy into those goals, how we measure the progress toward the goals, and how we reward our employees for achieving them.

Now let me tell you how we make absolutely sure at Continental Airlines that you know what's going on. And why if you don't know what's expected of you, if you don't know what's going on, *that's your own fault.*

When I took over this airline in 1994, we published an occasional, unpredictable employee newsletter. Employees received little information from us, and what they did learn from us often turned out to be inaccurate. They asked repetitive questions at staff meetings because there was always a lot they didn't know, and what they had already been told might have changed in the weeks—or hours—since they had been informed.

It's very different now.

Give Us Five Minutes and We'll Give You the Company

The biggest difference is probably bulletin boards. Soon after we introduced the Go Forward Plan in early 1995, Ned Walker, a former television journalist, who is the vice president of corporate communications, and I decided that the best way to get the word out was to install bulletin boards in every break room, every hallway, every common room. Every office common area throughout Continental's network around the world now has a bulletin board. There are 600 or so of them out there, and they're updated every day.

These are special bulletin boards, and every one is exactly the same. On one side of the board, on a simple 8½-by-11-inch sheet of paper, is a monthly update displaying color charts of the on-time percentages and the other operational performance goals measured by the U.S. Department of Transportation—not just the current month's, but at least a year's worth of measurements, so that anybody interested can see not only how we're doing but how that compares to last month and last year. It gives those numbers both in straight percentages (81.8 percent of flights on time) and in comparatives (we ranked, say, second).

How'd we do with baggage last month? Check the board. How are we shaping up on complaints? Check the board. We got our on-time bonus last month—what was our exact ranking? Check the board; it's right there. If we didn't get the bonus, how much better would we have had to do in order to get it? Check the board; it's right there. We told everybody they were being measured on these factors, so it seems only reasonable to keep people posted on how we're doing, don't you think?

The other side of the bulletin board features a daily news update. And look at that title carefully—that's *daily*. Every weekday, five days a week, all year long, our employee communications department sends out another update that's posted on every Continental bulletin board around the world. It tells employees what's up: perfect attendance awards, new destinations, updates on any negotiations with employee groups or possible corporate partners, code-sharing agreements and their ramifications. Anything we know, employees know, *every single day*.

To make sure that none of us lose our focus, one corner of that daily news update shows how we're doing on our metrics: the previous day's on-time arrival percentage, month-to-date mishandled baggage ratios, our stock closing price, and items such as load factor.

Thus, every day—*every day*—we update our employees on everything we know. Our employees know that every day they'll get an update on how they're doing. They know where that will be—it will be on the bulletin board in the break room. They know how it will be organized—it will have headlines on the left, text on the right, and a little box of numbers at the bottom in the corner. They know that if they're asked to fill in on an unusual route and end up in the break room in the airport in Guam, there will be a bulletin board and it will have exactly the same information as the one they are used to in Newark.

If I go into a staff room and find a bulletin board that isn't updated, I purely raise hell. That bulletin board has no value if it's not up to date, and any supervisor who isn't making sure that bulletin board is updated is missing the point of how we work here. It doesn't usually take more than one reminder if someone's gotten a little slack.

We have a guy on the corporate communications team who has the responsibility of writing that daily update, and it goes out at 4 P.M. every day. He's a newshound—he has his own sources, he hears everything, he makes sure it's right, and he gets the word out. That's how we want it: If people are asking about it or talking about it or wondering about it, we want to tell them about it.

Our employees know they can count on information. If they have five minutes in a break room, they'll be able to read that bulletin board and be up to date on everything at Continental Airlines.

Okay Then, One Minute

And it's not just bulletin boards. That information goes out on company voice-mail and e-mail lists. It goes out on faxes. It goes out on my own weekly voice-mail messages and is available on the other 800 numbers employees can call when they have questions. So if you're an employee and you don't have five minutes to stop in the break room, you can always call, for free, from your hotel room.

In 1997 we took that information-sharing philosophy as far as current technology will let us. Figuring that people might not have five minutes to stand around reading bulletin boards in break rooms but they probably have 45 seconds to microwave a coffee or grab a soda, we found a way to reach them in those few seconds. In crew break rooms and office hallways all over our network, we installed LED display newsboards. You know those running newswire signs you see in Times Square and at the stock exchanges? We now have those being installed all over our network, along with numeric data that keep a constantly updated display of Continental's daily percentage of on-time flights. It's connected to our monitoring equipment, so employees know our on-time percentage literally as soon as the people in the control room do. It keeps a running tab on our stock price, too, as well as any other notes and headlines people need to know, from weather at airports we serve to news affecting the company.

So every time an employee steps into a break room, he or she gets a momentary update of Continental news, kept current by our corporate communications staff. How's that contract talk going? How about that transportation bill in Congress? What's our on-time percentage? See the sign? Now you know.

Keep It Simple

The point behind all this communication is that the employees know what's going on in the company. That means they spend less time worrying and more time getting the planes to land on time, which is the goal.

So everything we tell them we have to say in ways they can hear. What we're telling them is all the things that are important to us all. We're giving them all the information we have so that they don't have to spend a lot of time hanging around the water-cooler speculating about what's going to happen. We want them to be able to work comfortably and thoroughly on the projects we've all agreed on.

The main project is getting our airplanes where they're going in a clean, safe, and reliable way. So one of the things that's on every daily news update on every bulletin board and every e-mail and voice-mail update is how we're doing. And everybody knows that how we're doing is measured, above all, by whether those planes are landing on time.

We don't measure how we're doing by return on equity, by market share, or by some other business-school guideline that our employees may not appreciate or be able to find a personal connection to. In the first place, the person taking your call at our reservations center may not know what the total equity is. In the second place, how does the way he or she books the reservation have anything to do with the equity of the company?

However, everybody makes a 100 percent correlation between what they're doing and the corporate goal of having a product we're proud to sell. Being on time is a measurable step toward that goal, and the reservation agent can certainly see that advising the customer to check in 30 minutes before departure affects that. Everyone knows they've got direct input into the company's success. We measure it and define it for them, and we communicate it every way we can.

That's also why, when we talk about the Go Forward Plan, we talk about it in the same way every time. The four elements of the plan—Fly to Win, Fund the Future, Make Reliability a Reality, and Working Together—always occur in the same order, whether they are being discussed at meetings, posted on bulletin boards, or appearing in company publications. There isn't an employee of Continental who can't rattle off the four elements of the Go Forward Plan in his or her sleep.

And that's how we want it. They don't have to think about it—they know it. They know their connection to it. They know our company goals. They know where they fit. That's good communication.

The point of any communication is to get a message across. So you've always got to ask yourself: Who am I trying to reach? What will they understand? When we're looking for goals for an entire company, we make sure our employees know what we're going for: to get the planes on time, not to aim for a certain return on investment. Goals such as certain equity or debt ratios or interest percentages work fine for the accountants, just as striving to repair a specific number of engines or reduce the number of seconds before the phone gets answered are goals set for particular departments. But when it concerns the whole company, we need a companywide goal—something that employees can immediately identify.

It's Not All Good News, Either

The same rules apply when the news is bad. In fact, good and honest communication is probably most important when the news is bad. I think we gained more respect and trust from our employees in the early days by telling them the truth when the truth was unpleasant than we have in subsequent years when the truth was easy to tell because it has been pretty pleasant.

We didn't say, "We're going to have to reduce costs, so a certain percentage of jobs will . . . ," and kind of mumble it away like that.

We said, "We're in trouble, and the Los Angeles maintenance base will have to be shut down." If you do it that way, everybody knows where they stand right from the onset, and they can either start making arrangements to transfer or look for new jobs—or they can convince us that they can make those operations run profitably. That's what our employees did in 1995. I bet they at least appreciate our straightforwardness in communication.

We have continued our policy of honest communication, as, for example, when we don't make our on-time percentage goals and we don't get to give out the corresponding bonus. That happened in November 1997—a bad month, during which we got hammered with a couple of storms, a few other things went wrong with our operation, and we just didn't quite get the job done. Let me tell you, I didn't want to withhold the on-time bonus during the Christmas season of our most successful year ever. But that's how it worked out: We didn't make the goal; we didn't get the bonus. We said so right up front, on voice mail, on e-mail, on the bulletin boards. I didn't try to bury the news. The truth isn't always fun, but if you work for Continental, you know you can get the truth about your company, and you know where and how to get it— *always*.

Make It Readable

Magazines, TV shows, newspapers, and public relations companies spend millions of dollars every year trying to figure out the best way to get people to pay attention to their publications and productions. They learn that people are more likely to notice something if it's well designed, and they learn what that means; they figure out how many pictures people like to see in publications. They figure out what kind of paper to use and how to make an attractive reading experience for their target audiences. They determine how to make somebody pick up a magazine or newspaper or newsletter and read it. Then people go to work for businesses that send out 40,000 copies of something you wouldn't pick up in a doctor's waiting room if the only other reading material available was *Highlights for Children*.

That's how it used to be at Continental. In the first place, we didn't give our employees much information. In the second place, when we did give it to them, it was in boring and unattractive newsletters that you couldn't blame them for not reading.

The vice president of corporate communications, Ned Walker, and his team changed that. In the same way that we filled our workplaces with messages about what was happening and what we wanted to happen, we started filling employee mailboxes at home with the same information, in readable, pleasant formats.

Ned and his group started a magazine called *Continental Quarterly*. A full-color, nicely designed publication, CQ is mailed directly to employees' homes, where people will have a few more minutes to leaf through it, and where family members can take a look at it as well. With detailed stories about big changes—a new baggage resolution center, new reservations systems, new planes— and stories about the ways different departments work, CQ helps carry the word on how the team's doing to family members at home. I was once at an employee picnic, where an employee's wife came up to me and said, "I didn't know you guys had ordered new 737s!" She had learned that from CQ.

The last page of CQ is usually a listing of every phone number employees and their families might need to get or share information: all the work-related hot lines (for safety, aircraft appearance, operational performance, ground safety, and so on); the voice-mail number employees can call from every country we serve; the hot lines for benefits and 401(k) information; human resources numbers; and numbers for travel services such as hotels and car rentals. The point is to make sure that employees have all the information they need and that whatever Continental-related questions they have are answered as quickly as possible, wherever the employee might be.

We also publish a monthly newsletter called *Continental Times*. It, too, is printed in four colors on glossy paper, so that employees will actually read it with pleasure. It summarizes the previous month's performance according to the Department of Transportation measurements, surveys the actions taken under the Go Forward Plan during the previous month, and keeps employees abreast of any other pertinent developments, such as when I or Greg Brenneman will be visiting different stops for employee meetings or things that have changed or been added to the planes, food, ticketing process, or management team.

It's worth pointing out that our corporate communications staff is smaller than those of many other similarly sized companies—we have fewer than 20 people putting out all the publications, daily updates, and other information I'm telling you about in addition to handling our community affairs and media relations. They can do all that because we hire the best people and because we try to give them the resources they need to get their jobs done. But also, they can do it because they don't have to spend a lot of time fighting us for information. *We encourage them to get all the information they want.*

As I've emphasized throughout, we've completely changed the way information is handled in this company. Unless it's dangerous or illegal for us to share it, we share it. And now if somebody stands up and asks the same old question in one of our employee meetings, we can say, "Buddy, where you been? We answered that last month, and it's been on voice mail, on e-mail, on the bulletin board, in *Continental Times,* and in *Continental Quarterly.* And the answer is, we have an alliance, but we're going to function as an independent airline, and we're still not merging with Northwest!"

Nobody in this company needs to stay up late at night worrying about what might happen. We've told them what's going to happen, and they know they can believe us. Now, if you don't know, it's *your* fault—and that's good. Not only does it make it easier for employees to know what's going on, it makes it part of their responsibility to know what's going on. That keeps them on their toes.

For example, I was at a meeting in 1997 where someone stood up and asked whether we were going to open a crew base in Tampa. I don't know where the person got that idea—it was something I hadn't heard. So I asked, "Where'd you get that idea?"

He replied, "Well, I've heard it around."

I took a deep breath. I said, "Okay. How long have you worked here at Continental?"

He said, "Twelve years."

"In those twelve years," I asked, "about what percentage of rumors running around here have you found to be false?"

He paused for a second, then finally said, "I guess around 99 percent."

I responded, "So why would you spend any of your time asking me about something that you know has a 99 percent chance of being nonsense?"

He said, "Well, Gordon, I just gotta know."

I shook my head. Everyone at the meeting laughed, and I said, "Look, the answer is no. But damn it, if it was yes, I would have told you. I tell you everything every week. We tell you everything about this airline, every single day. No, if you haven't heard it from us, it just isn't happening."

I didn't chew him out. It's important to make sure that people know they can ask any questions that are on their minds. However, I think most of our employees know this by now: If there's something that affects them, their jobs, and the company, we'll tell them about it.

And Read What We Tell the Customers

Another reason we're so communicative with employees is so that when customers have questions or problems, employees have the answers to give them. Say, for example, a rumor gets started that we're pulling out of Raleigh-Durham. If employees are asking about it, it's sure that customers are going to be hearing about it, too. They'll ask their flight attendants or gate agents or pilots, and it's great for the employees to be able to say, "If that were happening, we'd know about it. So if we don't know about it, you can rest assured it's not happening."

Therefore, we try to make sure that our employees want to read even the in-flight magazine, *Continental*, also recently redesigned. In the front of that magazine now is a section called "Continental Notebook," which gives passengers—and employees—information on new partners (hotels that offer discounts to OnePass holders, for example), new routes, and special accomplishments of the company or our employees. It's just one more way that we can let everyone know we're all working with the same goal in mind.

Of course, the magazine contains a tear-out, postage-paid card for customers to fill out and tell us how we're doing. Our 800 number is also listed for customer input. In the same way that we solicit input from our employees, we also solicit it from our customers. Just as we get as much information out to our employees as we can, we also want to get it out to our customers. We want them to share information with each other.

When you have nothing to hide, communication is a great thing.

Communicating with Customers

As I mentioned, I sometimes get voice mail, e-mail, or letters that irritate me. Some come from customers who had a great flight that landed on time and their baggage was there, but there was turbulence and a Coke spilled on them, and that's our fault. Some come from employees whose crew meals weren't to their liking, and that's our fault.

It can get kind of wearying now and then, when we've made so much progress. We're always going to have flaws, but we've come so far in such a short time. It can be frustrating to feel like I'm working so hard, giving everybody a way to reach me and our top management team, and then all we get in response are these nitpicky problems.

When Greg and I are dealing with employees, we often use the aforementioned line about the Clearasil in 55-gallon drums to clear up the company blemishes. But, more than anything else, I remind myself of the following: You asked for it.

I can get kind of cranky and I might wish the complainers would leave me alone once in a while, but I can't really complain that they're coming to me—*because we're the ones who told them to come to us with their problems.* We're the ones who instituted the 800 numbers. We're the ones who put the postage-paid cards in the in-flight magazine. We're the ones who said that communication is key to getting us all working together as a team.

So when the problems seem to be coming from every direction and I just wish they would stop, I have to remember: I asked for it. Hearing about the problems is much better than not hearing about them and letting them fester. And I tell all our employees the same thing.

Remember the woman with the lapdog I told you about in Chapter 6? You run an airline, you're going to run into people like that. When the gate agent and I were standing outside that air-plane waiting for the passengers to board so the plane could finally take off, we kind of chuckled over that lady, and I said the same thing to the gate agent: We asked for this.

This is a nutty business, carrying people around from place to place. When you run 2,100 flights a day, and you do everything in your power to get people to buy tickets on them, you're going to do business with a lot of people, about 3 million every month. Being human, these people are going to be involved in a lot of unusual situations. So you are going to run into the occasional woman with a dog who won't get off your plane. You have to solve the problem, and you may have to ask that customer not to come back, but you can't be surprised that she showed up. We asked for it. And I try to make sure everyone at Continental remembers that.

However, that said, I often remind my employees of something equally important . . .

The Customer Is Not Always Right

That's a popular line with my friend Herb Kelleher right now, and it's an important concept.

I've said a lot about getting everybody to feel like they're on the same team, and I'm going to tell you a lot more about it in the next chapter. One of the key concepts is getting the customers and the employees to realize that they're on the same side, not oppos-ing sides. If the planes get to their destinations on time; if they're clean, safe, and reliable; if the bags get there; and if the price is reasonable, sure, we'll win because we'll sell a lot of tickets. But the customers will also win because they're getting what they want. We're all on the same side.

Sometimes customers forget that, and when they do, the thing to remember is to back the employee. As the leader, the manager, I have to remember that my team is watching and looking to me for direction. So if we've had some kind of screwup and a plane is late, we're going to do everything we can to solve the problems that causes—help customers make their connections, help those who have missed them find other connections, and so on. That's our job, and that's what we told the customers we'd do for them. We owe it to them.

I tell the employees to remember that line about the blemishes and the Clearasil in 55-gallon drums and to use it with customers who are irate because their flight didn't go perfectly. But when we run into customers that we can't reel back in, our loyalty is with our employees. They have to put up with this kind of stuff every day. Just because you buy a ticket does not give you the right to abuse our employees.

We don't forget that this is not an equal relationship. We are selling the customers a service, and we need to accommodate their reasonable needs and frustration. Customer satisfaction is what we're selling. Defusing customer problems, communicating with customers, finding out what went wrong and how to fix it are big parts of what we do.

However, as I said, we run more than 3 million people through our books every month. One or two of those people are going to be unreasonable, demanding jerks. When it's a choice between sup-porting your employees, who work with you every day and make your product what it is, or some irate jerk who demands a free ticket to Paris because you ran out of peanuts, whose side are you going to be on? You can't treat your employees like serfs. You have to value them.

Your employees need to know that. People will take a lot of abuse without complaining when they know that you're behind them and that if they reach their boiling point you'll stand up for them. Then every insult they ignore, every complaint they coolly handle is a choice. But if they think that you won't support them when a customer is out of line, even the smallest problem can cause resentment. And that goes just as much for what a supervi-sor has to take from a disgruntled employee as it does for what an employee has to take from an irate customer. When we say, as part of Working Together, that everyone deserves to be treated with dignity and respect, we mean that—and we act like we mean it.

When employees know they have to take only as much abuse as they're comfortable taking, in fact, they'll take more. When I was a Navy officer stationed in Hawaii, I told my wife, T. J., I wanted to get her a car. She said, "No, Gordon, you'll be at work, I'll be at home. I won't really need a car." I said, "No way. Without a car, you'll feel stuck at home. With a car, you may not leave home any more often, but you'll have the choice." It's the same thing with our employees. They know that if they're being abused by a customer to the degree that they have to stand up for themselves, we'll stand behind them. That way, every second of anger they absorb to solve a problem, every time they just smile rather than lash out at a rude customer, it's their own choice.

Here's an example. A Continental flight attendant once was offended by a passenger's child wearing a hat with Nazi and KKK emblems on it. It was pretty offensive stuff, so the attendant went to the kid's father and asked him to put away the hat. "No," the guy said. "My kid can wear what he wants, and I don't care who likes it."

The flight attendant went into the cockpit and got the first officer, who explained to the passenger the FAA regulation that makes it a crime to interfere with the duties of a crew member. The hat was causing other passengers and the crew discomfort, and that interfered with the flight attendant's duties. The guy better put away the hat.

He did, but he didn't like it. He wrote many nasty letters. We made every effort to explain our policy and the federal air regulations, but he wasn't hearing it. He even showed up in our executive suite to discuss the matter with me. I let him sit out there. I didn't want to see him and I didn't want to listen to him. He bought a ticket on our airplane, and that means we'll take him where he wants to go. But if he's going to be rude and offensive, he's welcome to fly another airline. I thought our flight crew handled the situation correctly, and that was that. I was behind them.

In a way, that's what all this communication business is about—that your employees are important. They need to know everything about your business; they deserve to know what's going on. They *are* your business. They need to know that you'll stand behind them.

After all, nearly everybody's worked in a place where there was a new, flavor-of-the-month management strategy coming down all the time, manifested in posters about leadership, a bunch of new catchphrases, and lists of new rules to memorize and phrases to parrot when the big bosses were around—and it all leads to nothing.

What makes the Go Forward Plan different is that we mean it. All the things we talk about, we do. And all the things we do, everybody knows about. The lines of communication here are open from the customer straight up to me. Everybody knows what the goals are; everybody knows what the deal is.

I think that's the only way to run an airline.

Predictability,

or the Value of a Zippo

Twenty years ago, I used to smoke cigarettes, and I always used Zippo lighters. Like most people, I would take out a cigarette, flip open the lighter, and click it. Lighters being lighters, sometimes it would take more than one try to get a flame. But if that Zippo didn't flame on the third click, I'd stop clicking because that Zippo was out of fluid.

That's the predictability of a Zippo lighter. If it doesn't light by the third time, the lighter must be out of fluid. You know that because Zippo lighters are so reliable and predictable. Every Zippo you've ever used lights on the very first try just about every time. Same for the Zippos you've borrowed. Same for the Zippos you've seen friends and acquaintances use. Zippos are so predictable that when they don't work you don't wonder what the problem is—you *know* they're out of fuel.

And that is the value of a Zippo. You can buy lighters that are pretty, lighters that are sleek, lighters that are less expensive. But why do you pay a little more for a Zippo? Why are you willing to settle for a less fancy design? *Because it lights every time.* Its value lies in that predictability and reliability.

Consider the watches I talk about so often. What is the value of a watch? The value of a watch is that it's predictable. Every day you put on that watch, it keeps good time. If it says it's 11 o'clock and you have an 11 o'clock meeting, then it's time to go to the meeting. If it says it's noon and the meeting is scheduled to be over at noon, you can get up and leave the meeting, because it's the *meeting* that's late, not the watch.

The watch's value lies in its predictability. Other words for that are *dependability* and *reliability*, but they all amount to the same thing. You know that that watch, or that Zippo, is going to work.

When I came to Continental, the company was no Zippo lighter, and it certainly wasn't a watch that worked. The company defined *unreliability.* Our planes came and went as they happened to. Meetings started late and ended whenever the manager running them that day finally started boring even himself. Promised pay raises, bonuses, schedule changes, and promotions may or may not have come, depending on an almost limitless number of factors, including everything from the weather to the whims of whoever seemed to be running the place at the time.

That's no way to live. One of the things people most want is predictability. Don't get me wrong—I mean predictability in the things that *can* be predicted.

Predictability Is Valuable to Your Customers

Predictability is valuable not only in an airline. Why do people go to McDonald's? Because they know, from Houston to Moscow, what's going to be on their Big Mac. They know exactly what they are going to get. Why do they go to the Gap? Because they know the kind and quality of clothes they'll find there in any mall in the world. Those are predictable places. People know what they're going to get. That's their value.

Not that there's anything necessarily wrong with being unpredictable. However, when you're looking for that, you don't go to McDonald's or the Gap.

Or to Continental Airlines, because most people don't want unpredictability from an airline.

The essence of providing the service that we provide is being on time. We figured that out when we provided the on-time bonus to our employees, and they proved it when they started bringing in the planes on time and the customers started coming back.

We won the J.D. Power award twice and were chosen Airline of the Year basically because we went from being unpredictable to being predictable. People know what to expect from us now. They know that if we say our planes are leaving at 9:00 A.M., then that's when they'll leave; that if we say the plane gets in at 11:00, it gets in at 11:00. People love that, and, as a result, we're doing better.

Of course, our suppliers love it, too—we pay on time, we file orders on time, we tell them what we need, and we know what we're talking about. We're easy to service and easy to work with, so they love us and accord us the benefits in price and service that come with that.

Naturally, Wall Street loves us as well. The bond rating agencies love us. We're very predictable. We've made our numbers for eleven straight quarters now, starting with the second quarter of 1995. What's not to love?

But there's another group that loves us for being predictable.

Surprise! Predictability Is Valuable to Your Employees

One of the things some businesses don't recognize is that predictability is every bit as valuable to employees as it is to customers.

Think about this for a moment. Employees have lives just like anybody else. If I come in late, what will happen to me? If I do well, what will happen? What day will my check come? Will the plane be fueled and cleaned and ready to fly when I get on it? Will we be home on time? All of these are questions of predictability, and one of the reasons our employees are happy now is that all of these questions get the right answers.

Now try to put yourself in the place of an employee working for the old Continental, an airline where the planes were not predictable and neither was anything else, and you just never knew what might happen. So you were a flight attendant going to work in the morning, flying out to and back from some other city. Your daughter, Suzy, had a dance recital at 6 P.M. that night. Should be no problem, you wanted to say, since your plane was scheduled to get in at 3 P.M.

Only here's the problem: You knew from past experience of working at this less-than-stellar airline that there was *no way* of predicting whether that plane would really be in at 3 P.M. or anywhere near it. The planes landed whenever they happened to; for that matter, the whole company came and went however it happened to that day. So you had to say to Suzy, "Well, honey, I'll try my best to be at your recital." And then you spent all day wondering whether you'd actually get to go home when you were scheduled to go home. Even if everything worked out and you did make the dance recital, it was a bad day because you were constantly worrying about it. To say nothing of how it affected the way you dealt with customers and coworkers. That unpredictability wrecked *your* day—and maybe Suzy's, too, which probably meant even more to you.

If Continental couldn't even do job one—get the planes in on time—what else about the company could be predictable? The answer was, not much. Meetings started and finished with no real relationship to their schedules. Most employees had no idea what would really get them promoted and what would get them fired at this airline. It was completely unpredictable, and they just learned to keep a low profile as a way of staying ahead of things.

This went from the lowest echelons, where you had no idea whether the trash was going to be emptied on time or your paycheck was going to arrive when it was supposed to (and you even had to worry about whether the check was going to clear), to the top, where management strategies changed almost by the week, and so did management personnel.

Employees hated coming to work. This was reflected by their absenteeism and their on-the-job injuries. It showed in the letters they wrote me, and it showed in the things they told me when I was out with them. And one of the key reasons they hated coming to work was the unpredictableness of the environment. They never knew what it was going to be like when they came to work for the day—who was going to be in charge, what direction the culture was going to take, what kind of crazy marketing program would be implemented this week, whether it would be a relatively calm day or a chaotic one, whether they were going to be able to get back in time for Suzy's dance recital. It was all up in the air.

We Made Continental a Predictable Place to Work

It's not up in the air any more.

Remember that Go Forward Plan I've mentioned about a million times? We formally introduced the Go Forward Plan in January 1995, just two months after I took over. And if you go into one of our biweekly management committee meetings after you read this book, you'll find that we still structure the meeting according to the four basic elements of the Go Forward Plan. It's been that way every two weeks for more than three years.

Working at Continental Airlines is completely predictable now, and that's part and parcel of all the changes we made. In fact, this may be the biggest and clearest change. The first thing employees would say to you if you asked them what's different is, "We know what to expect now."

I don't think you can put a value on that. I think it means the world. Just as customers wouldn't value us if we weren't predictable, how could our own employees value working at a place that was completely unpredictable?

That goes for a lot more than just an airline. I don't care if you're flying planes, packing meat, or printing newspapers. Getting a newspaper to the door a half-hour earlier might not be of value to a customer who wasn't getting up any earlier to read the thing. Using that same example, if the newspaper showed up at any random time, day or night—whenever the deliveryperson got around to dropping it by—it would lose most of its value. The customer, who leaves for work at 7:30 A.M., subscribes to the paper because he knows it's going to be there by 7:00 every morning. This customer may not care whether it's there by 6:00, but if it's going to get there any time after 7:30, it's not going to do much good.

If you went to a dry cleaner that said it was open until 6:00 P.M., and you got there at 5:45 only to find it closed, would you return to that dry cleaner? If your paycheck was routinely incorrect, would you be happy? Would your landlord? Would your credit card company?

The same thing applies to that watch I'm always talking about. It's not much good if it runs some days, doesn't run other days, and is accurate only now and then. What makes that watch valuable is that it tells me what time it is, and it's always accurate. It's no good to me to know what time the watch says it is if the watch isn't predictable.

Life is full of unpredictability—it's the way the universe is. *That's why making at least one part of your life predictable is so valuable.*

Therefore, at Continental, we now have a predictable place to work. What's our goal? Same as it was last week, last month, last year: to run a great airline, primarily by getting clean, safe, and reliable planes in on time and secondarily by other specific means, determined and measured according to the job you have.

As a Continental employee, what are your specific goals and what are the measurements? Same as they were last week and last month—whether you work with baggage or phone calls or finances, you know what's expected of you, how it's going to be measured, and how it relates to the Go Forward Plan. What happens if you make it? You're rewarded, in a way you expect. If not? Same thing—you know the consequences. They're predictable.

What day do you get paid? Predictable. If you come to work an hour late, what will happen? Same thing that always happens.

If you have a meeting scheduled for noon, what time is it going to start? Well, it's going to start at noon, whether you're a baggage handler or the chief financial officer. And if that meeting is scheduled to finish at 1:00 P.M., can you schedule a lunch engagement for 1:15? You bet you can. In the first place, the meeting's going to be over on time. In the second place, if it is one of the very few that run late, all you have to do is stand up and leave at 1:00. Everyone else in the meeting who has someplace else to be will be doing the same thing. That's what I do, and that's what I've told everyone who works for me—and everyone who works for them—to do. That's how we do business at Continental now. We start when we say we will; we finish when we say we will. And if we're late, we don't expect anybody else to accommodate our mistakes. We no longer expect our employees to run an on-time airline when we can't get our own meetings to start on time. We have schedules and we live up to them.

Is today the last working day of the month? Then Greg and I must be holding an employee open house somewhere. We always do.

People who work for Continental know what to expect now, and they love it. Their absenteeism and on-the-job injuries have decreased. Turnover is lower. And now, when I talk to Continental employees at airports, they high-five me, they wave at me, they thank me for how well things are going. They write me letters saying that, and passengers in turn write me letters telling me the employees are great. I probably get 30 letters a week praising a Continental employee who went above and beyond the call of duty for some passenger.

When I get those letters, I write a note back thanking the passenger for the comments. I send a copy of the letter, with the praise highlighted, to the employee, along with a personal, handwritten note thanking him or her for the good work. The positive attitude feeds on itself. Believe me, when employees didn't like coming to work, we didn't get those stacks of appreciative letters. It's a great feeling.

Like Everything Else, Predictability Starts at the Top

In the same way that I changed the atmosphere at Continental to one of more collegiality by opening the doors of the executive suite, by sitting in the middle of the boardroom table instead of at the head, and by instituting casual days, I had to set the tone for predictability if I wanted the company to really be that way. So I start my meetings on time; I live up to my promises; I make sure that, where I'm involved, we do exactly what we say we're going to do.

Maybe the most visible way I do this is through voice mail. Every Friday I talk to the employees via a voice-mail message, which the employees can call on an 800 number to hear what's up. I've been doing this every week for four years. I do it because it's important that the employees have a number to call to get basic information, updated weekly, on how Continental Airlines looks from my knothole. And I do it because it's important that I show them, by putting on that message every Friday at around 5 P.M., that things around here are going as they expect, as predictably as they should be.

I realized this most forcefully one time when I forgot to do it.

I was in the middle of negotiating Continental's partnership with Air France in 1996, which was a very important new partnership for us. It meant a lot. One Friday during this time I was just running from morning until night, and I somehow forgot to record the voice-mail message at 5 P.M. That evening I was having dinner at the Ritz-Carlton in Houston with the then-chairman of Air France, Christian Blanc—it was a sort of celebratory dinner.

Ned Walker, Continental's vice president of corporate communications, listens to the voice mail every Friday evening, just so he knows what I've said to the employees. He usually helps me prepare what I'm going to say anyway, so it's a kind of check for him. It's just part of what he does.

That Friday, he called the voice mail at around 7 P.M. and heard the same message I had left the previous Friday. He knew where I was, of course, and he called the Ritz-Carlton, asking for me. The hotel staff explained that I was in a very important dinner and could not be interrupted. Ned told them that Mr. Bethune would want to be interrupted, that this was a very important message, from Ned Walker, involving voice mail. He finally convinced the poor person at the desk to bring me a message saying it was Ned on the phone, about voice mail.

As soon as I got the message I knew exactly what Ned wanted. I politely excused myself from the table, and I went to the lobby of the Ritz-Carlton. First, I thanked Ned for reminding me that I had forgotten the voice mail. Then I called and left a voice-mail message from the pay phone in the lobby.

When I checked my own voice-mail messages later that evening, there were two messages from employees—they were worried that something had happened to me. In fact, once when traveling overseas I actually forgot to record the message until Saturday morning.

That time there were five messages from employees who were worried that I was sick or something.

That's predictability.

The Benefits of Predictability

The employees aren't the only ones who benefit from this predictability. The whole company does.

For one thing, the peace of mind and satisfaction employees get from not needing to worry about what might happen next at work makes their lives easier, which means we can all rest easier and work better. But another way that it improves their performance—which helps the whole company—is through the virtue of repetition.

Everything's predictable, at Continental, right? That goes right down to the order of the elements of the Go Forward Plan. If we have a meeting, we're going to start with the Fly to Win goals and projects, proceed with Fund the Future, continue with Make Reliability a Reality, and finish with Working Together. The market, the money, the product, and the people, in that order every time. I tell people it's like the Boy Scout motto—everyone who's ever been a Boy Scout can recite those 12 items from memory, decades later. A scout is trustworthy, loyal, helpful, friendly, courteous, kind, obedient, cheerful, thrifty, brave, clean, and reverent. You just know that those are part of what being a scout is supposed to be. It's the same with the Ten Commandments or the multiplication tables. I like to think our employees will be able to recite the elements of the Go Forward Plan for the rest of their lives.

Now that's not just rote—that's so that we don't have to wonder what's next. If you're in a meeting, you know when it's going to be your turn to talk and what you're going to need to prepare. You know we're not going to forget your portion, so you don't have to spend half the meeting worrying about whether you will get your turn. Instead, you can focus on the other presentations and actually participate in the work being done.

And remember—the elements of the plan are not listed in order of importance. People ask which is the most important, and

I say, "Which is the most important part of a cake? Is your liver more important than your lungs? You have to have all the elements, or you're in trouble."

It's like practicing a jump shot in basketball. If you never know where the ball is coming from or where your teammates will be, you're going to always need to keep an eye on the basket, and if you get half a chance, you're going to throw up a shot. Not the best way to score points or win games. But if you know that there will be certain plays that feed the ball to you at a certain spot for a certain shot, you don't have to spend so much time worrying about the specifics. You can just do your job and let the shots come to you—which they will, predictably.

Predictability Fosters Creativity

This is important: Instead of fostering rote repetition, predictability fosters just the opposite. It fosters creativity and autonomy.

In planning and strategy, you know that all our goals are going to relate to the Go Forward Plan, but within that loose structure, you're free to come up with anything you can. Employees develop the ability to quickly figure out how their work relates to company goals and they get to the point where they practically do that in their sleep. That is the point where creativity is freed, because they're naturally focusing on what's important to the company, and then whatever ideas they have will be applicable.

That sounds a little conceptual. Think of Continental's most obvious goal—making our planes operate on time. Every employee on every flight knows that the goal for that flight is to land safely at its destination, with all passengers and bags, within 14 minutes of its scheduled landing time. That's it.

But how they get there is their own affair. If a couple of passengers are delayed on a connecting flight from Chicago, the captain and first officer, in possession of a flight plan, weather report, and schedule, can make their own decisions: Delay the flight and catch up in the air? Send the passengers on the next flight? Wait and see for 5 minutes, 10 minutes, 20 minutes?

If the captain and first officer find themselves waiting for passengers for particular connecting flights time after time—or if the schedulers notice that—then maybe it's time for a different fix, involving a five-minute change in departure time for the connecting flight, if that will work.

The point is that the predictability of a smoothly running workplace *fosters* creativity rather than destroying it. Knowing that everything has to happen on time just frees the mind from having to worry about the same little stuff that should always be taken care of—Will the plane be clean? Will it be in on time? Will there be meals?—and allows it to worry about the special case.

Return to the example of the basketball player. Those set plays and that system she's been taught by her coach don't limit her— they free her. Knowing the system is running—knowing the ball will be moving around and setting up different players according to plan—she doesn't have to think about what to do every time she gets the ball. That comes naturally. Thus the player can be more aware on the next level, and she can be creative. If something remarkable happens—her defender gets lost; a lane opens up to the basket—she can take advantage, because her eyes are open to that instead of being focused on where the ball might be. She *knows* where the ball will be, so she's free to think creatively.

Predictably, a Concluding Example

You knew there would be a final example of the value of predictability, didn't you? Almost every chapter has ended with a final quick example. So you expected it.

Okay, here it is.

Our reputation for predictability has spread even farther than we expected. When I first took over at Continental, we had a problem with our customers contacting the U.S. government—the Department of Transportation—to tell them how bad we were.

Not long ago, I was asked to speak at NASA about the changes we had undergone at Continental. As I spoke, I told the NASA people how impressed I was with what they do because of the complexity of their task. I said I was flattered that they'd ask me to talk to them, when, after all, they put people on the moon and send stuff to Mars. Then NASA director Dan Golden asked me about the size of our operation now. I told him we flew about 2,100 flights a day. He said, "And you gotta do all those within 15 minutes?" He continued, "We don't do 12 flights a year—we're kind of impressed with you."

That's the value of predictability. People stop complaining to the government about you, and the government starts complimenting you.

The true value of predictability is demonstrated by the fact that every single flight—2,100 times a day—is a chance to bust your tail. Every flight is a chance to make the evening news, to lose luggage, or to just come in late. Every payroll is a chance to screw up an employee's check. Every meeting is a chance to forget something, to start late, to finish late, to do the wrong thing.

Every time you try to light the Zippo, there's a chance for it to fail. Remember from Chapter Seven the psychology of perfect attendance? All you have to do is fall down on the job a few times and the value of that predictability is gone.

But when you don't fall down on the job, when you just stop making those mistakes and this continues over a long period of time, you become predictable. Your stockholders and investors value that, your customers value that, and your employees value that. And you reap the rewards.

Predictably, I like it that way.

12

What Gets Measured
Gets Managed

One of the great things about being a big shot is you get to hang around with other big shots and talk about all the fascinating stuff we big shots like to talk about. Which explains a conversation I had one day while watching a Houston Astros game from the owner's box in the Astrodome with Astros owner Drayton McClane.

Baseball is a great game, and watching from the owner's box is a great way to see it. You're closer than just about anybody else except the umpire, and you get to watch each player doing his job—every little shift of the infield, every throw to first by the pitcher, every signal by the catcher. Each action has its own importance, but they all add up to something much greater—they add up to a team pursuing a goal together.

In case you hadn't noticed, the Astros haven't exactly been winning the World Series every year, though they did make the playoffs in 1997. McClane and I were sitting in his box, watching the game. Instead of baseball, he naturally got me talking about business success. I told him that my team and I had changed the culture of Continental—we had changed the behavior of a group of 40,000 people. McClane wanted to know how we did it.

I said, "Okay, Drayton, I'll tell you how to change the behavior of your ball club." I said, "Try this: Before the next inning, go out to the pitcher's mound and talk to the pitcher for a minute. Explain to him that, starting right now, the rules are changed. Starting now, four balls are an out. Three strikes? A walk. Twelve straight balls and he's got three outs—he's pitched a perfect inning, he's retired the side, and he can sit on the bench and enjoy a cold drink."

Do you get that? Instead of strikes, balls are now the means of success for the pitcher. Balls retire opposing batters; balls win baseball games; balls win him the Cy Young award, a contract the size of the gross national product of a small nation, and a deal to endorse sports drinks and car dealerships.

After that, whatever signal the catcher sends, the first pitch that pitcher throws is going right over the batter's head and into the backstop. If that pitcher really understands how he and his team are rewarded, he's never going to throw another pitch over the plate for the rest of his life.

That's the simplest way I could think of to explain probably the most important management principle there is: What you measure and reward is what you get. More simply, what gets measured gets done.

The measurement in the baseball analogy is simple: The umpire gives you immediate feedback—strike or ball. The reward is clear: The pitcher has just been told that balls are the way to go. So that's going to work for him, and he's going to throw balls. That's how he wins. That's how he gets paid.

At the risk of oversimplifying, this is basically the key to running a successful business. You have to decide what constitutes success. If it's a fishing contest, are we trying to catch the heaviest fish or the longest fish? If it's a baseball game, what makes an out and what scores a run? If it's an airline, what are the indications that it is doing well? You have to explain to the people who work with you what those are, and the people have to buy into that. You have to measure that, and let them know how you're going to measure it. And you have to reward them if they succeed. That's it.

Of course, in the real world, this brings up an equally important point.

Define Success Right

You'd better get the right definition of success.

In the real-world Astros example, throwing a lot of balls would not lead to success, so any manager or team owner who defined success that way (and rewarded it) could change the behavior of his team, but the team wouldn't win any games. They wouldn't be successful.

This is one of the most common problems in businesses. *Businesses fail because they want the right things but measure the wrong things*—or they measure the right things in the wrong way, so they get the wrong results. Remember? Define success the way your customers define it.

Before I came to work at Continental, the company wanted to be a successful airline. But it measured only one thing: cost. That made Continental an airline that ran on low cost, paid its employees poorly, and delivered a really, really crappy product. Amazingly enough, that did not turn out to be the way to success any more than throwing all balls and no strikes is. That was not what our customers wanted.

Don't forget, Continental got what it seemed to want at the time: By saying that cost was the thing that defined its success, Continental's management got everybody to focus on cost. That turned out to be the wrong thing to focus on, though, and they just couldn't get that through their heads. It was what they focused on, it was what they measured, and they simply believed that somehow it would lead to success. That's why, even before the organization almost gave up the ghost, even when it was still trying as hard as it could, Continental just couldn't find the key to success—because the key didn't reside in cost, and cost was the main thing Continental focused on.

And Measure the Right Stuff

Once you've focused on the right *definition* of success, you'd better find the right *measures,* too.

Your employees are very smart. They pay close attention. What you're measuring and rewarding, they're going to do. So even if you define success right but you still measure and reward the wrong thing, your employees are going to figure out what you're measuring and give you that. If we had said that our goal was to be a great airline that gets its planes to their destinations on time and treats its customers right, but we also said that we were going to measure that by checking attendance very closely and making sure that people followed the rules of the employee manual to the letter, we would have had the best goal in the world, but we would have ended up with very prompt employees who kept their noses in their manuals. And, probably, we would have had a pretty lousy airline.

Straightening out this airline wasn't just a matter of adjusting the flying schedule and the frequent flyer program. It meant changing the definition of success and giving people the incentive to do the things that would make it successful. It was saying that success means getting every plane to its destination on time, safely, and with the baggage—and *that's* what we'd be measuring and rewarding.

That completely changes the mind-set, as well as the culture. When you change your definition of success, you change the entire reason your company is in business. And when we changed our definition of success from being the cheapest airline in the sky to being the airline with the best service, the best value, and the best employees, absolutely everything about the airline changed.

We wanted an airline whose planes arrived on time, so we started measuring whether the planes were on time. We rewarded the employees when they were. Pretty simple. And that goes for every reward system at Continental—even for sneaky little goals and rewards that you don't explicitly state but are part of employees' everyday lives. In fact, it probably goes double for those.

We can talk all day about giving our employees guidelines and urging them to use their own judgment in facing and solving problems. We can talk all day about treating each other with dignity and respect, about communicating, about working together, about doing what is necessary to win as a team. But if we said all that and still promoted people who undercut their coworkers and pursued their own selfish interests at the expense of the team, people would notice. They'd say, in effect, "Did you see what Steve got? He got that by screwing everybody over, so I'm going to start screwing everybody over to get some, too."

So we don't do that. We promote people based on the fact that they accomplish the goals we set for them according to the Go Forward Plan—goals that bring our planes in on time, that keep our finances in order, that keep our phones answered and our frequent flyers happy, and that keep our employees happy. In reservations, we measure how long it takes to answer a customer's call, the duration of the average phone call, how many customers the employee serves. In baggage, we measure how long it takes a crew to load or unload a plane and how many lost-luggage claims they get per thousand bags. Every job has its metrics, and every employee is judged according to things we can measure.

Measuring keeps us from solving the wrong problems, too. We measure everything we can measure: flight times, number of times a flight is late, number of times the flights feeding that flight are late, and on and on. The more we know, the better we can find out what's really causing a problem.

That's why an airline is analogous, once again, to a watch. Each has a lot of moving parts, and each has to deliver its value for the whole to have value. Otherwise, it stops. Say a plane is routinely late out of Newark. We can check everything: In the last hundred planes leaving Newark, was the plane cleaned on time? Were the bags loaded on time? Did the plane arrive from its previous destination on time? Was it fueled on time? Was it catered on time? Was it loaded on time? Then we can figure out which part of the watch is malfunctioning, and we can fix the broken part without having to upset everything else.

For example, we discovered that a lot of planes leaving Newark for Houston during the late-afternoon rush hour were late. It didn't take too much checking for us to discover that we were doing everything right on our end, but that the air traffic was just so congested during those hours that the planes were being held up by the controllers. So we couldn't do anything differently as far as loading or maintaining the planes.

We did take action, however, trying to find the least-congested minutes to schedule our planes for departure. We also isolated those Newark flights, preventing them from being continuation flights that would then upset all kinds of schedules down the road. Flying out of Newark or any airport, there's only so much you can control. We have all kinds of operational and cost reasons for scheduling planes the way we do, but it might turn out that, from Newark during peak times, we should forget about the cost issues and focus on solving the operational problems.

The point is that measuring lets us determine exactly what we can and can't control. Then what we can control, we fix; what we can't control, we either change or isolate. By measuring, we know where to spend our time and energy.

Clarify the Goals and Metrics

Goals and metrics need to be clear to everybody. If the employees don't know exactly what you're measuring and exactly what you want, they are going to invent their own goals and metrics, and these may not be the ones you'd like them to have.

That's why we came up with the Go Forward Plan and why, to this day, every single thing we do at Continental Airlines is part of that Go Forward Plan.

That's not an exaggeration. If somebody brings up an idea in a meeting—a new way to advertise, a new way to program for sharing information, a new way to monitor behavior—we always ask the same thing: Which part of the Go Forward Plan does this relate to? For example, Chapter 9 mentioned the music videos played during boarding. The marketing executives got so caught up in the concept of boarding videos that they forgot that the whole point of the video was to improve Continental's overall product—to make flights better for our passengers. Management had to redirect marketing's attention to that. Which part of the Go Forward Plan were those singing whales supposed to enhance?

Every year we publish and distribute annual goals organized under the Go Forward Plan. General goals, such as increasing the percentage of business passengers or making our Newark hub the hometown airport for New York City, are then broken down into department goals. The goals are determined after all the managers and directors have sought input from everyone who will be implementing them—everyone has the chance to put their two cents in. By now you know how we do things at Continental.

That way, if someone suggests that we acquire a little airline in Tahiti, we can steer them back into the fold. There are only so many hours in a day, and we can only work on so many things. We agree on what those things are, under the Go Forward Plan headings, and off we go.

Thus, when a nutty suggestion comes up, we ask how it fits. If the person who made the suggestion can't answer that question, we politely ask him or her to rethink it until that's clear. Because if a change to our airline doesn't directly affect our operations, our costs, our marketing, or our employees, then the change probably addresses something we're not that worried about. It's probably working on the wrong stuff.

If you want to do something, you have to find the thread between what you want to do and our company goals as defined in the Go Forward Plan. I assure you that that doesn't prevent people from being creative. In fact, it does just the opposite: It encourages people to use creativity *before* they start asking for other people's time and attention. It focuses their energies on what we've determined is important. And it ensures that the ideas people bring to us in meetings will help us on our way toward running a better airline.

Too often companies set lofty goals such as return on equity. Can you tell me how a production worker feels about return on equity? Chances are, he or she doesn't even know what that is. So we need to get the person down there pushing the airplane or picking up the tickets to figure out that he's part of the effort to achieve the corporate goal. That person needs to know what is his or her measurable contribution and how he or she affects the outcome. That's why everything in operations can be reduced to getting those planes in on time—and it's all measurable. Employees never have to ask—it's obvious. Will this help us get the planes to their destinations on time? If so, then do it. If not, drop it.

It's simple. It's clear. And it's measurable. If the employees do it, they get a reward. That's why it works.

Define Success Reasonably

You have to define success reasonably, too. Giving people goals they can't possibly reach is not going to get you anywhere. Furthermore, making goals clear allows for surprises. People—from other departments, from other units of your business—can unexpectedly demonstrate that they can achieve specific goals, once these goals have been clarified.

For example, when I was senior vice president of operations at Piedmont, one of the mechanics came to me and said, "You know, I want to be a supervisor in the maintenance department, but I don't know how to apply. People get picked to be supervisors, but nobody knows how they get picked." I promised to look into it.

I discovered that when the maintenance department vice president needed a new supervisor, he would assemble the directors who reported to him. They would nominate the people who they thought could get the job done and choose someone and there you were.

I suggested that there ought to be a process by which everybody who wants those jobs can compete for them. The company should post the qualifications for an opening, thereby making it possible for anybody who wanted the job to try for it. We would define the goal and let anybody in the company try to achieve it.

So he reluctantly did that. It took a long time to come up with a list of qualifications. (I think they kind of liked picking supervisors in this secret way.) The list was pretty formidable: The supervisor had to be a licensed airframe and powerplant mechanic with five years of experience, the candidate had to have knowledge of the Boeing 727 and 737 airplanes, and so on including many years of Piedmont seniority.

I had to say something. "You know, this seems like a pretty hard goal to attain," I told him. "I can see 'should haves' and 'could haves' for a lot of these requirements, but these are absolutes. It doesn't seem like these requirements really make this goal attainable for anyone other than the usual suspects."

The head of the maintenance department didn't seem to want to budge.

I tried again. "Remember that guy who showed up a couple thousand years ago and did that water-into-wine trick?" He did. I continued, "I don't want to be blasphemous, but wouldn't it be great if he could show up here and wave his arms over the airplanes and they'd all be fixed, and we'd be ahead of every schedule? Wouldn't that be nice?"

The maintenance vice president admitted that would be fine. "Well," I said, "you couldn't hire him, because he hasn't worked here five years."

He got the idea. On the one hand, don't set goals that God himself couldn't fulfill. And on the other hand, don't set goals that *only* God could fulfill.

As another example, I mentioned that $65 on-time bonus we offer our employees. I noted that another airline plucked that number out of the air to copy us, and they determined similar goals and bonuses for their own employees. The problem was that they did this without doing all the base work—organizing their schedules and maintenance work, meeting with their employees to explain the new way of working, providing them with the tools to do the job—that made the goals attainable.

Thus, instead of working toward a new reward, their employees suddenly were failing at yet another thing. Far from improving their employees' situations, it worsened them. Dangling a carrot that nobody can reach is worse than dangling no carrot at all.

And about Those Rewards . . .

Finally, make sure people know it when they get those rewards.

It makes a pretty big impression on people when you give them bonuses. A *real* big impression. It's pure reward, and anything that sweetens the reward is going to make it more likely that people will keep doing what got them the reward. This is pretty simple, basic psychology, but it's true. Maslow knew this; Pavlov knew this. If an employee does a great job and gets a bonus, he or she is learning the same lesson.

Anything you can do to intensify that reward makes the message stick. That's what we did at Continental when we delivered on-time bonuses to our employees in separate checks. We made it as clear as possible exactly what the extra money was and exactly what it was related to. As their record since then shows, the employees got the message loud and clear.

This sheds lights on the claim by Continental's previous management that the company's poor performance was the fault of poor employees. This is like a psychologist making a maze with nothing but dead ends and no rewards, putting mice in it and concluding that the problem with the maze is stupid mice. At Continental, we didn't change the mice, we changed the maze. We took the same "mice" and ran them through a different maze—and our mice *won*. Our mice know exactly where the food is, they go right for it, and they get there faster than any other mice.

Of course, I'm not suggesting that our employees are like mice. The point is that we gave our employees clear direction and clear rewards and these employees turned out to be the best in the business. Nobody beats our team now.

Managers Are No Different

Continental's top managers, of course, don't share in the on-time bonuses. They've all got bonuses built into their compensation plans, and they've got clearly defined goals and metrics they need to meet to earn those bonuses.

However, that's only half of the bonus for top managers. As with the line employees, we want our managers to know that their success is connected not just to their own departments but to the success of the whole airline. So we split their bonus compensation in half. Half is related to the success of their own departments and half is related to the success of Continental as a whole.

And just as we send the employees special checks, we did what we could to make an impression on our executives. A good example of that is what we did in our mid-1996 managers meeting.

By July 1996, things were going so well at Continental that we knew we were going to beat our 1996 plan. At about that time we had our midyear managers meeting, which all Continental's managers attend. At this meeting, we discuss what's been going on and how we're doing. Well, I had checks cut for each of these managers. The meeting gathered 350 people in a big assembly room at a hotel, and we had assigned seats.

I was the opening speaker, scheduled before lunch. I stood up and said, "Before I tell you how wonderful you are and what a great job you're doing and all the other stuff I normally say, I want you to stand up." They did. I told them to stand behind their chairs and turn the chairs over.

Taped to the bottom of each chair was the appropriate manager's check—for 50 percent of his or her bonus.

I said, "This is because you've done such an outstanding job—because Continental is going to make its plan this year. Here's the money the company owes you for that success."

And everybody was delighted at this unprecedented vote of confidence, a bonus payment six months before it was due. It was the greatest thing ever.

And then I said, "That's 50 percent of your bonus. The other 50 percent is based on your performance with your own department—it's based on the Go Forward Plan and all the things you're expected to do within it, from communicating with your employees to improving their performance according to one measurement or the other.

"But if you expect that other 50 percent, you're gonna have to earn it."

And let me tell you, we got their attention. They gave me a standing ovation—although, I have to admit, since they were already standing behind their chairs, they sort of didn't have a choice. But the applause was genuine. They knew exactly what we were going to be measuring them on, and they knew exactly what would happen to them if they did what we expected of them. By rewarding them early, we showed both our confidence in them and our commitment to sharing rewards as they came in.

I like rewarding people early. It shows trust, and it's unexpected. It's almost like extending credit. And it creates tremendous incentive and loyalty. (Continental's executive vice president of operations, C. D. McLean said, "That keeps us focused like a duck on a June bug.") I do the same thing for the senior executives. We get—or fail to get—our bonuses on a quarterly basis at the top. Continental is not one of those companies that can get off to a slow start so that people think, "Oh, we'll get going and catch up later in the year." We've got the tires screeching and the throttle running full-bore right out of the gate.

The managers left that meeting like it was halftime of a championship game. They had come in expecting the usual corporate rah-rah, and they left with a check for half their bonus, which they weren't expecting for another six months. Nobody cruised on autopilot for the rest of that year.

In 1996, Continental executives were focusing on dignity and respect, and we were going to be measuring our managers by checking with their employees and coworkers to see whether they were saying what we wanted them to say and doing what we wanted them to do. When we checked, you bet they did.

Watch That Compensation—and Who Gets It

As I said before, a common mistake that businesses make is measuring the wrong things. Another mistake that companies make is measuring the right thing, but giving the reward to the wrong *people*.

A competing airline, for example, became aware of our practice of rewarding our employees for keeping the planes on time. They copied the idea—only they reward their *executives* if the planes are on time.

Now think about this. Who sees that the planes are on time? The flight crew, the mechanics, the gate agents—everybody, in short, who's not in top management. Sure, the managers are the ones coming up with the schedule that makes it all possible and they make the right moves on top. Everybody is involved in success. But no manager ever looked at a plane that was short 10 dinners and thought, on his feet, how to still get the plane out on time; no manager ever hustled through her job as a gate agent, ran down the stairs, and helped to load bags in order to get the plane out on time.

How are those employees going to feel when the reward for their hustle and their sweat goes to their bosses? Not too great. And I guarantee you that executives will find a way to get their bonus payments. They're smart—that's usually how they worked their way up to executive positions. So if you make the mistake of rewarding them for the work their employees are doing, they'll get that money, and it won't make the employees too happy. But if you make sure you're rewarding them for what they truly control—revenue, cost, communication, planning, problem solving, all the stuff they should be concentrating on as supervisors—they'll find a way to get that done, too. And that will increase the peace throughout the company.

So keep in mind: Measure and reward the right stuff—and the right people.

I'll Say It Once More: Goals, Measurements, Rewards

It's pretty simple, really. We have two major rewards for most of our employees: the on-time bonus that they get for every month they rank in the top three airlines nationwide in on-time percentage and the profit-sharing money.

As I've already told you, that on-time bonus has become so much a part of Continental's culture that, for any month in which we *don't* get it, every employee does his or her own analysis of the company to figure out what went wrong and how to get together to fix it. They *want* that money.

In addition, our employees look forward with great pleasure to every year's profit-sharing check—so much so, in fact, that often, when I visit a training class for flight attendants or other employees, the first question they ask me is when that profit sharing kicks in. They know about it—it's one reason they want to work for Continental. They *expect* the company to be profitable, and they *expect* to get a piece of that profit. That makes for a very motivated employee—and one who works differently.

Consider the poor flight attendants during Continental's troubled years. The flight attendants have to work a lot harder on a flight when the plane's full than when it's half empty. During the years before I came, there were plenty of half-empty flights because we were flying to places people didn't want to go. But there were plenty of full flights, too, when we had ridiculously low prices. However, those full flights weren't making any money, so the flight attendants were hustling like crazy for . . . well, for no reward at all. In fact, it was worse for them if the plane was full than if it was empty. This didn't always make for the most chipper flight attendants.

Compare that with a recent flight I took, where the cabin was full and, as usual, the passengers had plenty of questions and problems that kept the attendants hopping throughout the whole flight.

I stepped into the galley during the flight and saw one attendant take a breath and let out a sigh of frustration. "It's hard work," I said. "But don't forget—these full flights mean more in your profit-sharing check come February."

She gave a smile. "I know," she said. "Believe me. I know."

And then she went out and helped those passengers, making sure each one had a flight experience that would result in more tickets sold and higher profits for Continental—and more profit-sharing money for her.

She knew.

Never Stop Measuring

Things may be going well enough that you want to take your eye off the measurements, and I have a piece of advice for you:

Don't.

Remember that I told you that you can't B.S. an airplane? That if you're the type of manager who demands to be told what you want to hear, you'll eventually get someone to tell you your tank is full even if it's really half-empty?

That's just as dangerous if you simply decide not to check on the fuel. At Continental, we chose being on time as our major metric, and that worked for us. But being on time, as I've said over and over, was not going to be enough. That's still only one of the four parts of the Go Forward Plan. We were going to have to have employees who liked coming to work, we were going to have to do a good job of finding and serving our market, and we were going to have to get control of and manage our finances. If we decided that all we were going to measure was whether our planes were on time, that wouldn't have meant that employee morale, marketing, and finances weren't important. It just would have meant that we weren't measuring them.

It's just like flying a plane. If you decide to ignore the airspeed indicator, that doesn't mean that you don't have airspeed. It just means you're ignoring it. So if the airspeed gets lower and lower and you're straying toward a stall, you won't know it if you're not looking. And you know what? Even if you're not looking at the indicator, you'd still better stay above stall speed, because otherwise you're in big trouble.

The converse is true, too, of course—the converse is the *point.* If you *do* keep your eye on the indicators, as soon as a problem shows up you'll know about it and you can take action to fix it. If the speed's falling, you add throttle or tilt the nose down. You lose a little altitude, but you pick up speed. Once you regain speed, you can add power, climb again, and everything will be okay. You caught a problem in time because you were paying attention.

You also have to keep an eye out for the quality of your indicators—you have to learn how accurate your instruments are. For example, when I took over Continental in 1994, one of the first things I learned about its financial systems was that they weren't accurate. The daily forecasts were regularly off by as much as $5 million. When the company was running on an unrestricted cash balance of around $40 million, that was a pretty dangerous degree of variance.

There's nothing more disconcerting to a pilot flying an instrument approach than to have an altimeter that's erratic. When you're close to the ground, you don't have much margin for error.

That's how it was with Continental. Those $5 million forecasting errors could have killed us, so we spent a lot of time scrambling as a result. Now, when we have a cash balance of nearly a billion dollars, a $5 million error barely makes us blink—though we've improved our forecasting system so much that a $5 million error is very rare.

Our systems are better for one simple reason: We measure more, and we measure better.

It's that simple: Measure everything you can, every way you can. Then when something goes wrong, you very quickly figure out what's causing it. Our on-time percentage dips, so what's going on? We can figure out which flights are late that were on time last month, and why those planes are late. Was there a series of storms? Has one of the maintenance facilities failed to keep up? Has a particular part started to fail? Has the catering service started taking longer to serve the planes—maybe that's because we recently complicated our in-flight menus. The point is that there's a reason for everything that goes wrong, and the more we've measured, the faster we can find that reason.

Suppose there's a problem at a maintenance facility. What's going on there? Is attendance down, or are accidents up? Is there a morale problem? Maybe there was an outbreak of flu. Maybe a manager left and was replaced by someone who doesn't quite fit in. Maybe they were having a new floor put in, so everything was slowed down for a month.

Regardless of the problem, because we measure, we can figure things out quickly, and we can take actions. Because we track our measurements, we catch problems before they get out of control.

To Sum Up: Goals, Measurements, Rewards

It comes down, as ever, to simple human communication. The entire major psychological change in Continental since I took over can be summed up in that $65 monthly on-time bonus. We told our employees what good is, we showed them what good looks like, we told them we'd reward them if they did good. Then they did good, and we rewarded them. None of this should come as a surprise.

We measured things customers valued. That wasn't being done before. Further, we measured things the employees could truly control.

We made the stakes something the employees would win or lose on *together*, not separately. That was a significant change from the department-against-department environment Continental had come from.

We explained to the employees exactly how they were going to be measured and what the reward would be: If the planes were on time, they'd all get $65 a month as a bonus. If they weren't, nobody would. It was that simple. You can't overestimate how nice it is for employees to be told exactly what they're supposed to do. After a decade of not being exactly sure what was expected of them, they finally knew what they were supposed to do and what would happen if they did it. We actually came through on the reward; we didn't try to wriggle out of it or change the rules.

It's pretty simple. The employees did their jobs, and those of us in top-level management did a little bit more than say, "Gosh, thanks." We rewarded them. They came through again—and better.

And they've never looked back.

Crop Duster's Son

I talk and talk about what we've accomplished at Continental—how we took a broken thing and made it work, how we took a group of people who were dispirited and disgusted and enabled them to work together and win—and sometimes people get a little frustrated. Not because I talk too much, though I suppose that's possible. But people get kind of irate because they think it's easy for me to talk about making change—after all, I'm the chief executive officer of a huge company. Of course, I can make change, they figure. I'm at the top.

I try to gently remind them that I actually was not born the chief executive of a huge airline. I started off as a baby, just like they did—a baby brought up by a divorced mom in San Antonio, Texas, who was doing the best she could under tough circumstances. I wasn't born with a silver spoon in my mouth—not even a silver dipstick.

The first business lesson I recall learning was from my mom, and I applied it recently during a stop in Washington.

After a long day of speaking with legislators about changes in the airline ticketing tax structure, I was ready to go home. I waited in the crew lounge for my plane back to Houston. The flight was a continuation of one that had left from Newark, and it was about an hour late.

If you want to see discomfort, you ought to try hanging around the crew lounge of an airline when the CEO of the airline is in there and his plane is late. Nobody wants to make eye contact, everybody is worried, and nobody, of course, wants to say anything. What are they going to say? "Gosh, Gordon, great to see you, plus you get to stay a little longer because our famously on-time airline is screwing up?" Not too many employees are going to chat with you like that.

Finally, one of the guys said to me, "Doesn't it make you frustrated when planes are late like this?"

I said, "Yep, it sure does. And you know what I'm gonna do? I should throw a tantrum."

He eyed me suspiciously, a little concerned.

"Yep," I said. "That's what I'm gonna do. I'm gonna holler and kick my feet and writhe around on the carpet until I hyperventilate. Because things aren't going exactly the way I want them to. You know why I'm going to do that? Because remember those fits Hitler used to throw when the war wasn't going his way? Well, that's why he won the war. He threw those tantrums and that changed everything and he won. Right?"

By now, the guy was starting to get the point and he was laughing with me.

But that's the answer. That's what I used to do when I was a little kid. If I wanted chocolate ice cream and we didn't have any, I'd throw a fit and scream and carry on, and when I quit yelling there would be chocolate ice cream. Right? Well, maybe not.

I suppose tantrums might have worked if my mom had been the fretful type of woman, and she'd have dropped everything to drag me across town to an ice cream store to get me to stop crying. Fortunately for us all, she was not. She'd send me to my room and tell me that when I was done howling I could come back out.

So I learned two things early: One was that howling didn't help much when I did it. And the other was directly from my mom— that when somebody else was howling, it was going to work only if I let it.

So I gotta tell you—you haven't seen me waste too much time howling when I wasn't happy, and you haven't seen too many people who work for me get much by tantrums or howling either. That makes for a more sensible place to work. And it's quieter, too.

The Education of a Crop Duster's Son

I actually think the next important lesson I learned was in my first job.

My parents divorced when I was very young, and I was raised mostly by my mom and my stepfather. But after a while my dad showed up again, and when I was 15, he invited me to spend a summer working with him in Mississippi. That was kind of how we got reacquainted.

He was a crop duster, and I had a lot of responsibilities to help him out. I handled the 55-gallon drums of chemicals for spraying and hustled to refuel airplanes. I helped take care of whatever was needed at the time.

But my most important job was getting the landing field ready for my dad at the end of the day. The landing field was just a long, flat strip in a meadow—there wasn't anything paved, of course. He was flying long, long days to make as much money as he could during the growing season, so he'd take off before it was fully light and often come back to land after dark.

My job was to put a big smudge pot on the fence at the far end of the runway and park our big 1950 Plymouth at the near end, with its lights shining down the runway. That was our lighting system.

I'd get everything ready, wait out there in the middle of that Mississippi field in the dark, and here he'd come. I'd hear him first, and then he'd come into view in those headlights, kind of sideways. The J-3 Cub he was flying, those planes didn't have flaps, so to lose altitude you'd slip the airplane slightly sideways, increasing drag. That way you can lose altitude without speeding up.

He would often cross the near fence almost sideways, and then at the last second he'd kick the rudder and land. That was really cool. I remember one night he just barely made it, and he finally stopped with one wing over the fence at the far end of the runway. Man, he was glad to get out of the plane that day. I also saw my dad abort a takeoff once when a freshly overhauled engine blew up on him. I was horrified—I had always thought that engines just kind of worked.

I had to learn responsibility that summer. It was my job to get those lights set up out there, and if I didn't get it done, the consequences were going to be pretty bad. So I got the idea that sometimes you just have to get the job done. Sometimes there's no wiggle room.

That summer I learned not only that when you have a responsibility you'd better carry it out, but that there are a lot of jobs in which the consequences of screwing up were pretty drastic. Not just being a surgeon or the president, but being a pilot or a mechanic—or the guy who put the smudge pots out to light the runway. Everybody else can do their job well—the mechanic gets the engine just right, the chemical guy loads up the plane, the pilot flies perfectly—but if the guy who's supposed to park the Plymouth at the end of the runway falls asleep or lets the battery die or steps out for a beer, well, it would be a pretty bad day for everybody.

I learned what *working together* meant right then—to say nothing of making reliability a reality, which it sure had to be.

Negotiating with Mom

I learned some negotiating skills when I joined the Navy, at age 17, before I finished high school. I can explain my lessons through one bad negotiation and one good negotiation.

The bad negotiation came at the recruiting office. I was running off to the service with my cousin, and we weren't yet 18, so we had to get a paper signed by our parents. My cousin wanted to become a paratrooper, and the Army guaranteed him that assignment. That was not the assignment I wanted, but in speaking with the Army recruiter, I asked what kind of guaranteed position I could get. He told me I could get a position in the infantry, the artillery, or an armored division. None of that sounded too good to me, so I walked down the hall to the Navy office and asked the same question. I hadn't finished high school, and what could they guarantee me? He said, "Nothing." I said, "Okay." At least I had a *chance* of finding something I liked in the Navy, and that sounded better than a guarantee of something I'd hate in the Army.

So that wasn't the best negotiation I ever conducted—though I did a little better when I got home. I knew my mother wasn't going to like the idea of my going to the Navy before finishing high school. So I went up to the attic and got the family suitcase and I started packing.

My mom wanted to know what I was doing and I said, "I'm going to California, and I'll send the suitcase back when I get there. I wanted to join the Navy but I couldn't until I was 18 if you wouldn't sign the permission, so I'm going to hitchhike out to California and find some kind of work, something to do until I'm 18 and then I'm going to join the Navy."

She said, "Oh no you're not, you're going to fall in with the wrong kind of people and possibly be in jail or get killed."

So I said, "Well, Mom, if you really don't like that, I do have these papers that you can sign to let me join the Navy next week when I'm 17." I learned quickly that when negotiating it's good to have a couple of options to offer—and it's better if the option you want the other person to choose is the best option.

Five days after I turned 17, I joined the Navy.

It Won't Hurt to Learn Something

I joined the Navy, like many before me, basically to get away from home and out of school, where I was bored. When they asked me at the induction center what I wanted to get into, I chose aviation, for no other reason than that I had hung around engines and airplanes with my dad and that one of the guys I met in my recruiting group was going into that, too.

In about the fourth week of our training we met with a counselor and were asked what we wanted to specialize in. I didn't have the vaguest idea. Leafing through the book of choices, I saw "aviation fire control technician," which I later learned was a position using radar and computer systems to drop bombs from airplanes. I took aptitude tests, then I went to the counselor, and he said that would be fine.

I said, "Before you put that down, does it have anything to do with putting out fires?" That's how much I knew about what I was getting into. All I really wanted to do was get away from school and get away from Texas.

So naturally I ended up in the most exhaustive school in the Navy, to become an aviation electronics technician—in the Naval Technical School at Memphis, Tennessee. Naturally enough, I rebelled. We started out by taking a test. The officer in charge explained that it really didn't matter how we did on the test; it was just checking to see what we knew. I answered 250 questions in about 17 minutes, went outside, and smoked cigarettes in the shade for a couple hours. I had it great.

Later I had lunch with a friend of mine from when we were recruited. He worked on the deck of an aircraft carrier—he was the guy who pulled chocks out from underneath the wheels of the planes when it was time for them to fly. I thought that sounded kind of fun—not much responsibility, you kind of just hung around until you were needed, got to spend a lot of time doing nothing.

My friend set me straight. These guys worked 12- to 16-hour shifts, he said, and the shifts were pretty terrible. It was noisy and dangerous. These guys got hit by equipment and fell off aircraft carriers. These were not good jobs. I asked him, "Who gets these jobs?"

He told me, "Mostly guys who flunk out of this avionics school."

I graduated second in my class.

I like to think I don't have to learn a lesson twice. I think I got a pretty good taste of defining and measuring success right there, and I don't think I've ever lost it. Success for me in that position became avoiding a job like those flight-deck guys had, and the way to avoid it was to do well in school. I got the picture. So I did well in school. Pretty simple.

How Much Better Do You Have to Be?

My estimate? About 10 percent.

That's what I ended up figuring in my early days in the Navy. The Navy is a huge, bureaucratic environment, and everybody gets a pretty well-defined job. In that environment, most guys just sort of do their jobs and disappear.

I figured, how much better do I have to be in order to get the attention of my superiors and get the better assignments, the better jobs, the promotions? And I figured only about 10 percent better. In other words, not much better. In an environment where most people are happy to just do their jobs and stay out of trouble, making sure you do a little better, a little something extra, come to work a little more prepared, is enough to get you noticed and rewarded. So I started doing that. It worked, and I've never really had reason to question that. You want more attention, more money, more status, more respect? Do more. In most cases, in a world where most people just want to do what they have to, you'll be pretty surprised how little more you need to do to get what you want.

After all the usual early jobs doing this and that, which any enlistee goes through during training, I ended up as an electronics mechanic. And I have to say, I think being a mechanic was about the best thing that ever happened to me.

A mechanic does a job with a very low tolerance for bullshit. An electrical system either works or it doesn't. If it doesn't, your job is to fix it. Is it fixed? Then you did your job. Is it still broken? Then what the hell's the problem? Pretty straightforward stuff. I grew to appreciate that. It was another job that was measured pretty simply. I've already said that you can't bullshit an airplane. Well, you can't B.S. a mechanical or electrical system either—and I like that.

I had already learned from my friend from the flight deck that acquiring new skills was only going to help me, so I kept doing that, taking whatever courses I could and studying for whatever came next. The second thing I learned was the difference between my boss's job and my own.

He'd assign me to fix an airplane. As soon as I fixed that airplane, I knew the boss would say, "Go fix another one."

I got smart and decided the boss had a better job than me.

It came about that there was a test to become petty officer, second class. I took it and I passed. Then the maintenance shop needed somebody to be second shift supervisor, from 7 P.M. to 7 A.M., and there was only one petty officer, second class, around. So I became the boss of eight other guys.

Telling Other People What to Do—and How

Until then, these eight other guys had been my buddies. I hadn't been a model seaman by any means, and I had spent plenty of time looking for ways to goof off. We were all hoodlums together, messing around and trying to see what we could get away with. And then the Navy (those guys aren't so dumb) co-opted me. All of a sudden, instead of using my talents to get away with more stuff, it was my job to use my talents to become a very productive citizen— and to see if I could get those guys to be more productive, too.

Managing mechanics is a little different from being one. Being a mechanic, it's pretty easy to measure your results: Are you or are you not getting airplanes fixed? That works if you're managing mechanics, too, over the long haul. I mean, if someone isn't getting any airplanes fixed or is slower than everybody else, you kind of get the picture.

But with an individual airplane, if you want to screw off all night long without fixing it, if you just stand around scratching your head, nobody can claim you're not working—especially some lieutenant who doesn't know how the thing works anyway.

The point is that, if you get a mechanic mad at you, he or she is not going to fix the problem. And there's not going to be much you can do about it.

I was now in charge of eight mechanics and what they did, and I was going to be judged on whether they got their airplanes fixed. I couldn't fix the planes myself—I had to get them to fix their airplanes so that I could be a success.

I could have picked up a whip or maybe a big stick, or I could have tried bribing them. But I knew I had to figure it out, because that was my job—to motivate them to do their jobs.

Well, I just figure out what I had liked when I was a mechanic. What had made me want to do a better job? That was pretty simple. When I was being treated like a person inside that uniform, as though I had intrinsic value, I appreciated that and I worked harder. When some bonehead treated me like a cipher, like an interchangeable part, I was much less willing to find a solution to a problem, and I fixed airplanes more slowly.

The Navy's a pretty hierarchical place. I eventually became an officer, but I was with people who had three or four stripes, whereas I had only two. But you know what? I knew some third-class petty officers who were smarter than any of us, and they had no stripes. There's not necessarily a correlation between the number of stripes you have and what you can do. The dummies who think there is always get into trouble. I hope that's still the case now. I may be the highest-paid guy at Continental, I may have the biggest office and the most status, but there are 40,000 people in the company, and just about every one of them has something to offer that I don't. My job is making sure they all want to offer that. Otherwise, we have to drag it out of them, and my predecessors proved that that just doesn't work.

So as a new supervisor in the Navy, I figured I'd rather have willing workers. You get more out of them. I therefore treated them like I wanted to be treated—pretty simple stuff. I doubt I'm the guy who made it up, but it works.

I was only days away from being a mechanic myself, and I knew what motivated mechanics. It's a hard job, a job you have to train hard for. Mechanics are motivated internally, and they want to fix things. They applied for the job and went to school. These mechanics worked hard to learn how to fix airplanes, and they liked fixing airplanes. What they want more than anything else is to be left alone to fix things—unless they have a problem, and then they want you to help them solve that.

So that's what I did. And I noticed that my guys were fixing a lot of airplanes.

I also noticed that each guy liked to work on certain kinds of problems or had certain skills. George could fix computer problems faster than anybody else; Hank was the best diagnostician; Bob could patiently press through a problem that would have the others ready to give up in disgust. How much smarts did it take to figure out that when an airplane came in with a problem and had to be turned around in an hour, George was the guy? That when everybody was stumped, it was time to call Hank?

I started to see that we were a kind of team and that the team did a lot better when we asked everybody to do what they were good at.

I kept applying those lessons, and I kept doing better in the Navy. I kept climbing in rank and being put in charge of more mechanics and the kind of things mechanics do.

It's People

The higher I got, the clearer one particular lesson became. Regardless of the specific processes involved, no matter how many people I was in charge of, they were all still people. And focusing on their needs as people was going to make things go the best.

Again, I don't think I invented this, but I sure know it's true. Lose track of how the people you manage are feeling, and you're history. Keep it in mind and you probably won't go too far off course.

About the best experience of this I had in the Navy came after 19 years, when I had worked my way up through chief petty officer and chief warrant officer. I was a lieutenant; I had a commission; I was doing great. Our guys had done so well in some inspection or other that our commanding officer, whom I really liked, told them he was going to declare one of their working days a half-day off, which delighted the men, of course.

Not long after that, we had a readiness drill, in which the squadron had to scramble—jump up at 5 A.M. and show that they were ready for emergency recall. A drill like this makes sure the phone banks work, the trucks move, the planes are ready to fly, and everybody knows their jobs. So we did that, and we did real well. We were done by about 11 A.M. We had some kind of meeting scheduled, but after that we were done.

The commanding officer said, "Gordon, you know what? I'm going to cancel this meeting, and I'm going to give the men the rest of the day off, because I owe them a half-day off."

I said, "Skipper, you don't want to do that. That's not real smart. This is 11:30, it's gonna be noon soon, and they got in here at 4 A.M. or so. This isn't going to look like a half-day off to them."

He said I was wrong—the drill was extra, so they were getting half a day off, and I replied, "You know, you can do that, but the average guys, the guys in the third row of the review, can count—they've been here 8 hours. You're not giving them a half-day off, you're just not making them work 12 hours. They are going to be giving you the one-finger salute."

He said, "Oh, they wouldn't do that."

I said, "Let me tell you, they would, because I used to be one of those guys, and whenever we listened to B.S. we all looked at each other and shot the C.O. the shaft."

He sat for a minute. "You know Gordon," he said, "that's good advice."

And he gave the guys the rest of the day off, but he told them that it didn't count for the half-day he owed them.

You see? He was forgetting—those are people out there. The rule may say that a drill is extra, so they've only worked a half-day. But they're standing there—they *know* they've worked a full day. If they're spare parts, giving them half a day off might work. But they're not—they're people.

Never forget that. I try not to.

A Little Education Is a Dangerous Thing

One other thing I did during my time in the Navy was to get my high school degree, studying at a high school in Florida when I was stationed there.

Notice I don't say general equivalency degree. I got that first, of course, just to be able to continue advancing in my career (above a certain rank, you had to have two years of classes or a GED). But I didn't want an equivalent of anything; I wanted that degree. I started going to school at night; I had to take four years of English and math. In 1965, I got my diploma from Key West High School. I enrolled in community college then, but I was a little worn out and quit.

I didn't go back to college again until I got married and was stationed in California. I took courses at community colleges here and there. When I left the Navy in the late 1970s, I enrolled at

Texas A&M, because I knew I was going to eventually want to practice law in Texas. I got in about a year of full-time college before I got a phone call from Braniff Airlines that brought me back to airplanes.

Lessons from a Dying Airline

While I was trying to go to college, I got a call from someone who knew me from the Navy. He worked for Braniff, and Braniff was running into a lot of trouble with its operations and maintenance—they were having trouble with the nuts and bolts of running an airline (kind of like Continental when I took over 16 years later). He managed the avionics shop and was getting things done. His boss said, "What we need is another guy just like you." And he said, "I know one."

So I flew up the next week and got a job.

In the aviation division of the Navy, we weren't really in a marching-and-giving-orders kind of environment. The total costs of the division were ours to manage, and we competed for scarce resources within the Navy. We could try to make our areas work better in any way we could—say, by promoting morale to promote productivity or by trying to make our airplanes work reliably so they were on time. To be honest, it was almost like working at an airline after deregulation, but in a larger environment—the Navy—that still had a very regulation-era feel to it.

This left me well prepared for life at Braniff.

When I joined Braniff in 1979, it was one of the more well-respected names in aviation. It was the state airline of Texas, in a way. And I walked in there and I thought I was walking back into the Stone Age.

They were terrible people managers; they had a lot of resources that were costing them money and doing nothing. Deregulation had been in effect for a year, and suddenly they were under pressure to do better, which they hadn't had to be concerned about before.

About deregulation: Take a look around at the trucks that your utility company sends around. Do you see a lot of old, broken-down trucks, with workers in them who are trying to fix wires with whatever tools they can scare up? Or do you see a lot of expensive, new, well-maintained trucks containing the best tools money can buy? You see the latter, because that's a regulated industry. Utility companies are not competing with anybody, so whatever they need, they buy—and they convince the regulating agency that they need to buy it with your money, which they do.

That's how the airlines were when they were regulated. Then deregulation came along and everything changed. Companies like Braniff had a lot of trouble adjusting, naturally enough.

For me, that was great. There were a lot of opportunities to look good in that environment. My job—I was hired as an engine-repair manager—was to deal with labor and cost issues that had suddenly become important in a deregulated environment.

This was all new to Braniff's management. They were still running in a top-down, regulation style. Their people were dispirited; they were wasting all kinds of money in every process; a lot of things weren't measured. It was sort of a mess.

Optimizing Your Assets

One problem I discovered at Braniff involved engines that needed maintenance. There was an annual budget for engine overhaul, which was subcontracted to a third party. The rule said that we could spend only $\frac{1}{12}$ of that annual budget per month. Your department was actually docked money if you spent more than that in a particular month.

Engines tend to need maintenance when they need it, not according to some financial schedule. So we'd have a month in which a few engines needed overhaul, but we were only budgeted for two, so one would back up. And we didn't have too many months in which no new engines came in for overhaul, so the engines started to back up. When I came in, there were about 28 of those engines backed up.

Think about this. Those engines cost about $1.5 million apiece, and they were just sitting around. They're spare parts—but spare parts that don't work, because we can't afford to have them fixed. How much is it costing us to *not* have them fixed? If we sold the damn things and put the money in a savings account we'd at least get the interest on the money.

I solved that problem by contacting one of our overhaul suppliers. I asked them a question: What if we send you a whole bunch of these engines, and you get started overhauling them according to your own schedule, instead of on the 30-day deadline we are using now? That way you can take as much time as you want, use them for fill-in work, and have a little more control over your own work flow. The only catch is, we don't pay for the engines until I call you to ship them. How's that?

The suppliers were glad for the opportunity. It meant more work for them, and it meant more control for them. And they certainly didn't think we were going to send them engines and never ask for them back. So I did this as a way of getting those engines back into circulation.

In November 1979, a big ice storm hit Denver. We lost eight engines because of it. My son was undergoing surgery that weekend, so I wasn't around. Well, the vice president of maintenance tracked me down in my son's hospital room. He said, "I want you to get ahold of TWA and find out whether you can lease some engines, because we've got eight planes out of service and we need to recover for Thanksgiving weekend."

I said, "Sir, if you don't care about the budget, I can solve that problem for you." He told me to get to it.

So I called our supplier and I said, "Can we have eight of those engines you've had for long-term overhaul?" He said, "I'd be delighted."

We didn't miss a flight.

That's what planning and control of your operation is all about. The suppliers won because they got special terms on which to do their work; Braniff won because we put all those engines back to work; our passengers won because they didn't miss a flight—and then we all won again, because we got more customers, the supplier got more business from us, and our passengers got more reliable flights.

As it turned out, my boss later discovered how I had organized the engine overhauls and he ordered me to stop it. Unrelated to that, he eventually left. His place was taken by William Huskins, who became the senior vice president of engineering and maintenance, and he was kind of my mentor.

When Huskins took over, there was still some bad stuff going on. A lot of consultants were hired when Braniff first started having trouble, and they were spending a lot of money generating reports and not much else. Those of us disposed to complain were told in no uncertain terms that there wasn't any room in the organization for people who wouldn't get on board. So we kept quiet— not much communication at the old Braniff, but the guys at the top wanted it that way.

The late Bill Huskins came on board and within a couple of weeks he was getting rid of consultants left and right and finding financial problems and measuring them to get a real sense of what was wrong. Bill had been in charge of maintenance and engineering for Northwest Airlines for years and was well respected throughout the industry. He was an engineer, and his way to solve a problem was to figure out what was really happening (by measuring), figure out what needed to happen, and then actually do something about it. Much of what we did at Continental, I learned from Bill Huskins.

He also taught me to temper my thinking. I was a very aggressive guy, and I didn't have the experience or the polish he had. He showed me how to compete without running over people— how to make sure I treated everybody with the respect they deserved, even if I thought I was right about something and they were wrong—even if I *was* right. He taught me how to be cooperative instead of adversarial, how to get my way effectively. He taught me when to loosen up and when to tighten up. He was a true friend.

Huskins encouraged me to do two things: one was to finish college by continuing at night school, and the other was to get an airframe and powerplant (A&P) mechanic's license. He had an A&P license himself, and he was a licensed pilot, as well as an aerodynamics engineer. I never forgot the authority that gave him with the people we worked with and the people we supervised. He knew how the damn airplanes worked, so when he made a suggestion, it wasn't just some business school grad applying a formula. He had credentials.

I listened to him, and I followed his advice. The license came easily, since I had been doing that work since I was in the Navy. I still have that license today. I persevered at college, taking night school classes continuously for several years, and finally earning my degree, in general studies, from Abilene Christian University. Then I had some credentials.

Learning to Fly

Speaking of credentials, I learned a lesson from my father that I haven't yet mentioned.

As I said, he was a pilot, and he taught me some flight basics—how to hold a heading, altitude, and speed. He wanted me to take formal lessons and get my pilot's license. We had many airplanes, after all, and he wanted me to learn to fly.

Well, I showed him. I wasn't going to take any of his free flight lessons. I didn't want to be a pilot anyhow. I refused and, as I said, I ran off and joined the Navy.

The lesson I learned was this: Headstrong kids can sure be dopes.

In 1983, when I had left Braniff and was working for Western Airlines in Southern California, people would ask me, like they often do at airlines, if I knew how to fly.

And I'd say, "Yeah, I kind of do, because sometimes in the Navy you get a chance to hold the controls, or whatever." So I could kind of fly, which is a little like saying you can kind of drive. Well, do you have a license? I didn't.

There was an engineer who worked with me at Western, Roger Icenogle, and he taught flying at a little airport there. I told him I wanted to learn to fly. So we started flying a little Cessna 152 at the Hawthorn Airport. I got myself a private license, joined the local flying club, and goofed around Southern California flying airplanes.

Then I went to Piedmont Airlines, in North Carolina. I was the big-shot senior vice president of operations, and now all the pilots worked for me. We had a flying school out of one of our operations, and I thought I'd like to learn how to fly multiengine airplanes—because, hell, I'm working at an airline, I'm kind of interested, you know? So that was something else I knew how to do, another credential.

And another way to learn a lesson.

At Piedmont I got a job for a guy named Austin Goodwin, who had also worked with me at Western and helped teach me to fly. When he was going to move to North Carolina, he asked me if I wanted to fly his plane across the country with him. I said sure. I flew to L.A., and we loaded our stuff into his Piper Arrow and took off. We got as far as New Mexico, where we spent our first night.

The next day we stopped for fuel somewhere in North Texas, where we learned that, to the east, there was overcast, with low-level clouds. That meant we wouldn't be able to see the ground. Since we were not flying an instrument-flight-rules flight plan— we were sticking with visual flight rules, which means you have to see where you're going—we knew we'd have to find a hole in the clouds somewhere in order to land. We figured we'd be fine.

I was in the left seat for this leg, so I was flying the plane and Austin was navigating. We found out as we flew, from charts and from weather reports, that there was another big front moving from south to north, which was pushing us off our east-west flight plan. We were trying to stay ahead of it. Meanwhile, the clouds below us were getting higher and higher—and clouds started developing above us.

We found ourselves flying between two layers of clouds, losing track of where we were. We could see fine; we just couldn't see the ground. The weather was getting worse—it was bad enough behind us that we couldn't turn around, and it turned out that, for some reason, we had mistuned the radio navigation equipment. We really didn't know where we were.

We called in to the air traffic control center, but with only a visual flight plan, we weren't on anybody's list of people to watch out for. With the weather so bad, the controllers from the various airports had plenty on their hands as it was.

I said, "Austin, let's find a hole in the clouds and spiral down the hole."

He said, "No way, Gordon. We don't know where we are—we might spiral down into the middle of a valley and hit a mountain on the way down."

Good point.

We had about two hours of fuel left, so I finally said, "Austin, I want you to find someone on the radio and declare an emergency." Austin didn't want to do it. He said, "I just got hired by Piedmont. We've got ourselves into a fix, without instrument clearance, lost, and without charts we ought to have for wherever it turns out we are. I'm going to look like a dope."

I said, "Austin, this is my leg. I'm flying the airplane, and I want you to call somebody now. If somebody has a problem with their license it'll be me, and I want to know where the hell we are while we still have two hours of fuel left to do something about it."

So we called and squawked 7700, an emergency code, on the transponder. We found out where the nearest airport was. We got under air traffic control, and they gave us a heading to follow. We didn't have the charts for the airport, so they talked us through a nonprecision approach. It was foggy, so Austin was flying the plane from the right seat for the landing, because I had no instrument rating.

I remember popping out of the fog, just above treetop level, and discovering we were perpendicular to the runway. Austin set us down somehow, and the safety officer hustled over to check our licenses immediately.

We got to North Carolina without further adventure, but I got myself into an instrument flying curriculum and got an instrument rating. I had got myself into a predicament where I needed somebody else to save my butt, and I wasn't going to do that again. You don't want to depend on other people to save your bacon. It was a mistake, but I learned from it, and I'm a better pilot because of it.

That experience helps me when I'm dealing with pilots. We're part of the same club. I'm not just some suit. I'm a pilot, and I'm a mechanic. When we're talking about the best way to run an airline, they know that I know something. They respect what I've done.

We speak the same language. If I say, "Don't over rotate," when I'm talking about not getting the company moving too fast, they get the idea. For example, I was talking to some pilots once at a simulator during the early days of Continental's turnaround, when we had started showing profits but we still had huge debts. (Don't get me wrong, Continental is still paying the price for its decade of mismanagement, but this was when we were barely out of the blocks.)

One guy said, "Well, the company's doing better and we're doing better, but we've put up with this crap for a long time, and we're ready to do a lot better right now. Why can't we get the raises we want now?"

So I said to these pilots, "What's the pitch attitude of this plane at rotation?"

One of the pilots replied, "About 10 degrees, nose up."

I said, "What kind of rate of climb does that give you?"

He said, "Initially, about 500 or 600 feet per minute."

So I said, "How about if I told you that you're the pilot, and we trained you to fly, but that's just not going to get the job done? We need you to hold 20 degrees nose up, because we just plain want to climb faster?"

The pilot said, "That's not going to work. It's going to get 20 degrees nose up for a few seconds, then the airplane stalls and you won't have the altitude to recover."

I said, "Well, you've answered your own question then."

He got the picture—or, at least, he heard what I was saying. It's a good thing to know how the business you're in works.

Piedmont and Boeing

After leaving Western I ended up at Piedmont, which was a great little airline. It won the Airline of the Year award in 1984, during my tenure there. This airline was little, but getting bigger, and it did well because we focused on what was important.

Once again, I had been brought in because they thought I was the type of guy who could actually get some things done and not just talk about it. So I had a good time there. I had a lot of freedom, the company set the right goals, we did some great work, and I learned a lot about the business. It was pretty heady stuff, but, I'm sorry to say, the lesson I remember best from those years was the one about leadership I told you about back in Chapter 7. The guy running the company not only took his eye off the ball, we missed the boat so bad the company was actually sold out from under us.

That was one of the biggest disappointments of my life, and I vowed I'd never make that mistake.

After leaving Piedmont, I eventually ended up at The Boeing Company, which, for my money, is one of the best-run companies in the world—though it's as different as can be from a little company like Piedmont was.

When I first walked in the door at Piedmont in 1984 there was a rotary phone on my desk. I got those replaced pretty quickly. At Piedmont, I could do a lot of simple stuff like that on my own authority, which I think is the way to keep a company moving.

Boeing is sometimes just the opposite. I like to say that you can have only one guy in the left seat, only one captain on the plane. At Boeing the left seat is kind of a bench seat. Five or six guys all think they're in charge. It can be very frustrating to get anything changed there, because there's a committee meeting and a debate about everything.

It's pretty understandable why a company like Boeing runs that way—they make decisions there that last not years, but decades. If you design a new airplane, you're going to be producing that plane in huge quantities, filling billion-dollar orders according to government regulations, for tens of years. So that had better be a good airplane, and everybody who needs to think about it had better think about it before things get started.

Boeing was like a 767, whereas Piedmont was like a Piper Super Cub, and Continental is like a turbojet. Continental is big, but it's not as big and unwieldy as Boeing. Turning a 767 is just like turning a Cub—only you've got to think a lot further ahead. So you can see why Boeing has its somewhat stolid, creaky hierarchical structure.

I did well there and was very happy for a long time. The good thing about a structure like that is that it takes good care of you once you're inside it and you know what management wants you to do. I always said that if I had lung failure, The Boeing Company would probably breathe for me. But it was inevitable that the structure was going to start pinching me, and, of course, it did.

I remember blowing my stack eventually over a problem with answering machines. I was running a program that had about

14,000 people in it, and we used a voice-mail system for some 6,000 of those people. The system had been chosen by the company, and the provider charged $11 per person per month for the service. My responsibility, like that of everybody everywhere, was to reduce costs. It didn't take me too long to say, "How much would it cost us to buy an answering machine at Sears?" The answer was about $60, which was already a 50 percent annual saving over the existing system. Buying them wholesale, I knew we'd do a whole lot better.

So I put that in my plan and watched it get shot down by some corporate committee. I squawked about it and was told not to bring it up again. I brought it up twice more, embarrassing my boss at large meetings. To my mind, this was like putting that 350-pound jockey on the back of a horse. They were telling us to win a race, then slapping this huge guy on our backs. I said it was talking out of both sides of their mouths.

But, of course, I wasn't going to win—even though it's one of the best companies in the world, it's a big company, and I'm only one guy. I fought against a lot of stuff like that at Boeing, and when it was time for me to leave, I told Phil Condit, Boeing's president, my friend, and the man who hired me, "You know what? You need to get rid of some of the dead weight here, some of the corporate staff. You need to go get a pistol with a 16-shot clip, and you need to empty the damn clip." (By the way, this time and the time I needed to get the airplanes painted at Continental are the only times I've suggested shooting employees or coworkers. I've thought about it a lot more often, but those are the only times I've actually suggested it.)

Phil said, "Gordon, the answer to what Boeing needs is probably halfway between what you advocate and the way I see it."

So I said, "Fine then. Get an 8-shot clip."

All that said, though, I loved—and still love—that company. The first excellent lesson I learned there was to fly a 767. I had become a little bored with my first job, revitalizing the spare-parts business, and I knew I needed a new challenge. The sales department wanted me to learn to play golf so that I'd be better with customers. I told Phil I needed to do one of three things: Get a new job, learn to play golf, or learn to fly Boeing airplanes. Phil laughed and told me to learn the airplaines.

So I became type rated on the 757 and 767.

An amazing thing happened. All the Boeing pilots suddenly thought I was a great guy. I hope I hadn't given them any reason to think otherwise of me before that, but this really got their attention.

The lesson I've taken away from that is one I've always tried to apply since then: When you're working with people, the credential you want is the one that shows that you're valuable in their eyes. Whether you're the chief executive, a plane cleaner, a baggage handler, or a pilot, you have to prove that you're adding value to the team, that you know something, that you can do something, that you're going to be an asset—that it's better to have you here than not.

Know Your Business

In fact, that may be the best lesson I've learned as long as I've been in this business. As I've emphasized throughout, this business is about people, and you have to be willing to understand people. You've got to like people, or you're probably miscast as a manager.

But you've also got to know your business. You've got to know how an airplane works. As I once told Al Gore in a meeting, it kind of helps to know how a watch works before you try to fix it.

That's why I can hire a financial guy like Larry Kellner, our chief financial officer and a top lawyer like Jeff Smisek, who don't have much airline experience, and I can work with a president like Greg Brenneman, who comes from a financial and consulting background. These are guys with great business acumen and well-honed skills in their areas of expertise, and all quickly learned the basics of our business. I can be responsible for the airline stuff, because that's my whole background. In operations, I need someone like C. D. McLean, Jun Tsuruta, or George Mason—guys I worked with in operations at Piedmont. They're operating the airline; they'd better be airline guys. But in some of the more general areas—finance, corporate management—I can hire just the best people, and I figure I can be responsible for bringing them up to speed on the airline specifics. You can learn the basics.

I've likened running a company to being a coach. This is like drafting the best athlete and figuring you'll teach that athlete how to play the position he or she needs to play. If you know your sport, you can simply draft an athlete with talent—it will work out.

There are things that are fundamental to any business—such as not running out of cash. But in any business, a lot of what makes you succeed or fail is specific to the business. You'd just better know that. There's no substitute for it. The plane's on the ground, smoking? Well, why?

The engine quit. Swell—but why? Well, it could be pilot error or it could be an oil leak or it could be they forgot to put fuel in it—or it could be a thousand things. If you want to be in charge of making sure the planes stay in the air, you'd better have some idea about what keeps them up there in the first place.

The final story I'll use to illustrate that point comes from my days at Piedmont.

We were sitting in my boss's office one day in January, with this beautiful Carolina blue sky visible out the window, and we were looking at the previous day's numbers. We'd had a lot of late planes and a lot had gone wrong. My boss asked me, "How come we ran such a crummy operation yesterday?"

I said, "You know what? Electrical carts froze to the concrete in Chicago yesterday. Planes tried to taxi to the active runway in Cleveland yesterday but they could not get through the snow drifts.

"The whole world is not like it is outside your window. There are places we fly where in the morning all the water is frozen and so the airplane needs to be thawed out."

And then there are just bad days, sometimes, where things go wrong. It's still just people running your company, and you have to accept that. You get to know it by working—by fixing planes, by flying planes. Or by cooking pizzas or fixing watches or designing clothes—whatever it is that you do before you become powerful enough to tell other people how to do it.

Sometimes guys in the boardroom forget that. Did you ever notice how company picnics are scheduled in July and not January? Because it tends to be cold or rainy or nasty in January. Well, if you're a big shot with an office on the twentieth floor, it never rains up there in that boardroom. If you've been on the twentieth floor long enough, you might forget that it rains at all. Or if you inherit the job, you can sometimes get to the twentieth floor without ever learning much about rain in the first place.

I like being on the twentieth floor. I really do. I've worked hard to get here and I've learned a lot on the way.

But I'm glad I've had enough picnics outside to remember that it still rains sometimes.

Why You Just Read This Book

Remember the story about the ambulance in the valley that I told you in Chapter 5?

It speaks volumes about what it costs *not* to do some of those things managers like to decide are too expensive—what it costs not to change the oil in an engine, what it costs not to put first-class seats in an airplane or food on the flight. What it costs *not* to put cheese on the pizza.

But you know, I didn't make up that story. I read it in 1961 in *Approach*, a Navy aviation safety magazine. And I never forgot it.

The entire point of my writing this book is that maybe one of the examples I've given here, one of the stories I've told, will have the same effect.

This book contains as many stories as I can think of to illustrate why Continental Airlines is so successful. My hope is that in reading at least one of these stories, someone quickly learns a lesson it took me years to learn and that person might take some other broken company, or a broken division, or a broken store, or a broken family for that matter, and help to make it work. I want to tell you how it worked here—how it worked for Gordon Bethune and Continental Airlines. Then you can take what applies to you and make it work for you.

So let me capsulize what I've told you—or at least what I think I've told you. I'll kind of run through the chapters, and I'll remind you of what I said. And if your boss or your boyfriend says you really ought to read this book but you hate it, you can just read this chapter and you'll be able to discuss the book intelligently, and nobody will be the wiser.

1. Is This Any Way to Run an Airline?

Not when I took over. In fact, we sucked. We had terrible service, cranky employees, few and angry customers, and no money. Yet somehow, in the years since I've been here, with virtually the same people and the same airplanes and the same cities and airports, we've become the best airline in the sky. My point is that the principles behind the changes we made around here are so simple that your grandparents probably told you every one of them before you were in third grade. The problem is that people tend to forget them. I have written this book to remind you of them.

2. The Last Suppers, or Whose Problem Is It?

I raised for you the important first question behind any problem: Whose problem is it? I told you how my colleagues and I helped the people at Continental determine whose problem their imminent collapse was and what might prevent it. I explained how Greg Brenneman and I came up with the Go Forward Plan, which addressed every element of the problems at Continental—it had the market and financial plan that any turnaround scheme has. But it went further, addressing the company's real problems, the problems causing its marketing and financial problems: the company's lousy product and its miserable, unhappy employees.

The main point, for us and for any business, is that you can't just address one or two problems alone. Continental had a bad product and unhappy employees, so it didn't have customers and it didn't have money. All the financial or marketing tricks in the world weren't going to get the company anywhere. Companies succeed when they have a product people want and employees who like coming to work, and there just aren't exceptions. So Greg and I came up with a plan to make that happen at Continental.

Everyone seemed to think the Go Forward Plan was a good idea, but the company was so dysfunctional that even the best ideas weren't going to be implemented. We had a go-round with the board on who was going to be in charge, and I laid it on the line: Without a single leader in charge, none of Greg's and my good ideas were going to work. Continental needed a single leader. I believe the buck stops—and starts—with the person at the top. I stated my opinions strongly, and eventually I convinced the right people. I became the person at the top.

3. Fly to Win, or You Can Make a Pizza So Cheap Nobody Wants to Eat It

The first segment of the Go Forward Plan was pretty simple. We decided to stop doing things that lose money. We painted all our planes the same color, so that Continental looked like a real airline. We started to fly places people wanted to go. We restored our award-winning frequent flyer program, which we had recently dismantled. We apologized to the people we had alienated—travel agents, business partners, and customers—and showed them how we planned to do better and earn their business back.

Our belief was that we had focused long enough on lowering costs by taking away the things people want to buy in the first place. As I've said, "You can make a pizza so cheap that nobody wants to eat it." We put the cheese back on the pizza.

We started to run our business according to the row-five test—that is, anything new that we wanted to add (or old that we wanted to remove) had to be considered from the perspective of the average customer—the person sitting in row five—to see whether it would improve that person's flight, whether it would add value—value the person would pay extra to receive. Once we remembered to think like our customers, our customers started to like the way we think.

4. Fund the Future, or If There Ain't No Funds, There Ain't Gonna Be No Future

We knew that if we didn't get control of our finances, we were going to go bankrupt. We didn't want to do that. So we did whatever it took to change it. We renegotiated loans; we wriggled out of poor airplane lease agreements; we begged money back from suppliers. By honestly telling the people whom we owed money how we planned to improve, we made them our partners in improvement instead of our adversaries. By honestly telling our employees when—and why—we needed to postpone a wage hike, we defused their anger. By living up to our promise that it was a postponement and not a cancellation, we proved our honesty. We took a company that was hemorrhaging cash and stanched the bleeding.

We set up systems to accurately measure our money, replacing systems that left us confused about what we actually had. With better information, we made better decisions. Along with a better product, that enabled us to stop burning our cash and start earning cash.

5. Make Reliability a Reality, or It's Time to Act Like a Real Airline

Pretty simple stuff, here. We figured out that all the marketing and financial strategies weren't going to help if we still had a lousy product. So we fixed our product. Removing the company's old focus on cost savings and gimmickry, we simply focused on putting out a first-rate product. We measured that by figuring out what was most important to airline passengers: clean, safe, and reliable flights that reached their destinations on time and with their luggage. So we focused on that, using U.S. Department of Transportation measurements of the percentage of flights that were on time. Each month that we were in the top five nationally, we paid our employees $65 extra. Surprising nobody except perhaps their previous management, our employees found that once we showed them even the slightest incentive, they could bring those planes in on time better than anybody else.

And they did that. We made it easy for employees and passengers to let us know when reliability was a problem, and when we heard about it, we fixed it. When we became more reliable, our customers came back.

6. Working Together, or Which Part of This Watch Don't You Think We Need?

We asked a simple question about our team: Which part of this watch don't you think we need? The answer, of course, is that every part in a watch is important for the whole watch to work. We showed our employees that the airline was like a watch, and we all had to get our jobs done. From an environment in which people in different parts of the company openly feuded, we forged a team. In the same way that the employees either won their $65 on-time bonuses as a group or lost them, our entire company was going to succeed or fail together.

Given a product they could believe in, an environment in which success was encouraged and rewarded, and the finances to do their jobs right, the employees easily lost track of old feuds and found that they liked winning much better than fighting. We've been winning ever since.

7. Success Has No Autopilot

It's human nature to want to relax once things have started going well. We've spent the last couple of years fighting that tendency, and so far we've managed to resist. We raised the bar on success— changing from ranking in the top five in on-time percentage to the top three, though with a higher bonus for coming in first—and kept fine-tuning, eventually deciding that an 80 percent or better monthly on-time percentage was worth a bonus, too, regardless of where we placed.

We also kept our eye on the ball. We didn't stop cooperating internally; we didn't stop trying to listen to our customers to improve our product. We didn't just try to stay the course. We tried to keep improving. Every time we improve, our customers like it. So we keep trying.

8. How the Sickest Patients Need the Best Doctors, and concerning Tapeworms

And they're worth it. I explained how the best people are worth their pay if they're saving your company from going bankrupt. If you were having brain surgery, would you choose an inexperienced surgeon willing to work for less or the best one you could find? That's exactly what we did.

Once again, an atmosphere in which the best people are rewarded for being the best and where success is actually understood and measured makes for an atmosphere in which B.S. doesn't succeed. A lot of people who survived on B.S. before have now left Continental. Everybody seems to appreciate that.

9. Nobody Loses When the Whole Team Wins

I've discussed at some length how a good airline—or any good company—is like a good team. Everybody knows the main goal: winning. Everybody has a different job. Everybody works together. Everybody respects each other's jobs—the linemen don't laugh at the kicker because he can't bench-press 350 pounds, and the kicker doesn't laugh at the linemen because they can't kick. That way, when the players line up for a game-winning field goal that the linemen have to protect and the kicker has to kick, there are no subagendas, no linemen who would get more satisfaction out of seeing the kicker trashed than out of winning the game, no kickers who think it would serve those lousy linemen right if this kick sailed wide.

When everybody wants to win, you've got the best chance of winning and the best chance of quick recovery when you don't. Continental has become a work-together kind of place. We win now—we win because we are a team.

10. Keeping the Lines of Communication Open

Continental's employees know something special: If we know any-thing that affects their jobs, we'll tell them. And furthermore, if we tell them something, it's true. We share any information we have, in as many ways as possible—from newsletters to daily updates on bulletin boards, to e-mail, voice mail, and electronic signs all over our workplaces worldwide. Employees never have to go to the newspaper to get the straight dope on their workplace. If we know it, they know it.

We've created an environment where, if an employee doesn't know what's up at work, what the goals are, what's expected, what's happening, it's his or her own fault. We work so hard to get information to them, they'd actually have to work *not* to know what's up. Consequently, we're all on the same page. Of course, that communication works both ways—we listen as well as talk up here in the lofty heights of upper management. That's the only way to work.

11. Predictability, or the Value of a Zippo

Something people often forget is that in this stressful, madden-ingly unpredictable world, predictability is incredibly valuable. For our customers, we become more valuable the more predictable we are. The more consistently we land our planes on time and with their bags, the more likely passengers are going to want to be on our planes.

But this works internally, too. Employees who know exactly what's expected of them and exactly what the consequences of their actions are waste a lot less time worrying. They work com-fortably because they know what to expect. It makes for a better place to work. And that makes for better work.

12. What Gets Measured Gets Managed

This is perhaps the key concept in improving performance: mak-ing sure that everyone knows the goal, how the goal is going to be measured, and what the rewards are for achieving it. For Continental, the goal was flying on time, the measure was the Department of Transportation data, and the reward was that $65 bonus. Pretty simple stuff, but it's the solution. You've still got to define success correctly and measure and reward it appropriately, but if you do those things, you'll probably do pretty well.

Anyhow, we sure did.

13. Crop Duster's Son

I shared the path I followed to become the fabulous big shot I am now. Believe it or not, there were a few hard knocks on the way. And believe this: I learned lessons from those knocks.

The Last Time, I Promise: It's All about People

So here we are. I've said about as much as I can say.

But when all is said and done, the biggest change that we've made at Continental is simple. Remember the question I've asked over and over: Did you ever hear of a successful company that had a product nobody wanted and where employees didn't want to come to work?

That's what we've addressed. We've turned Continental into a place that puts out a product that customers value and where employees like to come to work.

Employees come to work at Continental not just to pay the rent. They come to work because they enjoy doing work, they enjoy being part of a successful company, a successful team, and they enjoy serving our customers. It's about value. Customers value our product, and employees value each other and our customers. When people feel valued, good things happen. It's that simple.

Because (may I remind you?) *business is people*. That's it. You need to know about the business you're running; you need to know how to do your job. But whatever job you're doing, and whatever kind of manager you are, everything you do is really just creating, developing, and maintaining good, healthy, honest, and straightforward relationships. Forget it for a second and something will remind you. Forget it for a month and your profits will fall. Forget it for a year and your company will stagger. Forget it for much more than that and you'll be going down for the third time—and you'd better hope somebody shows up to save your bacon.

My Credenza

I frequently tell people what it was like when Piedmont Airlines, a place I loved, was sold out from underneath us (I told you the story in Chapter 7). I personally wasn't going to get hurt financially by that sale. I had a five-year contract for my position. I had stock worth a lot of money—in fact, it was worth more because it was inflated by the sale.

But I wasn't happy, because I wasn't working just for money. I was working because I love to work, I love being around airplanes, I love working with people. I loved that airline and those people, and the whole thing had been destroyed for us. We were like a team that had been sold to another town or that had suddenly been disbanded. I was unhappy because my motivation at work—to do well because it's a challenge and it's the right thing to do—was suddenly taken away.

Although you can't think about that kind of emotional motivation all day long, you'd better never completely forget it.

Let me give you an example, I have a credenza behind my desk, and in the bottom drawer of that credenza I have hundreds of letters—letters from employees, letters from competitors, letters from partners.

Letters from people.

In a way, those letters show the progress Continental has made. And though I don't expect to turn down my salary any time soon, those letters are a pretty important part of why I do my job every day.

There are letters from employees thanking me for my part in saving their airline. Letters from civic and business leaders in cities we serve thanking us for improving their service and the quality of their lives. Letters from coworkers, past and present, thanking us because we are now doing so well. They tell me that they enjoy or enjoyed working with me, that they wish me the best.

On the tough days, I root through that drawer and I read one or two of those letters. They mean more to me than I can really express.

My employees at Continental gave me a motorcycle one Christmas, when it became clear Continental was going to make it. These were employees whose salaries were still below industry average, but who knew that the work I and the other managers had been doing had saved Continental from going bankrupt.

I love that motorcycle. That's kind of why I do what I do—and it's certainly why I continue to do it when I could probably retire if I wanted to.

Everything Connects to Everything Else

There's a point that I've made several times but that I want to make one more time before I shut up: None of this is piecemeal. I've mentioned that the Go Forward Plan happened all at once. We didn't say, "First we'll fix marketing, then finance, then the product, then employee morale." Every one of those things affects all the others, and balance is the key. It's like a plane. Are you losing speed? Well, you're probably gaining altitude then, so maybe you can drop the nose and get the speed back up. Or if you want that altitude, then you'll have to expend a little more fuel to keep up the speed.

It's all connected. No ingredient in a cake is the most important. Miss one, and the whole cake is ruined. If you take nothing else away from this book, I hope you take that. A traditional Japanese management principle says that quality, cost, delivery, safety, and morale are all connected; they are all important elements to success. You'd better pay attention to them all if you expect your company to do well in the long run. There's no substitute.

Basically, that's the Go Forward Plan. We have to make a product that people want and put it where the people who want it can get it (Fly to Win). We have to do that in a way that enables us to have reasonable costs and make a profit (Fund the Future). Plus we have to be good and on time (Make Reliability a Reality)—and we have to be safe and keep our employees happy and safe (Working Together).

If you want to be successful, you have to have a good product that's worth what it costs. It has to be delivered where it needs to be when it needs to be there, and it has to be delivered by people who are happy and safe making it. None of those can be left out of the equation. None.

Let Me Serve You

There's one final reason for our success.

We at Continental have learned the secret to winning. If you want to lead, you have to follow. If you want to command, you have to serve.

That's not just a bunch of mumbo jumbo cribbed from some New Age self-help book. That's just plain true.

The airlines are a service industry. We provide a service that people need. We carry more than three million people on our planes every month. We want to win. We want to make money. We want to be the best airline in the world. So to do that, what had we better be really good at doing?

Serving—serving people.

We'd better like people, and we'd better like serving them.

Which we do, and which I do.

The customer isn't always right—but the customer is the point. We've made that point every day in our airline since I took over. I have a little column that runs every month in our in-flight magazine, and every month I end it by thanking the people reading it for choosing our airline. I mean it's pretty simple: no customers, no airline. We provide value, and we need to thank our customers for buying it.

My goal, from the day I walked into Continental, was to get that sense of value into every aspect of our operation, from the top to the bottom. I wanted every customer to feel valued in every transaction, and every employee to feel valued every day. That makes the customers come back for more, and it makes the employees do better and better work. Tell them what you want, reward them for giving it to you, and get out of the way. That's my strategy in a nutshell.

And you know what? It's worked.

Here's the last story I'll tell you.

We're a service industry. That means our people work during all the times when everybody else is at home with their families. Like firefighters or police officers, we never stop providing our service, and it becomes even more important during holidays, when more, rather than fewer, people need us.

So I like to drop in to our crew rooms on Thanksgiving and Christmas and other holidays to thank our crew members for working, to thank them for carrying the load. It's one more way to show them I appreciate them and to remind them that we're all a team. I'm always amazed by the quality of our staff and the attitude they maintain during those busiest times.

The best example of this I've come across happened to a friend of mine.

He was traveling on our airline over Thanksgiving. He walked up to the check-in counter at the Raleigh-Durham airport at around dinnertime on Wednesday, the day before the holiday— possibly the busiest moment in the busiest travel day of the year.

Everybody was hustling, and he was feeling cheerful because he was going to visit family and had a couple of days off. He thought for a moment and realized that he could travel and enjoy his holidays off because all those people behind the counter were working so hard—no doubt on a day they'd prefer to be relaxing or at least traveling home like he was.

So, feeling expansive, he decided to compliment the staff behind the counter.

"Thank you," he said, gesturing to the busy concourse around him. "Thank you for working, that we may travel."

It was a nice thing to say. But the agent behind the Continental counter shot back at him in a second: "Thank *you*," she said. "Thank *you* for traveling, that *we* may work."

That's the company I've tried hard to build. That's what makes me proud to work with the employees of Continental Airlines.

And that's the point.

ACKNOWLEDGMENTS

How do you determine which ingredient is most responsible for making a successful cake—they are all so important . . . so, too, are the people listed below who each in their way have shaped this book into what it is . . .

My thanks go to:

The more than 40,000 men and women who are Continental Airlines—when this many people have a common focus and work together as a team, nothing can top them. They were always the best, and they showed everyone, including themselves, that no one could ever do it better.

Ruth Mills of John Wiley & Sons, who first encouraged me to take on this project, and then managed the process to completion.

Scott Huler, my accomplished coauthor, who organized and edited hours of narrative from me and members of my team.

Ned Walker, Continental Vice President, Corporate Communication, who kept me focused, coordinated every change, and provided real input to our tale.

My partner—Greg Brenneman—no one could ask for better. Without Greg's talent, focus, and energy, the change we accomplished could not have happened.

Our team, Larry Kellner, C. D. McLean, and Jeff Smisek—together we provided solutions and ideas that were superior to any of those capable by any one individual. These three are at the very top rank of their professions in the industry.

The sickest patients need the best doctors, and we called George Mason and Jun Tsuruta—longtime friends and accomplished operations professionals from my Piedmont Airlines days.

Bonnie Reitz, David Siegel, Richard Metzner, and Ben Baldanza—the first wave of talent to revitalize Sales, Scheduling, Marketing, and Pricing.

Fred Abbott, Tom Barber, Dave Barger, Bill Brunger, Rebecca Cox, Mark Erwin, Larry Goodwin, David Grizzle, Greg Hartford, Glen Hauenstein, Gerry Laderman, Debbie McCoy, Ralph Schulz, Barry Simon—longtime Continental executives who always knew things would be better if only they were allowed to help.

Mike Bonds, Mike Campbell, Jim Compton, Brian Davis, Nene Foxhall, Ron Howard, Jeff Misner, Mark Moran, Jim Ream, Holden Shannon, Jennifer Vogel, Janet Wejman—recruited for their expertise, they each enriched our pool of talent and demonstrated teamwork's success.

My assistant and coworker, Kay Jennett—I never had to worry about the details—thanks to Kay.

My family—T.J. and our sons Xavier, Michael, and Grady, and my mother, Pearl Elley Bethune, who in their own individual ways taught me a lot of what I know.

Thank you all.

Gordon Bethune

And from the coauthor Scott Huler:

Gordon Bethune is perhaps the easiest chief executive in the world to work with, and it was truly a pleasure helping him make this book. Next, of course, thanks to all the people at Continental Airlines, who answered so many questions with such grace and in every case have genuinely lived up to their reputation. Kay Jennett, especially, fits in whatever category goes above "indispensable." Ned Walker and Tammy Godwin went to extra lengths to help this project. Ruth Mills, the editor who recognized that Gordon should write a book and asked me to help him, has shown that apart from being a great friend she is great at her job. My agent, Ed Knappman, undertook the role of responding to rather than originating a project with aplomb.

So many of my friends and family helped by listening to me, reading portions of this book, and just offering general support. I won't list everyone, but Michael, Kate, Lisa, David, Liz, Tami, Lisa and Chuck, Joe and Kathy, and especially a veritable bucketful of Menconis were more help than they will ever know. Rachel and Vic get special credit for extra reading, and Michael, Lori, Ed, Lynn, and Sarah get special credit for patience and length of service. Catering provided by Leigh Menconi.

INDEX

287